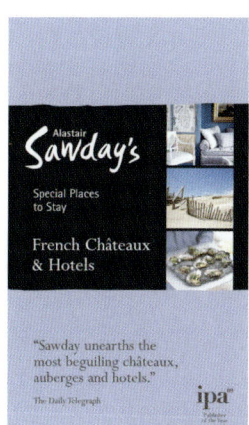

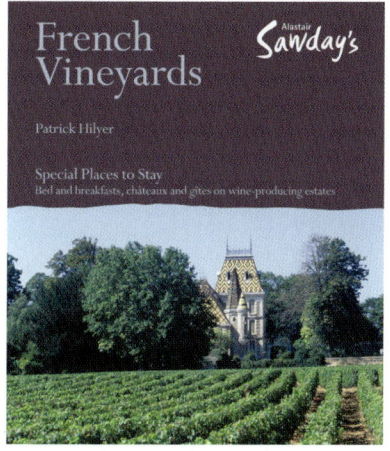

Alastair

Sawday's

Special Places to Stay

Fifth edition
Copyright © 2010 Alastair Sawday
Publishing Co. Ltd
Published in 2010
ISBN-13: 978-1-906136-24-6

Alastair Sawday Publishing Co. Ltd,
The Old Farmyard, Yanley Lane,
Long Ashton, Bristol BS41 9LR, UK
Tel: +44 (0)1275 395430
Email: info@sawdays.co.uk
Web: www.sawdays.co.uk

The Globe Pequot Press,
P. O. Box 480, Guilford,
Connecticut 06437, USA
Tel: +1 203 458 4500
Email: info@globepequot.com
Web: www.globepequot.com

*We have made every effort to ensure the accuracy
of the information in this book at the time of
going to press. However, we cannot accept any
responsibility for any loss, injury or
inconvenience resulting from the use of
information contained therein.*

Series Editor Alastair Sawday
Editor Nicola Crosse
Assistant to Editor Polly Procter
Editorial Director Annie Shillito
Writing Jo Boissevain, Ann Cooke-
Yarborough, Nicola Crosse, Monica
Guy, Rebecca Hargrove, Caroline Harris
Inspections Richard & Linda Armspach,
Helen Barr, Isabelle Brown,
Ann Cooke-Yarborough, Jill Coyle,
Meredith Dickinson, Penny Dinwiddie,
Janet Edsforth Stone, John & Jane Edwards,
Georgina Gabriel, Diana Sawday,
Susan Herrick Luraschi
*Thanks to those people who did a few inspections
or had a go at a write-up*
Accounts Bridget Bishop,
Shona Adcock
Editorial
Angharad Barnes, Jo Boissevain,
Roxy Dumble
Production Jules Richardson,
Rachel Coe, Tom Germain,
Anny Mortada
Sales & Marketing Rob Richardson,
Sarah Bolton, Bethan Riach, Lisa Walklin
Web & IT Dominic Oakley
Chris Banks, Phil Clarke,
Mike Peake, Russell Wilkinson

Alastair Sawday has asserted his right to
be identified as the author of this work

Maps: Maidenhead Cartographic Services
Printing: Butler Tanner & Dennis, Frome
UK distribution: Penguin UK, London

Alastair Sawday's

Special Places to Stay

French
Self-catering

4 Contents

The buildings

Beautiful as they were, our old offices leaked heat, used electricity to heat water and rooms, flooded spaces with light to illuminate one person, and were not ours to alter.

So in 2005 we created our own eco-offices by converting some old barns to create a low-emissions building. We made the building energy-efficient through a variety of innovative and energy-saving building techniques, described below.

Insulation We went to great lengths to ensure that very little heat can escape, by laying thick insulating board under the roof and floor and adding further insulation underneath the roof and between the rafters. We then lined the whole of the inside of the building with plastic sheeting to ensure air-tightness.

Heating We installed a wood-pellet boiler from Austria, in order to be largely fossil-fuel free. The pellets are made from compressed sawdust, a waste product from timber mills that work only with sustainably managed forests. The heat is conveyed by water, throughout the building, via an under-floor system.

Water We installed a 6000-litre tank to collect rainwater from the roofs. This is pumped back, via an ultra-violet filter, to the lavatories, showers and basins. There are two solar thermal panels on the roof providing heat to the one (massively insulated) hot-water cylinder.

Photo: Tom Germain

Lighting We have a carefully planned mix of low-energy lighting: task lighting and up-lighting. We also installed sun-pipes to reflect the outside light into the building.

Electricity All our electricity has long come from the Good Energy company and is 100% renewable.

Materials Virtually all materials are non-toxic or natural. Our carpets are made from (80%) Herdwick sheep-wool from National Trust farms in the Lake District.

Doors and windows Outside doors and new windows are wooden, double-glazed and beautifully constructed in Norway. Old windows have been double-glazed.

We have a building we are proud of, and architects and designers are fascinated by. But best of all, we are now in a better position to encourage our owners and readers to take sustainability more seriously.

What we do

Besides having moved the business to a low-carbon building, the company works in a number of ways to reduce its overall environmental footprint.

Our footprint We measure our footprint annually and use it to find ways of reducing our environmental impact. To help address unavoidable carbon emissions we try to put something back: since 2006 we have supported SCAD, an organisation that works with villagers in India to create sustainable development.

Travel Staff are encouraged to car-share or cycle to work and we provide showers (rainwater-fed) and bike sheds. Our company cars run on LPG (liquid petroleum gas) or recycled cooking oil. We avoid flying and take the train for business trips wherever possible. All office travel is logged as part of our footprint and we count our freelance editors' and inspectors' miles too.

Our office Nearly all of our office waste is recycled; kitchen waste is composted and used in the office vegetable garden. Organic and fairtrade basic provisions are used in the staff kitchen and at in-house events, and green cleaning products are used throughout the office.

Working with owners We are proud that many of our Special Places help support their local economy and, through our Ethical Collection, we recognise owners who go the extra mile to serve locally sourced and organic food or those who have a positive impact on their environment or community.

Engaging readers We hope to raise awareness of the need for individuals to play their part; our Go Slow series places an emphasis on ethical travel and the Fragile Earth imprint consists of hard-hitting environmental titles. Our Ethical Collection informs readers about owners' ethical endeavours.

Ethical printing We print our books locally to support the British printing industry and to reduce our carbon footprint. We print our books on either FSC-certified or recycled paper, using vegetable or soy-based inks.

Our supply chain Our electricity is 100% renewable (supplied by Good Energy), and we put our savings with Triodos, a bank whose motives we trust. Most supplies are bought in bulk from a local ethical-trading co-operative.

For many years Alastair Sawday Publishing has been 'greening' the business in different ways. Our aim is to reduce our environmental footprint as far as possible, and almost every decision we make takes into account the environmental implications. In recognition of our efforts we won a Business Commitment to the Environment Award in 2005, and in 2006 a Queen's Award for Enterprise in the Sustainable Development category. In that year Alastair was voted ITN's 'Eco Hero'. In 2009 we were given the South West C+ Carbon Positive Consumer Choices Award for our Ethical Collection.

In 2008 and again in 2009 we won the Independent Publishers Guild Environmental Award. In 2009 we were also the IPG overall Independent Publisher and Trade Publisher of the Year. The judging panel were effusive in their praise, stating: "With green issues currently at the forefront of publishers' minds, Alastair Sawday Publishing was singled out in this category as a model for all independents to follow. Its efforts to reduce waste in its office and supply chain have reduced the company's environmental impact, and it works closely with staff to identify more areas of improvement. Here is a publisher who lives and breathes green. Alastair Sawday has all the right principles and is clearly committed to improving its practice further."

Becoming 'green' is a journey and, although we began long before most companies, we still have a long way to go. We don't plan to pursue growth for growth's sake. The Sawday's name – and thus our future – depends on maintaining our integrity. We promote special places – those that add beauty, authenticity and a touch of humanity to our lives. This is a niche, albeit a growing one, so we will spend time pursuing truly special places rather than chasing the mass market.

That said, we do plan to produce more titles as well as to diversify. We are expanding our Go Slow series to other European countries, and have launched *Green Europe*, both bold new publishing projects designed to raise the profile of low-impact tourism. Our Fragile Earth series is a growing collection of campaigning books about the environment: highlighting the perilous state of the world yet offering imaginative and radical solutions and some intriguing facts, these books will keep you up to date and well-armed for the battle with apathy.

Photos: Tom Germain

My own self-catering treat this year will be in a wood-clad ski chalet that is as beautiful in spring and summer as it is in the winter. As the snow melts, the grass appears in all its post-hibernation luxuriance. Wildflowers pop up in their millions and a carpet of crocuses spreads its colours across the mountain side. The cows are brought up to the hamlet after their winter down in the valley, their bells tinkling and their udders heavy with the finest milk — destined for the great cheeses of the area.

It is deeply satisfying to be in a countryside that has hardly changed — apart from the ski-lifts — and where old farming traditions survive. But change is inevitable for most places and I am impressed by the speed with which people respond to it. A few years ago the French were cottoning on to the commercial potential in their lovely old houses but didn't always get it right. It is now easy to find places where you feel transported to a more attractive world. The biggest change, reflected in this book, is the sheer variety of places; we have over 100 new ones to show you.

City-breaks are more popular than ever, because short-haul flights are so cheap. (I wish their cost reflected their full environmental impact, but that will come soon and 'things' will change again.) More people to towns and cities means we have superb flats and apartments all over the country. French provincial cities, such as Toulouse, Perpignan, Bordeaux, and Montpellier (and many more) are leading the search for new ways of living in urban spaces. They are bold, imaginative and colourful — and culturally dynamic.

Another self-catering change has been the way owners no longer shove guests into a forgotten corner of the house, furnished with left-over furniture. 'Gites' are now more like people's own homes, with family pictures, books, games and good art. (I would like owners, too, to encourage guests to leave behind the olive oil and pepper, and even the spare meat and veg — the way you would do at home.)

The handsome old chateaux, of which we may dream, remain, equipped with labradors and (some) eccentric owners. Food gets better and better, with many owners becoming impressively green and providing guests with food from their own gardens. Lastly, one more change: we have more big houses than ever, and even more wonderful places to stay in ski-ing areas. Try them in the summer.

Alastair Sawday

Look on any French travel website, pick up any guide book about France and you're likely to be told that it is 'the world's most popular tourist destination'. And if the French Tourist Authority has massaged any figures to make this claim, no matter; holidaymakers flock there. Even through the recent recession-racked summer and in spite of the strong Euro the British have continued to find the country irresistible.

France has pretty much everything. Haul yourself up to the Alps for the best downhill skiing, snow boarding, cross-country slogging and dog-sleighing through snowy forests. Return in the spring to find a smothering of wild flowers, waving grasses and heavenly walks. The country's coastline caters for all-comers with its gentle white beaches for picnics and paddling to its wild Atlantic coast for crashing breakers, intriguing small islands and incredibly cool surfers.

Down at the expensive end of the Mediterranean there is still no place more convivial for people-watching than St Tropez, well worth the €5 you will fork out for a cup of coffee. Go on a Saturday to find a chic flea market selling vintage clothes and brocante, and, just beyond, stall after stall of pungent cheeses, charcuterie, soft fruits and crusty breads, roasted chickens, cakes and pastries. You just don't see people like this anywhere else: a monsieur in his 80s, dapper in a bright white suit with bell-bottom trousers and nifty scarf, middle-aged, fur-coated ladies with strutting pooches, boyfriends with tiny bottoms, and more perfect young skin than outside any nightclub; and that's before you get to the marina and the yachts. From these, crew members in uniform walk smart little dogs on diamante leads, many wearing coats sporting the boats' logos

Brittany and Normandy are awash with quaint fishing villages (quieter than any in Cornwall), glorious coastal walks along Grandes Randonnéess and the best mussels and oysters; try them with Nantais muscadet or a glass of calvados. The major rivers of France have carved great valleys through swathes of countryside for canyoning, canoeing, kayaking, white water rafting and boating through unspoilt scenery. Medieval towns perch on mountainsides and hilltops; potter around their cobbled streets, drop in on their markets, marvel at the battlements and ramparts, ancient churches and stupendous views. And, for those who like wild marshland there's the

Photo left: Château de Vaux, entry 80
Photo right: Bastide des Hautes Moures - Lodge Kaomi, entry 308

Camargue, famous for horses, bulls and flamingos (but mind the mosquitos).

Pretend to live in Paris, the city that has inspired generations of artists, and wonder at the architecture, the nightlife, the bustling brasseries, the impatient waiters... the parks, the markets, the metro and the magasins. During August it's pretty quiet as Parisiens holiday out of town which is nice in some ways but you miss out on the real Paris without its people and its smaller, quirkier shops and cafés. Check out information on free gallery times, or invest in a Paris pass allowing you free entry to the major art galleries and museums; the Louvre alone, magnificent palace of the old Kings of France, will take days if you want to see everything.

I could wax lyrical about the long hot summers of the south; the perfect cycling across Provence; the vineyards for wine tasting – even grape harvesting; the village games of boules. But you get the picture – France is diverse and full of space and not so full of people and cars; a marvellous place for holidays, and a mere hop over, or under, the Channel.

Armed with this book you can stay in a swish apartment in town, a love nest for two that clings to the mountainside, an alpine chalet with walks from the door, an island cottage. There are medieval houses that combine crumbling elegance with cutting edge design, grand châteaux in rolling parklands for vast family get-togethers, simple beach houses for the sportifs. Some of these places do meals too, in case you feel lazy and want to be cosseted and cooked for. There are gardens to wander, swimming pools to slip into – some solar-heated, some saltwater – markets to buy your supper in and oodles of corners to explore.

Once you have chosen the perfect bolthole for you, you have two choices. You can go and stay, not join in or even try to be French. You can shop in anonymous supermarkets and buy the same plastic-wrapped meat and vegetables that you can in Britain. You can ignore the locals, the music festivals, the markets, the shops, the friendly people who are so proud of their region and who understand its culture. Or you can open your mind and engage! Talk to the people around you, even if you have to use an embarrassing old school dictionary to do so. You will be given information that could transform your holiday: the weekly markets are often a joy, filled with unpasteurised cheeses and charcuterie, just-picked herbs, *champignons* and vegetables, cordials, ciders and wines and other *specialités de la region* you simply won't find anywhere else

If you go to France, make the most of France. Celebrate it. And wherever you choose to stay, I hope you enjoy being there as much as we have enjoyed discovering these Special Places.

Nicola Crosse

It's simple. There are no rules, no boxes to tick. We choose places that we like and are fiercely subjective in our choices. We also recognise that one person's idea of special is not necessarily someone else's so there is a huge variety of places, and prices, in the book. Those who are familiar with our Special Places series know that we look for comfort, originality, authenticity, and reject the insincere, the anonymous and the banal.

Inspections

We visit every place in the guide to get a feel for how the place ticks. We don't take a clipboard and we don't have a list of what is acceptable and what is not. Instead, we chat with the owner or manager and then look carefully, sensitively round the house. It's all very informal, but it gives us an excellent idea of who would enjoy staying there. Once in the book, properties are re-inspected every four years or so to keep things fresh and accurate.

Feedback

In between inspections we rely on feedback from our army of readers, as well as from staff members who are encouraged to visit properties across the series. This feedback is invaluable to us and we always follow up on comments.

Do let us know how you get on in these houses, and get in touch if you stumble across others that deserve to be in our guide. Use the forms on our website at www.sawdays.co.uk, or later in this book (page 375). Any poor reports are followed up with the owners in question, while praise is always a pleasure to pass on.

Subscriptions

Owners pay to appear in this guide. Their fee goes towards the costs of inspections, of producing an all-colour book and of maintaining our website. We only include places and owners that we find positively special. It is not possible for anyone to buy their way into our guides.

Disclaimer

We make no claims to pure objectivity in choosing our Special Places. They are here because we like them. Our opinions and tastes are ours alone and this book is a statement of them; we hope you will share them. We have done our utmost to get our facts right but apologise unreservedly for any mistakes that may have crept in.

You should know that we don't check such things as fire alarms, swimming pool security or any other regulation with which owners of properties receiving paying guests should comply. This is the responsibility of the owners.

Photo right: Chalet la Forêt, entry 264

Finding the right place for you

All these places are special in one way or another. All have been visited and then written about honestly so that you can take what you like and leave the rest. Those of you who swear by Sawday's books trust our write-ups precisely because we don't have a blanket standard; we include places simply because we like them. But we all have different priorities, so do read the descriptions carefully and pick out the places where you will be comfortable. If something is particularly important to you then do check when you book: a simple question or two can avoid misunderstandings.

Maps

Each property is flagged with its entry number on the maps at the front. These maps are a great starting point for planning your trip, but please don't use them as anything other than a general guide – use a decent road map for real navigation. Most places will send you

detailed instructions once you have booked your stay.

Ethical Collection

We're always keen to draw attention to owners who are striving to have a positive impact on the world, so you'll notice that some entries are flagged as being part of our 'Ethical Collection'. These places are working hard to reduce their environmental footprint, making significant contributions to their local community, or are passionate about serving local or organic food. Owners have had to fill in a very detailed questionnaire before becoming part of this Collection – read more on page 370. This doesn't mean that other places in the guide are not taking similar initiatives – many are – but we may not yet know about them.

Symbols

Below each entry in the book you will see some little black symbols, which are explained in a short table at the very back of the book. They are based on the information given to us by the owners. However, things do change, so please use the symbols as a guide rather than an absolute statement of fact and double-check anything that is important to you.

Children – The symbol tells you that children of all ages are welcome. If there's no symbol, it may mean there is an unfenced pool, a large boisterous dog, fine things, steep stairs or that the

Photo left: Maison des Cerises, entry 252
Photo right: La Peyre - Maison Bleue, entry 215

owners are aiming to offer a child-free break. If you are convinced that your impeccably behaved five-year-old can cope, the owner may allow you to bring her – but at your own risk.

Pets – Our 🐕 symbol tells you which houses generally welcome them but you must check whether this includes beasts the size and type of yours, whether the owner has one too (will they be compatible?) and whether you can bring it into the house or leave it in an outhouse. Your hosts will expect animals to be well-behaved and obviously you will be responsible for them at all times.

Quick reference indices

At the back of the book (pp. 376, 377) you will find a number of quick-reference indices showing those places that offer a particular service. Scan these pages if you are looking for places that offer short breaks, have swimming pools or are suitable for wheelchair users.

Photo: L'Auzonnet, entry 248

Facilities

If it is important to you that your holiday home has a microwave, dishwasher, TV, CD-player, barbecue or central heating in winter, check with the owners first. Most properties will have a washing machine or shared laundry; we try to mention where they don't, but again, double-check. Electric kettles are still a rarity in French-owned homes so if you can't manage without bring your own. You may also want to consider bringing a portable fan as they can be a godsend in high summer. If you have your own electrical appliances bring an adaptor plug, as virtually all sockets are for two-pin plugs that run on 220/240 AC voltage.

Prices

Prices are in euros and/or sterling, according to the wishes of the owner.

All prices are per property per week, unless we say otherwise. We give a range from the cheapest, low-season price to the highest, high-season price. Check with the owner and confirm in writing the price for the number in your party. Remember that in ski resorts, high season is February. Prices are for 2010 and may go up in 2011 so please check with the owner or on their website if they have one. A few properties offer a reduction if you stay for more than a week but don't expect any deals during peak season. Some places require you to stay a fortnight during these months.

The taxe de séjour is a small tax that local councils can levy on all visitors paying for accommodation. Some councils do, some don't: you may find your bill increased by a euro or two per person per day.

What's included?

Utilities – In most cases this covers electricity, gas and water. In some cases, the electricity meter will be read at the start and end of your stay and you will have to pay separately. In other cases, it will just be heating that's extra.

Linen – Where linen is not included, we say so alongside the price. You may need to bring your own or the owners may offer a hire service. Even where linen is included, towels often aren't, so check when booking.

Cleaning – Some owners charge for the cost of cleaning and you will have to pay this whether or not you are willing to clean the place yourself. At other places you can either clean up yourself or pay someone else to do it. In some cases the cleaning cost is deducted from the security deposit.

How to book

Our first advice is to book early and to check the owner's website to see if their place is available for your chosen dates. Once you have agreed on dates, the owner will normally send you a booking form or contrat de location (tenancy contract) which must be filled in and returned with the deposit and commits both sides. The owner will then send a written confirmation and invoice, which constitutes the formal acceptance of the booking. Contracts with British owners are normally governed by British law. Remember that France is one hour ahead of the UK and Ireland and people can be upset by enquiries coming through late in their evening.

One or two places in the guide can only be booked through the local Gîtes de France booking service but as most transactions are done by email nowadays the language problem, here or with non-English-speaking owners, should not arise.

Deposits

Owners usually ask for a non-refundable deposit to secure a booking. It makes sense to take out a travel insurance policy with a clause to enable you to recover a deposit if you are forced to cancel. Your policy should also cover you for personal belongings and public liability and, possibly, for taking part in adventurous sports. Many owners charge a refundable security/damage deposit, payable either in advance or on arrival.

Payment

The balance of the rent, and usually the security deposit, is normally payable at least eight weeks before the start of the holiday. (If you book within eight weeks of the holiday, you'll be required to make full payment when you book.) A few owners take credit cards, otherwise you will need to send a euro cheque, or a sterling cheque if the owner has a British bank account.

Closed

When given in months this means the whole of the months stated. So, 'Closed: November–March' means closed from 1 November to 31 March.

Photo left: Mas de la Boissière, entry 297
Photo right: Flop House Palace, entry 284

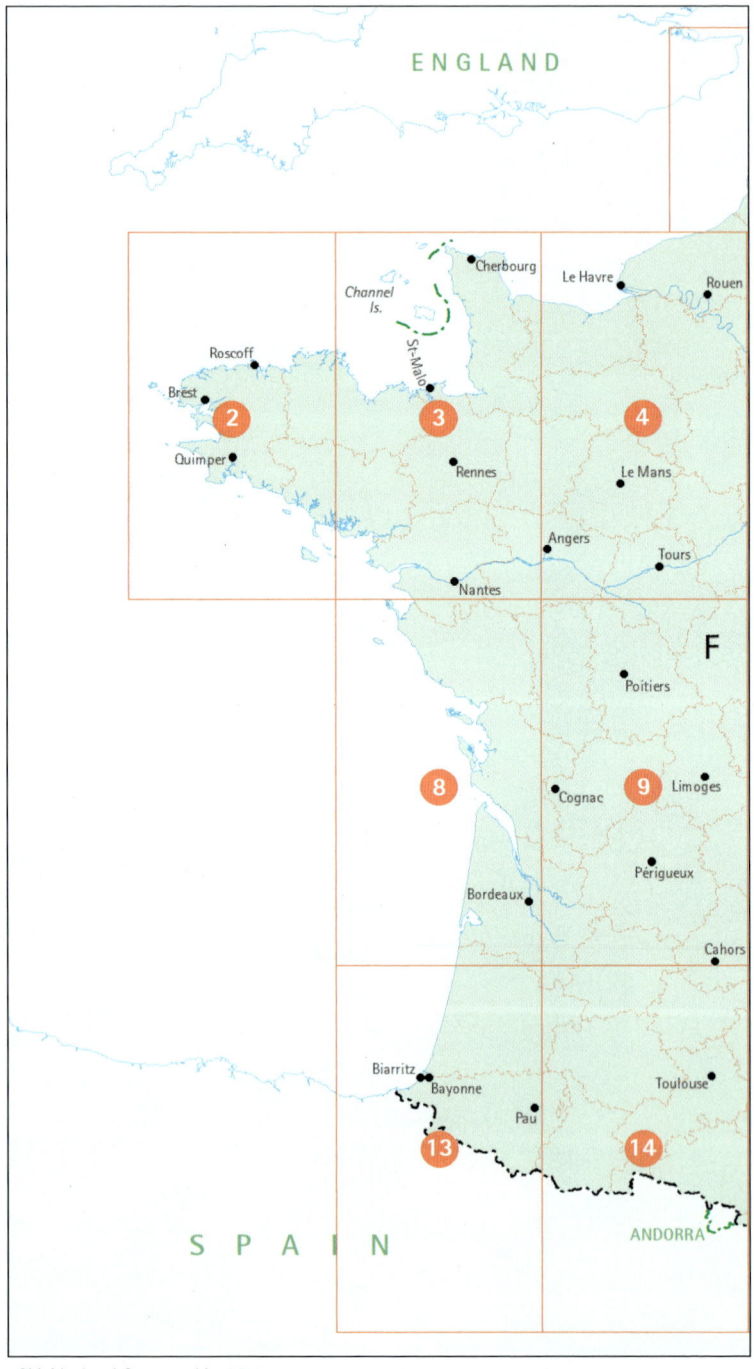

Medical & emergency procedures

If you are a European citizen, it's a good idea to have a European Health Insurance Card with you in case you need any medical treatment. It may not cover all the costs so you may want to take out private insurance as well.

To contact the emergency services dial 112: this is an EU-wide number and you can be confident that the person who answers the phone will speak English as well as French, and can connect you to the police, ambulance and fire/rescue services.

Other insurance

If you are driving, it is probably wise to insure the contents of your car.

Roads & driving

Current speed limits are: motorways 130 kph (80 mph), RN national trunk roads 110 kph (68 mph), other open roads 90 kph (56 mph), in towns 50 kph (30 mph). The road police are very active and can demand on-the-spot payment of fines.

Directions in towns

The French drive towards a destination and use road numbers far less than we do. Thus, to find your way à la française, know the general direction you want to go, ie the towns your route goes through, and when you see *Autres Directions* or *Toutes Directions* in a town, forget road numbers, just continue towards the place name you're heading for or through.

Photo: istock.com

Map 1

23

©Maidenhead Cartographic, 2010

Map 3

25

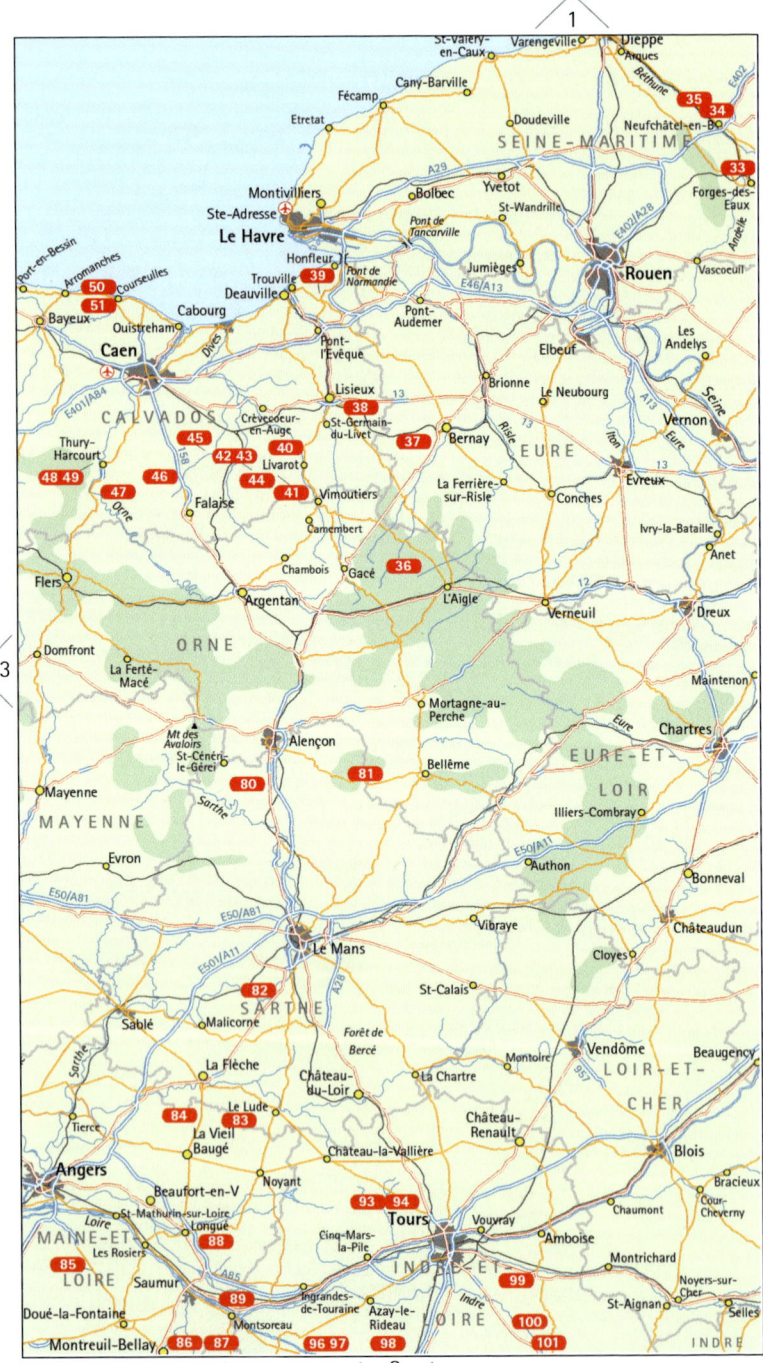

Map 5

27

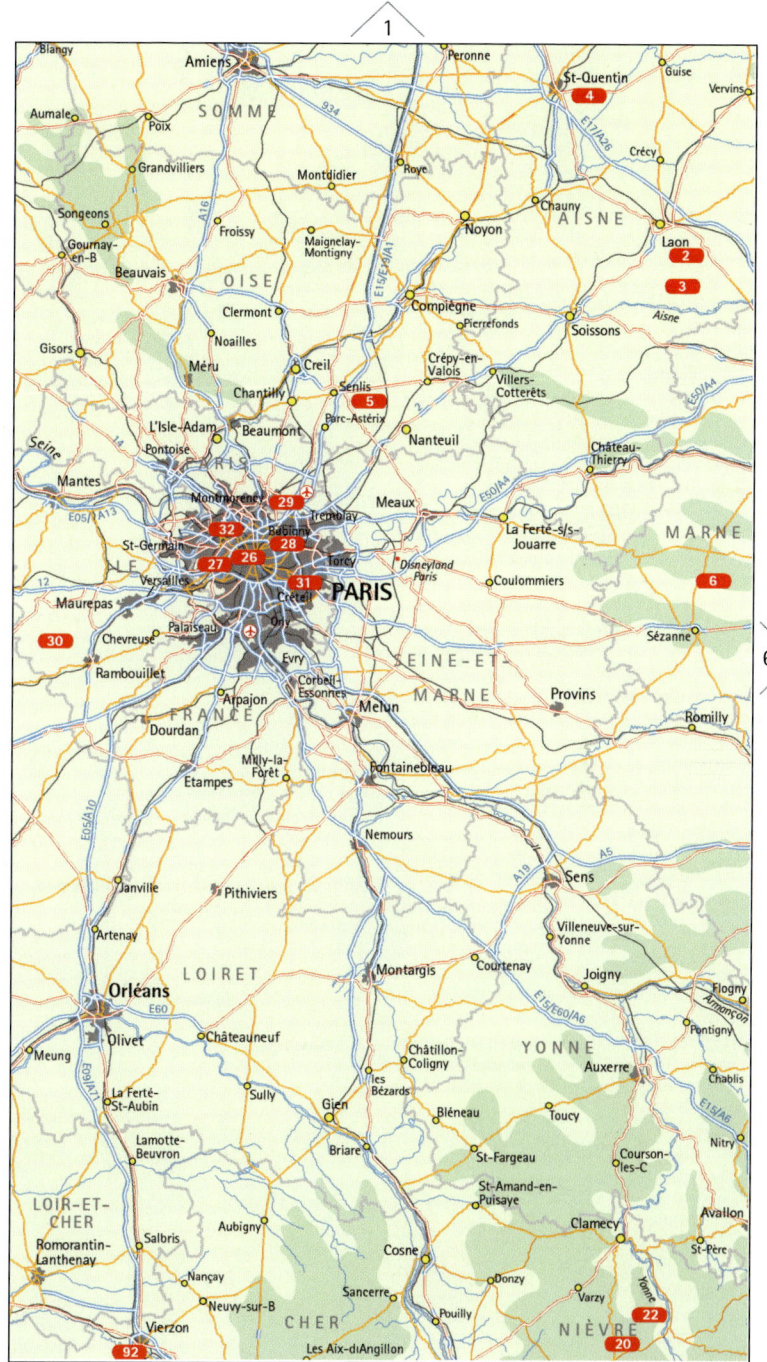

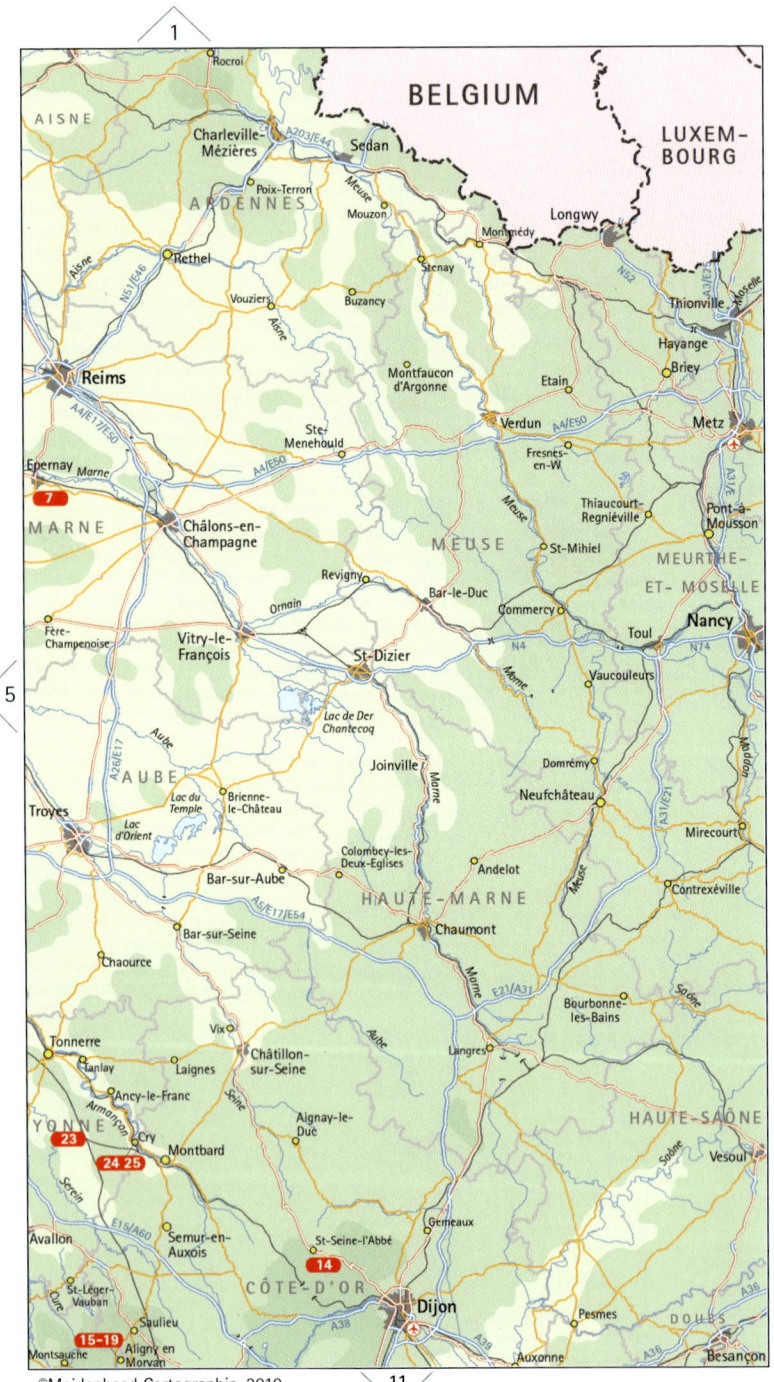

Map 7

29

©Maidenhead Cartographic, 2010

Map 9

31

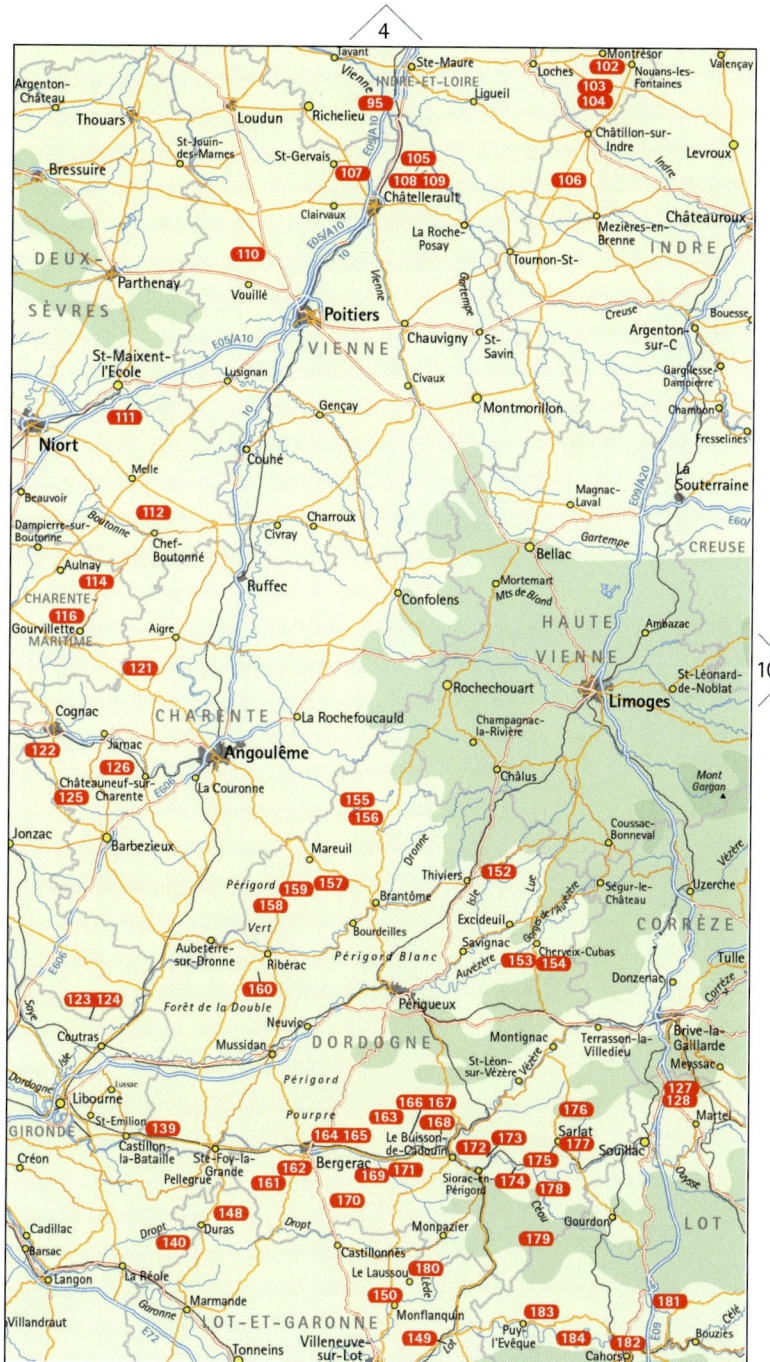

Map 11

33

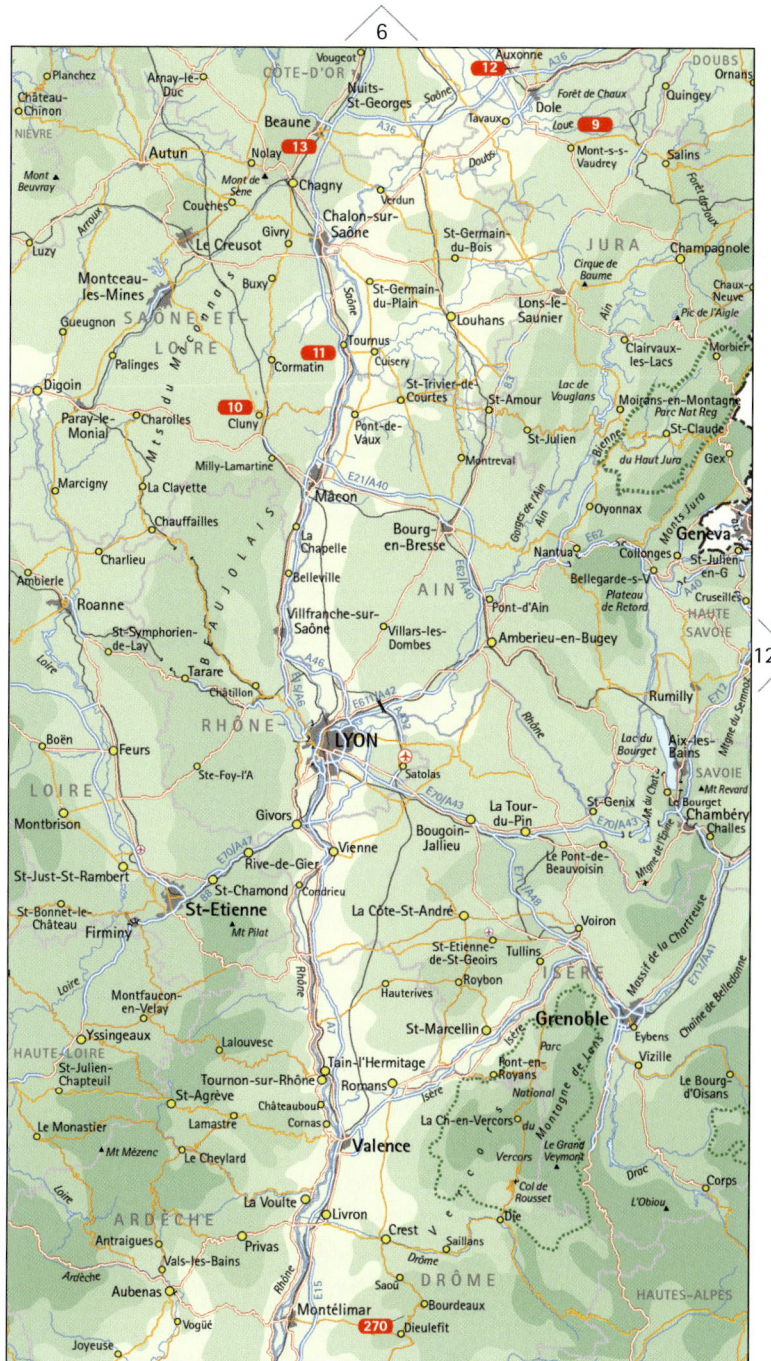

7

SWITZERLAND

Ornans
Mouthier   Morteau
DOUBS
Doubs   Montbénoit
Pontarlier
Cluse de
Joux
Les Hôpitaux-Neufs
Mont d'Or
Chaux-
Neuve

Lausanne

Lac Léman (Lake Geneva)
Evian
Thonon
Sciez   **260**
Abondance

Genèva

Mt Salève   Les Gets
Bonneville   **261 262**
Cluses   **263**

HAUTE
SAVOIE   Argentière
Chamonix
Sallanches   Servoz   **266**   **265**
Chaîne des Aravis   **264**   Chamonix-Mont-Blanc
Annecy   Thônes   Le Fayet   **267**
Sevrier   Combloux   Mont Blanc
Lac   Megève   Massif du Mont Blanc
d'Annecy   Flumet   Les
St-
Jorioz   Ugine   Contamines

11

Albertville   Conflans   Roignais
Bourg-St-Maurice

SAVOIE   Mt Pourri
Aiguebelle   Aime   Val d'Isère
Moûtiers
268   Grande
Casse   Bonneval
Parc National
de la Vanoise
269   Massif de la Vanoise   Bessans
Gorges Rousses   St-Jean-de-Maurienne   Lanslebourg
La Chambre   Arc
Avrieux
Modane
Valloire

ITALY

La Grave
ISÈRE   **277**   Le Monetier
La Meije
Chantemerle   **279**   Montgenèvre
Massif des Ecrins   Mt Pelvoux   **278**
276   Briançon
Parc National
Abriès
des Ecrins
Parc Nat Reg
Château-Queyras
du Queyras
Vieux
Chaillol   Guillestre
HAUTES-ALPES
Vars   Les Claux
Embrun
Gap   Barrage de
Serre-Ponçon

Map 13

35

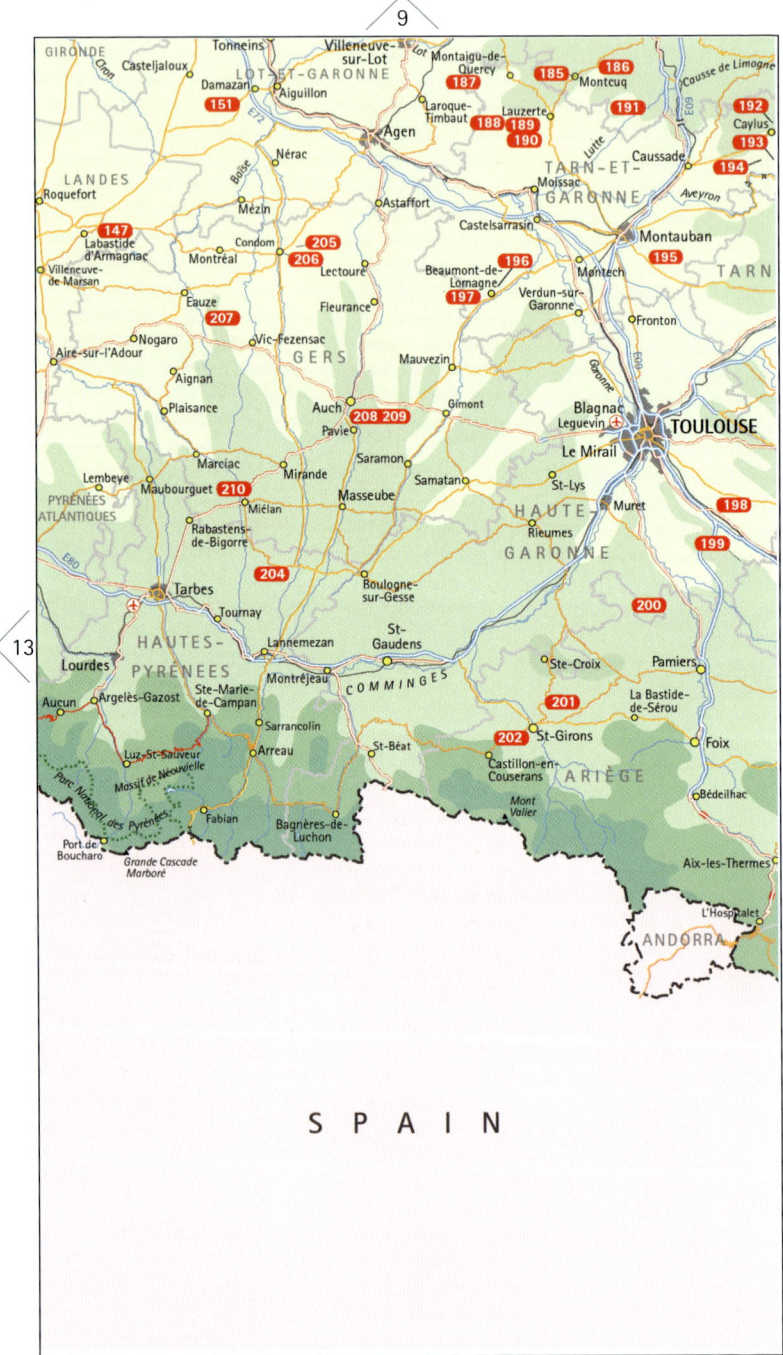

Map 15

37

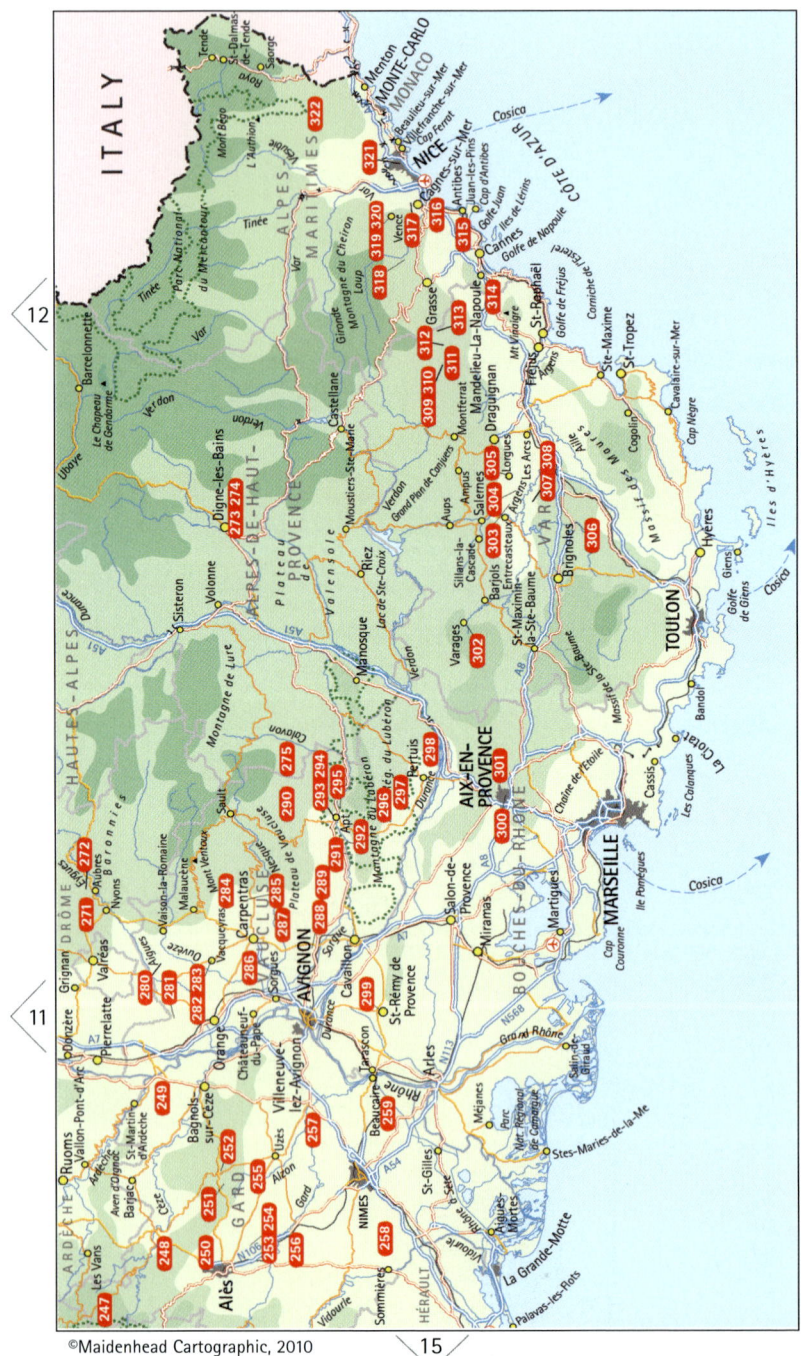

The North • The East • Burgundy • Paris – Île de France

La Maison au Ruisseau & La Grange

A treat to stay in these houses, so perfectly appointed and tickety-boo. The owners live in the charming old Picardian farmhouse, the creamy low-slung gîtes stand on either side, and a big immaculate square of grass lies in between, planted with shrubs and a lavender trim. A tennis court and a lattice-fenced, lounger-lined pool fill the area next to the larger of the gîtes, the Maison au Ruisseau, and all is as quiet as can be. No need to worry about the weather, both houses are airy, comfortable and cosy inside: you could happily hole up all week here. Downstairs spaces are open plan, furnished with new sofas and wood-burning stoves, fine fitted kitchens and every useful thing, from tennis rackets to tumble dryers. Pretty bedrooms are under the eaves; logs are on the house; heating is generously included. La Maison has a patio terrace furnished with green plastic table and chairs; both houses have barbecues and share the use of the lawned courtyard and pool. You are in a pretty little village – the neighbours' roofs can just be seen – while lovely walled medieval Montreuil is a 15-minute drive.

Price	£1,500–£1,600 each per week.
Sleeps	14.
Rooms	Maison for 8: 2 doubles, 2 twins; 2 bathrooms. Grange for 6 + 2 children: 2 doubles, 1 twin; 1 shower room, separate wc.
Meals	Restaurants 15-minute drive.
Closed	Never.

Tina Beattie
Sempy, Pas-de-Calais

Mobile	+44 (0)7866 362597
Email	thehouseinruralfrance@googlemail.com
Web	www.thehouseinruralfrance.com

Le Clos

At the end of the château-like farmhouse, itself part of an 18th-century farming estate, is this big, inviting, light-filled ground-floor gîte for two. The owners, wonderfully down-to-earth retired farmers whose family have been here for 300 years, occupy most of the house with their B&B guests. The living room is full depth, its kitchen neatly set within a breakfast bar surround, its furniture generous and fittingly old-fashioned: golden velveteen sofa and chairs, sturdy antique sideboard, a good sofabed. Red and white stripes hang at high windows and there's a fine stone fireplace for logs in winter. In summer, doors open to the scent of grass and trees coming over your own gravel entrance terrace. The powder-blue bedroom is traditional and cosy with views to church tower and apple orchard, new quilts and mattresses, a clean and simple shower room. Roam where you will, over the green pastures or to the pretty lake across the lane – take picnic and rod. There's a good little restaurant in the village and more in history-rich Laon. An authentic slice of old France. *Sawday B&B.*

Price	€350 per week. €150 per weekend.
Sleeps	2.
Rooms	1 twin, double sofabed; 1 shower room.
Meals	Meals on request. Restaurant 500m.
Closed	Mid-December to March.

Michel & Monique Simonnot
Chérêt, Aisne

Tel	+33 (0)3 23 24 80 64
Email	leclos.cheret@club-internet.fr
Web	www.lecloscheret.com

Moussy - Gîte de Verneuil

Deep in the country, surrounded by copses and fields, Verneuil is a peaceful, isolated little farmhouse. After the devastation of the First World War, when all that remained of the village were the wash house and church, this farm was the only one to be rebuilt. So you gaze on grazing cattle and rolling acres of peas, sunflowers, barley and wheat. In the walled garden are swings, a barbecue, tables and chairs under the weeping willow; in the outbuildings, the farm equipment. Your house is bigger than it looks and, with immaculate white-walled rooms and just the right amount of furniture, the whole place has a new and spotless feel. One end of the living room has pretty, original tiling and rustic dining table; the other, dark polished boards, an inviting sofa and wicker chairs. Black and white floor tiles gleam on the hall floor and the square, airy kitchen is designed for whatever you need on holiday. Upstairs are simple, pleasant bedrooms and a plain bathroom. There's a Sunday morning market nearby, many war museums, monuments and cemeteries to visit, and some fabulous walks.

Price	€180–€415 per week. Linen not included.
Sleeps	6.
Rooms	1 double, 2 twins; 1 bathroom, separate wc.
Meals	Restaurant 3km.
Closed	Never.

Bruno & Blandine Cailliez
Vendresse Beaulne, Aisne

Tel	+33 (0)3 23 24 41 44
Mobile	+33 (0)6 87 45 59 72
Email	blandine.cailliez@wanadoo.fr
Web	www.gitedeverneuil.fr.st

Château de Lucy

In champagne country, an 18th-century château with 19th-century extensions; your gîte is in the oldest part, which explains its fine well-proportioned windows and the handsome oak staircase in the hall. Requisitioned by Crown Prince Wilhelm and occupied by the Germans during both world wars, the château is now being revived by the English owners. You are surrounded by dense woodland and on the banks of the trout-rich river L'Oise — go fish for your supper! (Failing that there's a twice-weekly market in historic Saint Quentin.) Bedrooms are decorated in traditional French style, with polished pitch-pine boards, patterned wallpapers, good antique beds and pretty little chandeliers. The large bathroom has a claw-foot tub and hydrotherapy shower. In the light-filled living room are two black leather sofas, a dining table on which sits a generous hamper, a simple kitchen in a corner. Four pine steps lead up to a super-size terrace, your own private sunspot with a barbecue, chairs, tables and loungers. Fancy a meal out? There's a restaurant you can walk to, in little Ribemont.

Price	€450–€845 per week.
Sleeps	5.
Rooms	Wing: 2 doubles, 1 single; 1 bathroom, 1 shower room.
Meals	Picnic with wine €10 p.p. Restaurants 1.5km.
Closed	Rarely.

Amanda & Martin Stormont
Lucy, Aisne

Tel	+33 (0)3 23 04 02 98
Email	info@chateaudelucy.com
Web	www.chateaudelucy.com

Picardy

Les Petits Ponts

In a spectacularly peaceful walled village, a solemn time warp, here is a good spot if you want it all: you can spend half your days lazing in the forest in unpolluted rural peace, then rally the fleshpots of Paris and quench your raging thirst for fashion and urban culture for the other half. Oozing French charm, the terraced cottages are the well-converted outbuildings of a fine manor house (its splendid park hides behind: book some fishing and you'll walk through it). Guests have the use of a highly decorative, formal rose garden just heaving with roses – a place of peace, poetry & contemplation – and the yard in front with its towering lime tree. Each cottage has a newly built modern kitchen and sizeable bathroom, two good plainly-furnished bedrooms with brand new bedding, an antique chair or wardrobe, and wonderful old floors of flags or terracotta tiles (rugs on top for cosiness). One sitting room leads to the rose garden, a definite privilege. Forests, castles and the lovely River Oise, old villages, châteaux, including Chantilly and its horse museum, oodles of history and Paris just an hour away.

Price	€400-€700 per week. Short breaks available.
Sleeps	8.
Rooms	Each of 2 cottages: 1 double, 1 twin; 1 bathroom.
Meals	Auberge in village; restaurants 10km.
Closed	Never.

Mireille & Marc Doucède
Fontaine Chaâlis, Oise

Tel	+33 (0)3 44 54 08 17
Mobile	+33 (0)6 72 84 56 55
Email	mireilledoucede@yahoo.fr

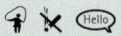

Auprès de l'Église

New Zealanders Michael and Glenis first discovered Auprès de l'Église ten years ago. Now they own it, share it with guests, do excellent table d'hôtes. Thanks to a previous artist owner, the 19th-century house has a very special atmosphere, is full of surprises – some walls are unadorned but for the mason's scribbles! – and has been gorgeously restored. The two upstairs bedrooms and bathroom are separated by a fabulous wall of bookcases and an attic stair, the ground floor has a French country feel and harmonious colours. Kitchen, dining and living rooms merge peacefully into one airy space that overlooks the courtyard and Oyes church. Sit out here in the sun and sip the wonderful local champagne as you watch the barbecue smoulder. Quirky brocante abounds yet the comforts are resolutely modern. Two more rooms and a shower lead off the hall, with crisp white cotton and huge beds. Charming Sézanne is a 20-minute drive and the marshlands (now drained but an unhappy surprise for the soldiers of the First World War) are a birdwatchers' paradise. *B&B also.*

Price	€1,000–€1,500 per week. Short breaks available.
Sleeps	8.
Rooms	2 doubles, 1 twin/double, 1 twin; 1 bathroom, 1 shower room.
Meals	Dinner, with champagne aperitif, €25–€30. On request.
Closed	Rarely.

Glenis Foster
Oyes, Marne

Tel	+44 (0)7808 905233
Email	enquiries@aupresdeleglise.com
Web	www.aupresdeleglise.com

Gîte de Cramant

A simple little cottage in a village in Champagne. It is distinctly homely, a little like a doll's house, one you can live in very comfortably. The Charbonniers, who do B&B on the spot, are a truly delightful couple and work hard to keep everyone happy (book yourself in for breakfast: it's a feast!). Cosy bedrooms are upstairs and share a neat little bathroom; the striped double has slanting ceilings and a couple of beams, the twin has small beds dressed in toile de Jouy duvets, perfect for children. Downstairs, an open-plan kitchen/living room with a tiled floor and neatly beamed ceiling – simply decorated, typically French. There's a round dining table, a fireplace (for decoration only) and lots of pretty china. Outside, a postage-stamp lawn is flanked charmingly on one side by an old stone wall up which creepers climb; iron-and-wood chairs, café table and barbecue invite meals outside. For restaurants and market you need to travel to Épernay (five kilometres). Sample the champagnes; if you overdo it, head for Reims and its cathedral to beg forgiveness. *Sawday B&B. Babysitting available.*

Price	€300 per week.
Sleeps	4.
Rooms	1 double, 1 twin, sofabed; 1 bathroom.
Meals	Meals on request.
Closed	Rarely.

Sylvie & Éric Charbonnier
Cramant, Marne

Tel	+33 (0)3 26 57 95 34
Email	eric-sylvie@wanadoo.fr
Web	www.ericsylvie.com

Les Hirondelles

Swallows and redstarts nest in the eaves, deer populate the forests, breathtaking views stretch across the valley to the Black Forest beyond. Your whitewashed gîte – a former barn – is plainly furnished, spotless and peaceful and clad inside with pine. Floors are carpeted upstairs and wooden down, the kitchen sits in a corner, the bedrooms are under the eaves, and central heating guarantees warmth in the cold months. In summer, walk into the mountains from the front door, in winter don your skis… the non-sporty may follow the Route du Vin and discover the area's wines. The front-line trenches from the First World War are a ten-minute drive away; some of the fiercest fighting took place here and you can see bullet holes in the main house where the English owner lives. In summer, the locals compete for the best scarecrow and you'll see them in all shapes and sizes in the local villages. Orbey, just up the road, has all you need, even a cinema. Try Munster cheese – one of France's most pungent – from the farm shop opposite, and don't miss the stunning medieval walled village of Riquewihr.

Price	€480 per week.
Sleeps	5.
Rooms	1 twin, 1 family room for 3; 1 shower. Extra folding beds.
Closed	Never.

John Kennedy
Orbey, Haut-Rhin

Tel   +33 (0)3 89 71 34 96
Email jhken1@aol.com

Franche Comté

Château d'Ounans

A generous, handsome and child-friendly place for tribal or work events in an unspoilt part of France. The huge kitchen alone deserves the 'château' label, its original flagstones carrying the latest equipment, its timber table perfect for casual breakfast or children's supper before the hovering fireplace. Or be elegant in the dining room through the arch. In the vast hall great ceilings and double staircase convey an immediate sense of place yet it's a family-kind grandeur. High gates close to keep children safe in the magnificent park, there's a big outdoor table for soft summer days, a grand piano and books in the salon, a separate library/telly room, bedrooms with space and pastel comfort but no overweening luxury, properly modernised bathrooms. The area is laden with history, fine buildings, pastoral landscapes for long walks — and few people. From the highest ridge, you can spy Lake Geneva. The river Loue, fresh and clear, is ideal for kayaking, fishing and swimming; Arbois produces a famous yellow wine; Arc et Senans houses the Royal Saltworks. *Shared pool. Skiing apartment available in Valmorel.*

Price	€1,000-€3,300 per week.
Sleeps	14.
Rooms	3 doubles, 1 twin, 1 triple, 1 room with bunks, 1 single; 2 bathrooms, 2 shower rooms.
Meals	Restaurant 3km.
Closed	Rarely.

Isabelle Chavelet Lasaygues
Ounans, Jura

Tel	+33 (0)3 84 37 09 00
Email	isabellechavelet@hotmail.com
Web	www.val-perriere.com

Le Nid - Rouge-Gorge, Le Pinson, La Chouette, L'Hirondelle

An artist-owner in a dreamy place, an 18th-century Burgundian house divided neatly into three apartments plus the former stables. There is an understated elegance here, as if everything has been designed but quietly so, mixing old stone floors, limestone walls, high beamed ceilings, colour in small doses – a crisp sense of light and space. In the largest living room, cream sofas, blue armchairs, books, candles and a big fireplace. Apartments have kitchens or kitchenettes; Rouge-Gorge's kitchen has a table and chairs to serve a multitude, and every modern thing. A broad stone staircase leads from here to a hallway and delightful bedrooms. Good art hangs on the walls – sketches, prints, watercolours – while Karen's sculpture is dotted about the grounds. The pool, its loungers and its relaxing lawn bathe in sunlight. Beyond, fields and woodland stretch across the hills. This part of France has been compared to Tuscany, only it's less busy, and your hosts, who do B&B in the house next door, will cheerfully help you discover the region. *B&B also. Shared pool. Creative groups welcome.*

Price	RG €735–€875. LP €525–€675. LC €425–€550. LH €495–€645. Main house (RG, LP & LC) €1,575–€2,025. Prices per week. Towels not included.
Sleeps	15.
Rooms	RG: 2 doubles; 1 bath, 1 shower. LP: 1 twin, 2 sofabeds; 1 shower. LC: 1 double, 1 sofabed; 1 shower. LH: 2 doubles, 1 single, 1 twin on mezzanine; 2 shower rooms.
Meals	Restaurant 4km.
Closed	Rarely.

Marc & Karen Keiser
Château, Saône-et-Loire

Tel	+33 (0)3 85 59 18 02
Email	info@lenid-france.com
Web	www.lenid-france.com

Burgundy

Château de Messey

Set in a magical hide-and-seek paradise of 90 hectares, Messey is the most welcoming, youthful, family-friendly place you could hope for. Against a backdrop of 16th-century château, buttercup meadows, duck ponds and working vines, the beautifully rustic vine workers' cottages stand round a grassed courtyard, leafy with weeping willow and wall-creeping shrubs. The stream that runs past has formed a lake on its way through: the play potential is endless. Each cottage has its own entrance leading to simple, country-pretty interiors. There are beams and space, exposed old stones, comfy wicker sofas and the occasional working fireplace. You will feel private inside and community-spirited outside, though you also have your own bit of garden or courtyard. Young Delphine and Markus live with their three children in one of the cottages and manage it all with charming efficiency. They can organise visits to the château's vineyard and wine cellars, of course; the rest of Burgundy is just beyond the gate. A deeply welcoming if sometimes busy place. *Sawday B&B. Unfenced water.*

Price	€370–€740 per week.
Sleeps	12.
Rooms	3 cottages for 2-6.
Meals	Dinner €30. Wine €7-€10. Restaurant 2km.
Closed	Rarely.

Delphine & Markus Schaefer
Ozenay, Saône-et-Loire

Tel	+33 (0)3 85 51 16 11
Email	info@messey.fr
Web	www.messey.fr

Château de Flammerans

'Glamorous' and 'gîte' co-exist here: in the grounds of a Burgundian château is an old farm building whose plain stone face conceals a houseful of riches. Enter a large, airy hall with a living room to the left, a kitchen straight ahead, a bedroom to the right and a staircase to the first floor. The subtleties of stone grey, sand beige and oak buff speak out across these simply elegant rooms, with patches of pure white in contrast and muslin flowing at every window. Bedrooms have irresistible stitched quilts on mosquito-net draped beds, handsome fauteuils on limed and planked floors. Bathrooms are fabulous, with their distressed marble from Provence, and bathrobes white and fluffy. Catherine is the lady of the house and mother of a young family, Guy is passionate about cooking and gives lessons in the château kitchen. The gîte garden area is open-plan, the swimming pool and orangery (with chic lounge/bar) are shared with the B&B guests, & the farm outbuildings are in the process of being restored. There are walks in the forest & charming shops in Auxonne. *Sawday hotel. Spa with hammam, power plate & Finnish sauna.*

Price	€1,650–€2,050 per week.
Sleeps	9.
Rooms	1 double, 1 triple, 1 quadruple; 3 bathrooms. Extra beds.
Meals	Dinner €45. Restaurants 6km.
Closed	Rarely.

Guy & Catherine Barrier
Flammerans, Côte-d'Or

Tel	+33 (0)3 80 27 05 70
Email	info@chateaudeflammerans.com
Web	www.chateaudeflammerans.com

Burgundy

Hameau de Blagny

In a hamlet of three houses, the 18th-century cottage with vines creeping up to its borders has privileged views: to one side, the grands crus vineyards of Meursault, to the other, those of Puligny Montrachet. You could not be more steeped in Burgundy. As quaint as the cottage appears on the outside, it is stunningly luxurious within. The limestone-tiled ground floor includes one bedroom en suite, a black and steel state-of-the-art kitchen, a living room with an open fire (plus charcoal sofas, round dining table, logs on the house) and doors to a small garden, terrace and pool, illuminated by handsome bronze lamps at night. Upstairs, under sloping overheads, two further rooms lie, each with sweeping vineyard and woodland views. A bold plum or red wall is offset by pale exposed stone and subtle lighting, superior mattresses top superior beds and showers are totally fabulous; baths for soaks, too. It is super high-spec, and much is included: unlimited electricity, basic dry grocery, maid service three times a week. The owner is a wine merchant and can arrange tastings and visits. Immaculate. *Further gîte for 4.*

Price	€4,000 per week.
Sleeps	6.
Rooms	3 doubles; 3 bathrooms, 3 separate wcs.
Meals	Restaurant 1km.
Closed	Never.

Jean-Christophe & Isabelle Thomas
Puligny Montrachet, Côte-d'Or

Mobile	+33 (0)6 09 30 15 87
Email	contact@hameau-de-blagny.com
Web	www.hameau-de-blagny.com

Gardener's Cottage - Château Les Roches

Next to the fairytale flourish that is the Château Les Roches, the 19th-century gardener's house has changed mightily. Now an un-rustic designer interior, with a couple of antique armoires for Frenchness, lies behind the simple dressed stone and slate, picking up those natural tones to give sober, supremely restful rooms. On the quarry-stone ground floor, the hyper-modern Aga-warm kitchen looks across to the black sofas of the living area. From there, a well-designed wooden staircase carries you down to chic bedrooms, quietly done in grey walls, white beams, subfusc bedcovers, top-quality mattresses and linens, and glowing metro-tiled bathrooms. French doors lead to private pale-gravel terraces. All three rooms have wood-burning stoves for winter cosiness and red curtains for a dash of colour. Do dine one evening with your generous young hosts and their B&B guests, taste their careful wine choices, hear the story of the house; you can book on Thursdays and Saturdays. The fort on the hill is one of the oldest specimens of medieval architecture in monument-rich Burgundy. *Sawday B&B. Children over 10 welcome.*

Price	€950 per week. €200 per day (min. stay 3 days). Includes welcome basket.
Sleeps	4.
Rooms	2 doubles; 2 bathrooms.
Meals	Meals on request. Restaurant 5-minute walk.
Closed	Rarely.

Tobias Yang & Marco Stockmeyer
Mont Saint Jean, Côte-d'Or

Tel	+33 (0)3 80 84 32 71
Email	info@lesroches-burgundy.com
Web	www.lesroches-burgundy.com

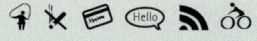

Burgundy

Domaine de La Chaux - Le Château

La Chaux is more village than domaine. Rent a small part of it – or the whole place for an anniversary or wedding. Madame de Chambure lives in the middle of it all, sparkles with energy and exercises a benign rule, delighting in bringing families and friends together. The peace enfolds you and the magnolias and ancient trees of the award-winning *jardin remarquable* are stunning. The Château, an old hunting lodge, is where Madame herself once lived and its vast warren of rooms has barely changed over the years, in spite of the addition of a new kitchen, modern plumbing and some elegant wrought-iron furniture. Two dining rooms, two salons, all with open fires: a warm, ample place for a large party. It has that wonderful French feel, with stippled, faux-marble walls, fine furniture from Louis XV onwards, polished parquet – an old-fashioned elegance touched with eccentricity. Bedrooms, bathrooms and a dressing room share the top two storeys; views swoop over parkland and hills; you have all you could possibly need, a library full of books, TV, table tennis, loungers. Restaurants are five kilometres away.

Price	€2,460 per week.
Sleeps	15.
Rooms	4 doubles, 7 singles; 3 bathrooms, 3 shower rooms, 3 separate wcs.
Meals	Restaurant 5km.
Closed	Never.

Pierre de Chambure
Alligny en Morvan, Nièvre

Tel	+33 (0)3 86 76 18 62
Mobile	+33 (0)6 10 07 10 18
Email	giteslachaux@gmail.com
Web	www.gites-lachaux.fr

Domaine de La Chaux - Moines & Roses

Moines is great fun and its monkish name is reflected in the décor of refreshing, monastic simplicity. Bedrooms on the second floor, in a row of monks' cells, have two wash rooms between them, each graced with three unmonastic designer basins set in granite. Showers are downstairs on the ground floor; the two main bedrooms have wcs and basins en suite. It's a big, delightful space where you could happily retreat for a week with friends. Warm colours, solid beams, terracotta floors, three staircases; you have a library and a living room with antique trestle tables and rush-seated ladderback chairs. A carved statue of the Virgin Mary stands in one corner, two cream-coloured fauteuils pull up by the fire. And what a hearth – it's big enough to fit a small tree and belts out quite a heat on winter days. Across a small meadow is Roses with four bedrooms (two in the attic) and another lovely fireplace. With its trestle table and wood-panelled walls it has a similarly medieval feel but is smaller and suitable for six. The gardens are *remarquables. Shared laundry.*

Price	Moines €1,720. Roses €720. Prices per week.
Sleeps	24.
Rooms	Moines: 3 doubles, 1 twin, 1 single, 1 family room for 3, 1 family room for 6; 2 shower rooms, 3 separate wcs. Roses: 1 double, 1 twin, 2 singles; 1 bathroom, separate wc.
Meals	Restaurant 5km.
Closed	Never.

Pierre de Chambure
Alligny en Morvan, Nièvre

Tel	+33 (0)3 86 76 18 62
Mobile	+33 (0)6 10 07 10 18
Email	giteslachaux@gmail.com
Web	www.gites-lachaux.fr

Domaine de La Chaux - Iris & Clématites

Every house in La Chaux has its own individual touch but there's one feature they all share (Lavande excepted): a huge fireplace stacked with logs. So winter stays are possible as well as summer ones; the wood is provided at extra charge. Ground-floor gîtes Iris and Clématites sit opposite each other, with a good stretch of grass in between — ideal for a family and grandparents on holiday together. Clématites' raised fireplace dominates the main bedroom, giving this pale-walled, red-tiled room an easy feel. The living area is open plan with the kitchen in the corner (with all you need, dishwasher included); the second, bigger bedroom has three beds. Iris, too, is terracotta-tiled, with russet-brown curtains and the odd bit of country furniture. Every house in the domaine has a barbecue and garden furniture, including loungers: summers are long and hot in the Haut Morvan. A visit to the Lac des Settons, the biggest man-made lake in Europe, will cool you down: sail, swim, waterski, windsurf or pedalo. And there's a magnificent *bateau mouche* for the less sporty. *Shared laundry.*

Price	Iris €280. Clématites €570. Prices per week.
Sleeps	6.
Rooms	Iris: double sofabed; 1 shower room, separate wc. Clématites: 2 doubles; 1 bathroom, separate wc.
Meals	Restaurant 5km.
Closed	Never.

Pierre de Chambure
Alligny en Morvan, Nièvre

Tel	+33 (0)3 86 76 18 62
Mobile	+33 (0)6 10 07 10 18
Email	giteslachaux@gmail.com
Web	www.gites-lachaux.fr

Domaine de La Chaux - Chèvrefeuille & Glycines

These two gîtes are a step apart – Chèvrefeuille (Honeysuckle) with its farmhouse feel, and the more modern Glycines (Wisteria), custom-made for wheelchairs: its rooms span the ground floor of the last stone cottage in a row of four. Chèvrefeuille has two storeys and a charming outside stone staircase; floors are new and tiled, furniture a mix of newish and old, and the kitchen is simple. Note, this is an outdoorsy place and the grounds are more beautifully tended than the gîtes. But there's masses to do: table tennis on the estate, trout-fishing in crystal-clear creeks beyond, kayaking on the River Cure. You are right in the middle of the miraculously unspoilt Morvan National Park, distinguished by vast forests of beech and oak, moorland and lakes. Criss-crossed by rapids, the area is a dream for white-water enthusiasts; the walking, too, is exceptional. Take maps, go off the beaten track and look out for red and roe deer, wild boar and badgers, buzzards and woodpeckers. In the gentler, more pastoral northern sector there are carpets of wild flowers in spring. *Shared laundry.*

Price	Chèvrefeuille €720. Glycines €720. Prices per week.
Sleeps	12.
Rooms	Chèvrefeuille: 2 doubles, 1 twin; 1 bathroom. Glycines: 2 doubles, 2 singles; 1 shower room, separate wc.
Meals	Restaurant 5km.
Closed	Never.

	Pierre de Chambure
	Alligny en Morvan, Nièvre
Tel	+33 (0)3 86 76 18 62
Mobile	+33 (0)6 10 07 10 18
Email	giteslachaux@gmail.com
Web	www.gites-lachaux.fr

Burgundy

Domaine de La Chaux - Lavande & Vitis

The latest addition to the Domaine's stable is Lavande. It occupies one end of a long, low, L-shaped building at the far end of which lives Madame, the remarkable owner of La Chaux. The gardens, now listed among Burgundy's finest, are superb (gigantic sequoias, Lebanese cedars, banks of rhododendrons, four lakes) and the population of this rural enclave soars to 67 in summer, including Madame and her son. (He and his wife are new co-managers, brimming with plans.) Enter an open-plan living area, whiter than white, with a charming easy chair-ed mezzanine under super high rafters; step down to fresh bedrooms with vintage terracotta floors. The kitchen is compact; the terrace is charmingly flagged; everything sparkles. With sidelong glances to the château from its safe and secluded garden is Vitis – a dear little cottage. Expect a sitting room, a separate kitchen/diner, stairs down to bedrooms and a door to the garden. The fireplace has a carved pitch-pine surround, black and white tulips dominate a white wall, rush mats soften old terracotta and the kitchen is white and pristine. *Shared laundry.*

Price	€570 each per week.
Sleeps	8.
Rooms	Lavande: 1 double, 1 twin; 1 bathroom, 1 shower room, separate wc.
	Vitis: 1 double, 1 twin; 1 bathroom, separate wc.
Meals	Restaurant 5km.
Closed	Never.

Pierre de Chambure
Alligny en Morvan, Nièvre

Tel	+33 (0)3 86 76 18 62
Mobile	+33 (0)6 10 07 10 18
Email	giteslachaux@gmail.com
Web	www.gites-lachaux.fr

La Villa des Prés

The scent of sweet hay and tack would once have pervaded this old stable block on a lovely estate with breathtaking views; and this nifty, brick-arched building saw life, pre 1910, as a posting stage. Today you shed your boots and bikes in the old stable room, where rich-red Burgundian floor tiles and wonderful old stalls and troughs are still intact, and trot softly up the wooden stair. Once the stable boys' quarters, this apartment has an altogether funkier 1970s feel than the classic décor of the Dutch-owned manor house and B&B next door. A modern kitchen opens into a rattan-chaired eating spot with an open fire place. Lose yourself in the big smart bathroom, soak up the dreamy views from the bed: there's an English garden and sweeping parkland to wander. Until the French Revolution, Benedictine monks would toil and rest in this deeply peaceful place; their centuries-old vegetable garden has been recently restored. Bees still bumble, eggs and fruit wait to be plucked, and the pond bubbles with frogs and fish. Take long lunches and tour Romanesque churches, châteaux, vineyards. *Sawday B&B.*

Price	€415–€475 per week.
Sleeps	2.
Rooms	1 double; 1 bathroom.
Meals	Restaurant 8km.
Closed	Mid-September to mid-April.

Kees & Inge Stapel
St Révérien, Nièvre

Tel	+33 (0)3 86 29 03 81
Mobile	+33 (0)6 51 18 89 67
Email	villa-des-pres@orange.fr
Web	www.villa-des-pres.com

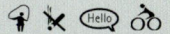

Le Pavillon du Château de Prye

In a magical situation looking over age-old trees to copse-crested hills, and the madly moated neo-Gothic château just visible across the vast estate, this compact, sweet-turreted 18th-century gate house is ideal for those seeking real rural isolation: shops and all things 'civilised' are a fair drive away. Outside, the endless green grounds are yours to roam alongside the fine Charolais herd; inside, the tone is red and white with the odd burst of blue, good furnishings and nice old pieces such as a pair of carved wardrobe doors on a built-in cupboard and the deep-carved Henri IV sideboard that dominates the dining room. There is comfort and personality, wonderful original satin-finished terracotta flooring and decent crockery, a neat black and check sofa before the open hearth. In the bathroom you will find soft white towels, deep blue tiling and a leafy view. The walking is exceptional, the vineyards are not far and country pursuits abound. The open-minded young owners at the château are altogether charming. *Sawday hotel.*

Price	€355–€440 per week.
Sleeps	4.
Rooms	1 double, 1 twin; 2 bathrooms, separate wc.
Closed	Rarely.

Magdalena & Antoine-Emmanuel du Bourg de Bozas
La Fermeté, Nièvre

Tel	+33 (0)3 86 58 42 64
Email	info@chateaudeprye.com
Web	www.chateaudeprye.com

Domaine de Drémont

For nature lovers not city slickers, a beautiful 17th-century Burgundian farmhouse sitting alone in its valley, reached by tree-lined driveways, surrounded by majestic views. Quietly charming young owners, green farmers of sheep and Charolais cattle, live with their children at one end; guests live privately at the other. Downstairs find a neat, slim kitchen, two simple antique-filled bedrooms, and a sitting room with fine oak beams and atmospheric fireplace, velvety sofas and bold-fabric walls – big but deliciously convivial. Up the outdoor stone stairs is a charming, rambling family suite under whose lofty rafters hangs the old two-foot-deep monastic farm bell, now delightfully spotlit. Tapestry-covered armchairs, country armoires, patchwork spreads, cowhides on honeycomb tiles… all is spotless, and steeped in character. The garden has a big grassed, enclosed terrace and a natural spring water feature under which you may bathe, and the owners will happily show you around the farm. Ancient peace, a peerless setting and Vézelay an easy drive.

Price	€980 per week. Short breaks from €140. €20 extra per day in July/August.
Sleeps	9.
Rooms	2 doubles, 1 family suite for 5; 1 bathroom, 2 shower rooms.
Meals	Restaurants 8km–16km.
Closed	Rarely.

Ghislaine Bentley
Anthien, Nièvre

Tel	+33 (0)3 86 22 04 54
Email	mg.bentley@wanadoo.fr
Web	www.dremont.fr

Entry 22 Map 5

Burgundy

Le Cottage

In a pretty and unspoilt old Burgundian hamlet with quaint houses and a small chapel in the centre you are surrounded by flat agricultural plains. You stay tucked away behind a high wall and wooden gates in an independent long, low cottage built of pale field stone. There is a perfect little kitchen, bright white with red wraparound tiles, a swishly decorated living room with a wood-burner, pale fabric sofa and chairs with red and black scatter cushions, and a long dining table with high-backed modern chairs and a beamed ceiling. A back door leads out to the garden with a little pergola-covered terrace. One bedroom is on the ground floor with light colours, seagrass matting and a handsome Asian bedspread. The other two are upstairs with skylight windows and are more or less open-plan to each other – perfect for families. The bathroom is luxurious and brand new with double hand basins and a huge rounded bath tub. Find plenty of advice about street markets, fishing, cycling, vineyards, monuments and medieval villages. Good restaurants abound – or stay at home and fire up the barbie.

Price	€420–€650 per week. €310 per weekend. Linen €14 p.p.
Sleeps	6.
Rooms	1 double, 1 family room for 4; 1 bathroom.
Meals	Restaurant 4km.
Closed	Never.

Corinne Collin
Noyers sur Serein, Yonne

Tel	+33 (0)9 51 90 89 29
Mobile	+33 (0)6 85 84 21 67
Email	corinne.collin@lecottage.fr
Web	www.lecottage.fr

The Gate House

Adorable, white-shuttered, independent and with a secluded feel, the little gate house sits in a walled garden with a gate that leads to a boat and a river — will it be trout for dinner? From the apple-treed and rose-tossed garden you step into the hall, then the large and lovely kitchen and living area. There are simple white walls, rush matting on a flagged floor, four windows full of light, modern furniture, old country pieces, stacks of logs for the wood-burner and, in winter, a just-lit fire. On the same level are the bedrooms: duvets and linen on good new beds, bright wicker furniture, boat prints on fresh white walls, garden flowers. No access to pool or park — just a romantic, cosy and comforting little house on the edge of a honeysuckled village in the heart of Burgundy: one of the best. And you should go on at least one wine tour while you are here and sample some of the area's finest burgundies and chablis; the House Book comes with all the information. *Ask about painting/wine/walking/bridge holidays. Can be let with La Maison du Château.*

Price	£290–£540 per week.
Sleeps	4.
Rooms	1 double, 1 twin/double; 1 bathroom.
Meals	Restaurants 2-minute walk.
Closed	Rarely.

Lady Susanna Lyell
Cry sur Armançon, Yonne

Tel	+44 (0)1582 840635
Mobile	+44 (0)7794 132091
Email	info@lmdc.co.uk
Web	www.lamaisonduchateau.co.uk

La Maison du Château

The charming 18th-century manor house on the edge of the quiet village seduces all who stay. Its English owners fell in love with it and its 24 acres and took on the lot: chestnut avenue, grass tennis court, trout river and all. You could almost spend your entire holiday exploring the grounds; there's even a boat to row to your own small island. Large, luminous rooms have enchanting park or meadow views and captivating art on ochre walls. Floors are oak parquet or pale stone with slate inlay, curtains are linen and white, there's a gracious hall with an elegant staircase, the kitchen has two ovens and enough china for a huge party. A stone fireplace and an antique washstand grace one bathroom, beds are beautifully dressed, sofas are merry with throws. The barn houses two en suite bedrooms, a grand piano, a long period table, colourful rugs on a planked floor: as generously embracing as all the rest – and stone stairs to take you down to the safe, enclosed pool with teak loungers, barbecue and fridge. A brilliant local chef is yours to borrow. *Ask about painting / wine / bridge courses. Can be let with Gate House.*

Price	From £2,400 per week. Price includes cook's services, ingredients extra.
Sleeps	17.
Rooms	6 twins/doubles, 2 doubles, 1 single; 7 bathrooms.
Meals	Full board, including wine, available.
Closed	Rarely.

Lady Susanna Lyell
Cry sur Armançon, Yonne

Tel	+44 (0)1582 840635
Mobile	+44 (0)7794 132091
Email	info@lmdc.co.uk
Web	www.lamaisonduchateau.co.uk

Martinn

A gem of a pied-à-terre, right there in the middle of old Paris. The quiet, neat and secluded cobbled courtyard, hidden behind a huge old heavy wooden coach-entrance door, is your introduction to Martine's ground-floor flat. The door opens straight into the small, uncomplicated and attractive bedroom with its purple tafetta bedcover, set of pretty watercolours and Japanese prints; beyond are the gorgeous bathroom – with full bathtub and fine 'salad-bowl' washbasin – and the living room; all are well-furnished and beautifully decorated. The whole compact place has every modern-living item you could require and the corner kitchen is equipped for real cooking. The neighbourhood teems with restaurants, busy brasseries & pavement cafés, fashionable shops and peaceful semi-pedestrian zones. A snazzy yet intimate and peaceful place to be, in the thick of things and within easy strolling distance of the Pompidou centre, the Louvre, the well-kept secret that is the Palais Royal garden and the whole of the Marais district. And the manager of this hideaway for two is a most charming, helpful woman.

Price	€680 per week.
Sleeps	2.
Rooms	1 double; 1 bathroom.
Meals	Restaurants within walking distance.
Closed	Mid-November to mid-February.

Martine Jablonski-Cahours
Paris

Tel	+33 (0)5 62 96 01 07
Mobile	+33 (0)6 23 55 34 82
Email	info@mart-inn.com
Web	www.key2paris.com

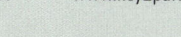

Studio Eiffel

Between the monumental solemnity of the Invalides and the iconic airiness of the Eiffel Tower, set two courtyards back from the road, the unfussy Studio Eiffel is well lit for a first floor with a leafy, birdy tree peering over the neighbour's wall and everything you could need to be properly independent. The living space contains a good red-quilted bed on parquet flooring, a couple of pretty pieces of painted oriental furniture, a writing table, an eating table between the two double windows and, in the foot of the L, a proper fitted kitchen. The cleverly designed little shower room comes complete with pink towels, slippers and shelves for your things and there's a door between the hall and the living room to guarantee total quiet from the staircase. With nothing pretentious or over-studied, it is a neat and ideally central little space for putting your feet up after tramping from 15th-century church to 20th-century pyramid to ephemeral fashion house while, just round the corner, bustling rue Cler provides market stalls, people-watching cafés, laughter and local life. *Also studio flat in Montmartre.*

Price	€750 per week. €119 per day. Minimum 5 days.
Sleeps	2.
Rooms	Twin/double studio; 1 shower room.
Meals	Restaurants nearby.
Closed	Never.

Valérie Zuber
Paris

Mobile	+33 (0)6 30 93 81 35
Email	studiodamelie@wanadoo.fr

L'Appart de la Folie-Méricourt

Pascal and Pascal, who live next door, are the most attentive owners you could hope for and their 'Paris pads' are young at heart and sweetly done with a 1970s feel. The climb up to L'Appart has its rewards. Across the front windows, a fancy wrought-iron balcony offers colourful little garden tables and chairs for you to sit among the flowered window boxes and watch the world go by on the pavement below or the pigeons fly over the rooftops. There's more vibrancy inside: the twin/sitting bedroom (beds or divans) is lime green and pink, the room beyond has a red theme, the decorative touches are ethnic African and most attractive. You will find a mass of high-tech equipment plus DVDs, and a bright, crisp and well-supplied kitchen with your breakfast basics, homemade jams included, ready for you, all in the deal. You are in a good, authentic part of Paris, neither synthetically sophisticated nor grimily down-trodden, with shops, cafés, restaurants and entertainments of all sorts. And lucky to have such nice friendly neighbours: the owners. *Five floors up, no lift. Two other flats available.*

Price	€105 for 2, €125 for 3, €140 for 4. Prices per day, breakfast included. Min. stay 2 nights. Reductions for longer stays.
Sleeps	4.
Rooms	1 double, 1 twin/double; 1 bathroom. Two extra beds.
Meals	Restaurants nearby.
Closed	Never.

Pascal Minault
Paris

Tel	+33 (0)1 77 15 69 54
Email	folie.mericourt@noos.fr
Web	www.appartement-hotes-folie-mericourt.com

8 rue Campagne Première

Behind Montparnasse, beneath the chestnut tree that spreads over the cobbled alley, you will find what looks like a garden shed. Enter: the shed turns into a smart dark grass-papered hall, beyond it a blue-plush, white-walled double-height indoor 'garden' full of happy plants and northern light from the sloping glass roof, and generous living space for two. It is the nicest, most unexpected Parisian hideaway imaginable; totally sheltered from road noise, highly original and delighting in a tiny, pretty kitchen. Up a steep staircase, the bedroom looks into the living room: three cottage windows light its beige, green and brown quietness. The owner's oriental origins show discreetly through in Chinese prints and vases, in her taste for rich dark colours and unobtrusive class. After the bedroom comes the study – big glass writing table, single divan and… deep-freeze; then the laundry – useful washer/dryer – and the splendid black and white bathroom that gives onto a leafy courtyard straight from a provincial backwater. A secret cocoon, restaurants galore, the whole of Paris to hand.

Price	€1,000 per week. €3,000 per month.
Sleeps	2.
Rooms	1 double, sofabed; 1 bathroom, separate wc.
Meals	Restaurant 20m.
Closed	Never.

Alice de Chambure
Paris

Tel	+33 (0)3 86 76 10 10
Email	alicedechambure@orange.fr

Domaine des Basses Masures

There are riding stables nearby so you can saddle up and go deep into Rambouillet forest: it encircles this peaceful hamlet. Madame, who is friendly and informal, takes care of the fine horses that graze in the field behind the house – do introduce yourself. The house is an old stables: long, low and stone-fronted, built in 1725 and covered in Virginia creeper and ancient wisteria. Madame lives in one end and does B&B; the gîte is at the other end. It is a homely little place with a cottagey feel. Whitewashed bedrooms, carpeted, cosy and up under the eaves, have roof windows and the odd rafter, new beds dressed in crisp cotton and fat pillows. In the sitting room downstairs there's a cheerful blue sofa that opens to a bed, a big oriental rug, modern wicker armchairs, an open fireplace and white-painted beams. The back windows look over the surrounding fields. The kitchen, more functional than aesthetic, has a round dining table and is very well equipped; it leads into the garden, with outdoor furniture. Versailles is 20 minutes, Paris 45 and there's excellent walking from the door. *B&B also.*

Price	€750 per week.
Sleeps	5.
Rooms	1 double, 1 triple; 2 bathrooms.
Meals	Restaurants nearby.
Closed	Never.

Madame Walburg de Vernisy
Poigny la Forêt, Yvelines

Tel	+33 (0)1 34 84 73 44
Email	domainebassesmasures@wanadoo.fr
Web	www.domaine-des-basses-masures.com

Entry 30   Map 5

Paris Riverside

Could this be the perfect mix? Your own 'country cottage' for quiet seclusion in a bushy bird-filled garden, the magnificent Marne river flowing broad at the bottom of the road for tree-lined walks and boating, the little town shops five minutes away – and Paris just a short train hop. Behind a typical 1890s country house (an actor, he used to come from his Châtelet theatre on horseback), the converted stablehands' rooms are now two sweet and modest bedrooms in mushroom and white with a superb new shower room, and the 1950s extension is a large friendly living space lit by three good windows, warmed by a generous fireplace and furnished for comfort but no clutter. In quiet, unflashy colours, all the fittings are new, the kitchen has everything, the top-quality convertible sofa is supremely comfortable. Make it your own for a week and you have the best of both worlds, town and country. The young owners, both professional musicians, are most attentive: toys in the cupboard if children are staying, advice, bikes on loan. *German spoken. Station 3-minute walk, Paris 20 minutes by train.*

Price	From €700 per week.
Sleeps	4.
Rooms	1 double, 1 twin, sofabed; 1 shower room, separate wc.
Meals	Restaurant 500m.
Closed	Rarely.

Aurore & Olivier Doise
La Varenne Saint Hilaire,
Val-de-Marne

Tel	+33 (0)1 48 89 34 47
Mobile	+33 (0)6 01 97 13 45
Email	olivier.doise@free.fr
Web	parisriverside.fr

Entry 31   Map 5

Neuilly Studio

Hugging the edge of the city, Neuilly is seen as either an honorary 21st arrondissement or the most urban-chic of suburbs, in the city but not of it. On the ground floor of a large house in a secluded close, your deliciously independent studio has the signal privilege of a cosy, attractive garden. Two walls of sliding window bring the deck and greenery into the square white room. You enter your den via a diminutive kitchenette (fridge, kettle, induction hotplate, microwave). The little shower room, newly done in primrose yellow and grey Moroccan tiles, leads off it and a glazed door opens onto the living space. Here, the bed is a comfortable daytime sofa, there's a big writing table and a director's chair, bookshelves… a cultured atmosphere. The room becomes smaller when you open the sofabed, of course, but it's easy to handle. A journalist and singer of Russian origin, the owner greets you with quiet, relaxed courtesy, observed by her ginger cat and her daughter's puppy. Privacy, peace, easy transport and a high-class residential atmosphere: a special place to stay in Paris. *Ask about B&B.*

Price	€85-€115 per day.
Sleeps	2.
Rooms	Studio room with sofabed; 1 bathroom.
Meals	Restaurants within walking distance.
Closed	Rarely.

Catherine Galitzine
Neuilly sur Seine,
Hauts-de-Seine

Tel	+33 (0)1 47 22 91 14
Mobile	+33 (0)6 13 52 60 37
Email	galitzinecatherine@yahoo.fr

Normandy • Brittany

Le Gaillon

Two hours from Calais, on the crest of a hill in deep countryside, a solid little farmhouse just right for a family or close friends. Red terracotta tiles run throughout the ground floor; there's a sitting room with fine oak ceiling beams, old-fashioned easy chairs, a brick fireplace with logs in winter, piles of DVDs, books and board games. In the dining room, a refectory table for eight, a patterned rug, a huge mirror; in the light, well-equipped kitchen, a table for six and a further fireplace. The master bedroom is also on this floor, with its feather-filled duvet and pretty patchwork quilt, and so is the one large shower room that the household shares. Then up well worn stairs to a long, large, uncluttered sleeping space under the eaves – white, open, airy, all beautiful gnarled timbers and endless views. Stow most of the party up here and they'll be happy. Fencing keeps the frisky cows framed in their buttercup meadow, leaving you the run of the big garden. As dusk falls, you can sit, chat and barbecue as the poplars rustle and the fairylights twinkle like fireflies. Good value, gorgeous views.

Price	€320–€900 per week. Short breaks from €200.
Sleeps	7.
Rooms	2 doubles, 1 triple, sofabed on mezzanine; 1 shower room, separate wc. Cot.
Meals	Restaurants 10-minute drive.
Closed	Rarely.

Mr & Mrs P Slack
Forges les Eaux, Seine-Maritime

Tel	+44 (0)1435 866688
Email	info@legaillon.com
Web	www.legaillon.com

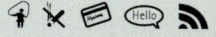

23 Grand Rue - La Grange

A launch pad for touring Normandy's cider, cheese and calvados regions, a pure and simple low-rise gîte that shares the owners' drive. Retired English wine pro Peter and vivacious Madeleine do immaculate B&B in the main house, and are more than happy to provide a pre-booked breakfast or superb table d'hôtes supper should you develop self-catering malaise. Your little cottage has its own tiny patch off the main garden, framed by lime and hazelnut trees behind which lie hills dotted with apple orchards and pastures. Expect a fresh, bright and prettily no-nonsense décor. There's a spotless little bedroom and, by arrangement, a double sofabed in the open-plan living area, alongside a wood-burning stove and a charming, well-equipped eat-in kitchen; the shower room is big enough to fit an armchair (good for the not-so-mobile). The road takes you straight into medieval Mesnières-en-Bray for a peep at a fairy-tale château and you can reach Rouen or Dieppe in 30 minutes. The wonderful Avenue Verte, a 45km-long path and cycle route, lies outside the door. *Sawday B&B.*

Price	From €250 per week.
Sleeps	2.
Rooms	1 twin/double, double sofabed; 1 shower room.
Meals	Dinner €25.
Closed	Rarely.

Peter & Madeleine Mitchell
Mesnières en Bray, Seine-Maritime

Tel	+33 (0)2 32 97 06 31
Email	info@23grandrue.com
Web	www.23grandrue.com

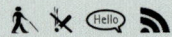

Château Le Bourg

The 1860s petit château has tall windows, a grand position in the middle of a small village and was once owned by the mayor of Dieppe. You get the top floor to yourself and with it the best views – of the village, church and surrounding low hills. The interior comes in comfortable, homely-château style: high slanting ceilings (you are up under the eaves), stylish fabrics, vibrant quilts, polished floorboards. The odd timber runs from floor to ceiling and there are skylights and dormer windows. The master suite is vast, the other rooms smaller, one with a mural, and the beds are the best. A spacious sitting room has sunny yellow walls, comfy sofas and more colour. Leonora, a retired lawyer from Hereford, is a talented cook and you are welcome to join her for sumptuous dinners – *bistrot* or *gastronomique*. Relax in her dining room decorated in the grand style: old oils, period wallpaper, candelabra on a polished table. And there is a garden to share, with barbecue and trees for your children to climb. Beyond, horses graze the meadows and the market town of Neufchâtel is close. *Sawday B&B.*

Price	€500 per week.
Sleeps	6.
Rooms	1 twin/double, 2 twins; 1 bathroom, 1 shower room.
Meals	Dinner, with wine, €20–€40. On request. Restaurants within 9km.
Closed	Never.

Leonora Macleod
Bures en Bray, Seine-Maritime
Tel   +33 (0)2 35 94 09 35
Email leonora.macleod@wanadoo.fr

La Poterie

In the grounds is a dairy where camembert was once made. It evidently did rather well for the owner made enough money to build himself this big, mid-19th-century house. It stands by a quiet road, backing onto open countryside, with an airy and impressive interior. The long, inviting sitting room has windows on three sides and an abundance of books, videos and games; the immense oak table in the green-and-white dining room seats fourteen. Cooking for that number shouldn't be too daunting, given the superbly designed kitchen and a dresser sometimes packed with local organic produce – paté, honey, jam, cider (plus price lists and honesty box). White bedrooms have their original parquet floors, two windows and beds made up with pretty white linen. Sue and Dan have worked hard to make this a great place for families: there's an enticing selection of bicycles and tricycles, doll's prams, garden toys, a paddling pool – even a mini-snooker table. The dairy is being converted into a separate gîte (to serve as a games room) and there's an excellent fishing and swimming lake in the village a short hop away.

Price	£950–£1,600 per week.
Sleeps	14.
Rooms	5 doubles, 2 twins; 1 bathroom, 1 shower room, separate wc.
Meals	Meals on request. Restaurants 2-minute drive.
Closed	Never.

Sue & Dan Gascoyne
Saint Evroult Notre Dame du Bois,
Orne

Tel	+44 (0)1206 790828
Email	info@lapoterie.co.uk
Web	www.lapoterie.co.uk

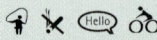

La Baronnière - La Maison Verte

It shares a boundary with The Guest House (see entry 38) yet the two entrances are a kilometre apart. Here you have a typical Norman cottage set in a smallish square garden (not especially flowered but entirely safe for children), far from the madding crowd. The hamlet is surrounded by fields; hedging camouflages you from the property next door. The ground floor is a well-converted, open-plan affair: comfy chairs and sofa with throws and cream cushions, white walls with good and varied pictures, pale beams, terracotta floors, a wood-burning stove and a large dining table; the well-fitted kitchen appears behind five crooked timbers. One newly-decorated large bedroom on this floor has its own french doors to the garden and a downstairs shower that doubles as a laundry room. Upstairs are chocolate beams and bedrooms in the attic – such cosy spaces with hanging rails and an agreeably large bathroom with shells round the bath and a prettily tiled floor. Book in for delicious dinner chez the owners; it's a meadow walk past black-headed sheep to the stream-fed lake and the charming old manor house. *Sawday B&B.*

Price	€600–€850 per week.
Sleeps	6.
Rooms	2 doubles, 1 twin, single on landing; 1 bathroom, 1 shower room, 2 separate wcs.
Meals	Meals on request.
Closed	Rarely.

Christine Gilliatt-Fleury
La Chapelle Hareng, Eure

Tel	+33 (0)2 32 46 41 74
Email	labaronniere@wanadoo.fr
Web	www.labaronniere.com

Normandy

La Baronnière - The Guest House

A 200-year-old barn in the grounds of a manor house; twenty-two rambling acres and a forest to insulate you from the world. The barn once stood elsewhere; the Fleurys dismantled it piece by piece, then reassembled it 20 paces from the lake. It is a stunning timber and brick building, renovated with boundless verve and sublime style. Pristine white walls soak up the Normandy light, exposed beams and sandblasted timbers stand out like ribs. Uncluttered bedrooms have garden views, trim carpets, new wooden beds, maybe a hi-fi; outside are barbecue and terrace. The English owners run painting and cookery courses and you can gorge on a four-course feast at the manor house if you don't wish to cook. They'll do your shopping, too, before you arrive; just ask. Visit Monet's garden at Giverny or the tractor-pulling championships in Bernay in June! Or stay put and watch the geese on the lake. Later you will fall asleep to the sound of water: the stream that feeds the lake tumbles over a sluice gate close by. Too much camembert and calvados is inevitable – why resist? *Sawday B&B.*

Price	€500-€750 for 3 bedrooms; €750-€1,000 for 4 bedrooms. Prices per week.
Sleeps	8.
Rooms	2 doubles, 1 twin; 1 bathroom, 1 shower room, separate wc. Extra en suite double with separate entrance.
Meals	Dinner, 4 courses with wine, €50. On request. Restaurant 5km.
Closed	Never.

Christine Gilliatt-Fleury
Cordebugle, Calvados

Tel	+33 (0)2 32 46 41 74
Email	labaronniere@wanadoo.fr
Web	labaronniere.com

L'Atelier

Through the Norman gateway into the sun-drenched courtyard: Liliane and history embrace you. One of the jewels of ancient Honfleur, the complex was first a convent, then fishermen's cottages, later a *cidrerie*. Now this quarter is a conservation area and all has been properly restored. On one side of the enclosed yard, the side where the apples used to be pressed, Liliane does B&B and above a small art gallery she has created an immaculate gîte. Privately off the street, up a steep narrow stair, is a charming light contemporary space with pure white walls, woodwork painted a soft grey, a sweep of pale parquet. There's an elegant blue sofabed, a suave leather armchair with footstool to match, walk-in cupboards, music, books, games, TV. At the far end, separated by pale grey standing timbers, is a well-kitted-out kitchen; a fig tree taps at the window from the courtyard below. The bathroom is next door; the bedrooms are on the second floor: good curtains, crisp white bedcovers on new wrought-iron beds. Honfleur is at your feet and charming Liliane knows the town intimately. *Sawday B&B.*

Price	€750 per week. €140 per day. Parking €9 per day.
Sleeps	4.
Rooms	1 twin/double, 1 twin, sofabed; 1 bathroom.
Closed	Never.

Mélina & Liliane Giaglis
Honfleur, Calvados

Tel	+33 (0)2 31 89 42 40
Email	coursaintecatherine@orange.fr
Web	www.coursaintecatherine.com

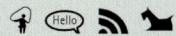

La Boursaie - Le Trou Normand

Even the ducks and chickens live in a half-timbered cottage. No modern building disrupts the black and white beauty of this tranquil farmstead, clustered around a large grassy courtyard, sitting in a fold between rolling hills. Waiting for you is a basket of cheese, home-produced cider, bread, jam, fruit and eggs in this tiny private cottage for two where once calvados was distilled. Set into the hillside with views that sail over orchards of apple, cherry and pear: find cream walls, tiled floors, a fire in winter and blue toile de Jouy on the sofa downstairs; steep stairs lead up to low cruck beams and minute windows in the bedroom. There's archery, table tennis and a huge lawn for kids, a sandpit and play area for tinies; and you can enjoy your own well-furnished piece of garden. Tour du Pays d'Auge footpath runs almost from the door; there's riding on the beach at Deauville – a half-hour drive – and Camembert is not far either. The cheese's creator, Marie Harel, whose promotion campaign included sending free samples to Napoleon, is commemorated in the next-door village of Vimoutiers. *B&B also.*

Price	€390–€560 per week.
Sleeps	2.
Rooms	1 double; 1 shower room.
Meals	Meals on request. Restaurant 1.5km.
Closed	January.

Anja & Peter Davies
Livarot, Calvados

Tel	+33 (0)2 31 63 14 20
Email	laboursaie@wanadoo.fr
Web	www.laboursaie.com

Les Petits Matins Bleus & Les Pommiers

Les Petits Matin Bleus was once a distillery, where apples became calvados in an alembic on the fire. Now, this romantic little red-and-black brick cottage has French windows leading to a neat, paved terrace and your own garden complete with pergola, climbing roses, vines and a long gentle view south to the bucolic Auge countryside. The living room is homely and uncluttered with cane chairs and a sofa, French books and DVDs, and bedrooms have a feel of genuine country France with painted beams, pictures and the odd bit of antique furniture. Large family parties can spill over into Les Pommiers, or couples can rent it for a weekend with breakfast included; the ground floor apartments can join up. Studios are comfortable and compact, each with a well-stocked kitchenette with breakfast bar and stools, fitted carpets, pretty lamps, TV and patio or balcony. Anne's welcome includes organic cider, fresh flowers and a breakfast basket with homemade jam and brioche. She pays special attention to elderly guests and provides everything for the very young. Treat yourself to a grand day out at the seaside. *Themed weekends.*

Price	€800 per week. €400 per weekend, including breakfast.
Sleeps	13.
Rooms	Les Petits Matins Bleus: 1 double, 1 triple; 1 shower room. Two cots. Les Pommiers: 4 studios for 2; each with bathroom.
Meals	Dinner, with wine, from €20. On request.
Closed	Never.

Anne Bourbeau
Sainte Marguerite de Viette, Calvados

Mobile	+33 (0)6 09 94 28 78
Email	maisondhotesnormandie@gmail.com
Web	www.petitsmatinsbleus.com

La Ferme de l'Oudon - Les Tulipes

The Vesques' farmhouse has a dovecote and is partly 15th-century. Although the days of farming have long gone, clucking hens survive, as do the ducks who sail upon their pond with highfaluting grace. Monsieur and Madame are the nicest people, keep horses, do B&B in the main house, cook brilliantly and provide picnic baskets on request. Madame is learning English with the local Chamber of Commerce, Monsieur runs an interior design company, and his work is on view in the old dairy to stunning effect. Les Tulipes is a charming, sunny, two-floor conversion that has been carried out with imagination and a consummate eye for detail. Enter to find an open-plan living area where contemporary furniture, warm fabrics and a luxurious tomato-red kitchen are off-set by ancient timbers, mellow tiles and creamy exposed stone. One bedroom is up, one down, there are terraces for summer, a wood-burner for winter, a bathroom with beautiful multi-coloured tiles, an enclosed garden with table tennis and barbecue, an indoor pool, a potager to pluck from and bicycles to rent. *Superbe! Sawday B&B.*

Price	€790–€990 per week. €500 per weekend in low season.
Sleeps	4.
Rooms	1 double, 1 family room for 3, 1 single on mezzanine; 2 bathrooms.
Meals	Dinner €39, on request. Restaurant 2km.
Closed	3-23 January.

Patrick & Dany Vesque
Berville l'Oudon, Calvados

Tel	+33 (0)2 31 20 77 96
Mobile	+33 (0)6 11 72 91 59
Email	contact@fermedeloudon.com
Web	www.fermedeloudon.com

La Ferme de l'Oudon - Le Pressoir

Another enchanting farm building at L'Oudon, another fine restoration. This was the old cider press, its ground floor now a vast, light living space, comfortable and contemporary. You find big leather sofas, beautiful floor-to-ceiling curtains and an ultra-chic wood-burning stove. A gorgeous kitchen/diner leads to a private garden; there's a big, bold, sunny bedroom and the paved and furnished terrace is as inviting as all the rest. Walls are white plaster or light-gold stone, floors are pale-tiled, there are old beams and joists and new windows to pull in the light. Ascend the staircase with tiled treads to a mezzanine with sofa and two skylit bedrooms under the eaves, one large, both delightful. Bathrooms shine. The charming Vesques give you cider, homemade jam and farm eggs on arrival, and everything is included in the price, from linen to logs. Twice a week there's table d'hôtes – a chance to meet the B&B and other guests over a civilised meal. The orchards, rich pastures and half-timbered manor houses of the Pays d'Auge are yours to discover. *Sawday B&B. Indoor pool.*

Price	€990-€1,290 per week. €580 per weekend in low season.
Sleeps	8.
Rooms	2 doubles, 1 twin, 2 single beds in alcoves; 2 bathrooms.
Meals	Dinner €39, on request. Restaurant 2km.
Closed	3-23 January.

Patrick & Dany Vesque
Berville l'Oudon, Calvados

Tel	+33 (0)2 31 20 77 96
Mobile	+33 (0)6 11 72 91 59
Email	contact@fermedeloudon.com
Web	www.fermedeloudon.com

La Ferme de l'Oudon - Le Lavoir

The latest of Patrick and Dany's sparkling ventures is a restored wash house – a delicious bolthole for two. Its veranda laps at the edge of a lively pond where nature frolics and recycled water babbles: a delight to ear and eye. Trot down the new brick path and through the fenced garden to find an unexpectedly lofty, light-drenched room with a clean sweep of stone floor. A weaving hangs above a pale stone fireplace, a *chaise-hamac* is suspended from a beam, there are cream curtains at sliding glass doors, bright red towels in a chic shower, a kitchen that is a joy to use and a metal spiral stair winding up to a bed that tucks itself – and you – under the eaves. You get your own decked veranda with a Japanese feel, and seven hectares of fields, gardens, ponds, potager, horses and hens to share with the others. There is also table d'hôtes – delicious, twice-weekly, huge fun. Under construction are a large eco pond so you can swim with the frogs (purification ingeniously taken care of, thanks to special plants) and a hammam, indoor pool and fitness centre. Amazing! *Sawday B&B.*

Price	€590–€790 per week. €150 per day.
Sleeps	2.
Rooms	1 double; 1 shower room.
Meals	Dinner €39, on request. Restaurant 2km.
Closed	January.

Patrick & Dany Vesque
Berville l'Oudon, Calvados

Tel	+33 (0)2 31 20 77 96
Mobile	+33 (0)6 11 72 91 59
Email	contact@fermedeloudon.com
Web	www.fermedeloudon.com

Coeur de Combray

This lovely 18th-century mini-manor in Normandy's bucolic Calvados region once served a camembert fromagerie. They don't make cheese here now, but Stuart, Emma and teenage son Lexus have created a restful and beautifully equipped retreat overlooking the rushing river Laizon. There are five gîtes here, from the multi-family-scale Cider Press to cosy, couple-friendly Canon. All have lustrous wooden floors, traditional French furniture, deeply comfortable bedrooms and spanking new kitchens. Eco-friendly air-source heat pumps fuel underfloor heating; bins for compost and recycling let you do your bit. Each property has its own garden thanks to RHS-trained Stuart; even with a full complement of 35 guests, it never feels crowded. Over a stone bridge you'll find a swimming pool with sunbeds and a tree-fringed lake where guests can swim, row or fish for carp, tench and trout. If you're keen to mingle, the friendly Gordons organise go-karting, boules and barbecues on summer Thursdays. If self-catering feels too arduous, Emma will cook for you, using home-grown and local organic produce. *Laundry on site.*

Price	€250–€1,180 per week. Short breaks available. Towels not included.
Sleeps	35.
Rooms	5 gîtes: 1 for 12, 1 for 8, 1 for 5-7, 2 for 2-4.
Meals	Restaurant 6km.
Closed	Never.

Stuart & Emma Gordon
Ernes, Calvados

Tel	+33 (0)2 31 20 67 19
Email	stuart@holidaysincombray.com
Web	www.holidaysincombray.com/

Manoir de Laize - Le Pressoir & La Grange

Apples used to be pressed for cider and calvados in the medieval *pressoir*. Across the lawns, pretty with blossoming apple trees in the spring, is the farmhouse where the owners live; Madame is more than happy to provide an evening meal from local and seasonal produce. Inside the Pressoir, much country charm: ceiling beams, tiled floors, soft colours, antiques and plenty of space. The lovely light living area is open plan, with a well equipped kitchen in the corner; French windows lead down a step to a walled suntrap patio with barbecue. Upstairs: new beds dressed in crisp white linen, a bathroom filled with soft towels. Books, toys, games – and central heating for winter cosiness. More open-plan living in the adjoining La Grange, with its lime-washed stone walls, new carpeting and harmonious colours. The whole place is brilliant for families: a superb games/art room with easels at the ready, a fenced pool, a stream to dam. Soak up the setting, paint a picture, stock up at the weekly market, cycle or canoe down the gorge, pick wild flowers in spring and your own salads from the potager. *Babysitting available.*

Price	€500–€1,200 per week.
Sleeps	13.
Rooms	Pressoir: 2 twins, 1 family room for 3; 1 bathroom. Grange: 1 double, 2 twins; 1 bathroom, 1 shower room.
Meals	Meals on request. Restaurant 5km.
Closed	Never.

Claude & Jean-Michel Guyon Despagne
Fontaine le Pin, Calvados

Tel	+33 (0)2 31 20 87 35
Email	manoir.de.laize@gmail.com
Web	www.manoirdelaize.com

Le Cottage

An unusual, taller than wide 1920s granite house on the edge of a small and pretty village through which the river Orne flows; the locals think it is haunted! This is a real home from home, filled with books, pictures and fine china. You have the run of the house: a large kitchen diner with a good round table leads to a conservatory and then the garden. The long sitting room is opposite with its Art Deco fireplaces – one at each end, but only one working – another big, polished table, squashy sofas and plenty of books. A handsome pitch pine staircase with rich red painted walls takes you to bedrooms – all leading off a central corridor of polished floorboards dotted with fine oriental runners. First floor rooms have marble fireplaces, rough plaster walls and good antique furniture, mostly 19th-century. Walls are covered with a pleasing mix of pastels, water colours and collected prints. Both bathrooms are a good size; one has a lovely view to the garden behind. There are plenty of places to eat traditional French food, the brave can try canyon-style rocky cliff climbing, and the hiking trails are marvellous.

Price	£750 per week.
Sleeps	10.
Rooms	2 doubles, 2 twins/doubles, 1 twin; 1 bathroom, 1 shower room.
Meals	Restaurants within walking distance. Table d'hôtes on request.
Closed	Rarely.

Elizabeth & Andrew Bamford
Clécy, Calvados

Tel	+33 (0)2 31 68 19 08
Mobile	+33 (0)6 15 07 05 39
Email	info@clecycottage.com
Web	www.clecycottage.com

Château La Cour - Le Jardin

Up a stone staircase, through a small door and into an unexpected world of grand windows, oak-panelled doors and elegant rooms. Lesley and David, who have wisely chosen to settle in France, are the friendly lord and lady of this 13th-century château in deep countryside, with views stretching over the Suisse Normande. Your apartment, a private and discreet three-room suite, is light, spacious and gracious – from the parquet corridor with floor-to-ceiling windows to the oak-panelled doors and the richly coloured curtains falling in folds to the floor. If you think the bedroom is swish – king-size bed, stacks of cushions – just wait until you see the bathroom; gleaming white with brushed chrome, its roll top bath has space enough to perch a G&T. The living area, a soft, roomy space of sofas, hi-tech lights and natural linen with a dining table by the window to feed your daydreams, has a futuristic corner kitchen, a showpiece of stainless steel and gadgets. Flowers, welcome groceries, binoculars for birds, hosts who love to spoil… Sawday *grand cru*. *B&B also*.

Price	€750 per week.
Sleeps	2.
Rooms	1 double; 1 bathroom.
Meals	Restaurants within walking distance.
Closed	Rarely.

David & Lesley Craven
Culey le Patry, Calvados

Tel	+33 (0)2 31 79 19 37
Email	info@chateaulacour.com
Web	www.chateaulacour.com

Le Moulin du Pont

Nothing but the sound of rushing water and rustling trees. Despite its mature gardens and its graceful good looks, this luxurious house was built in the 1970s on the site of a mill. Everything is designed to capitalise on the setting. Water flows under the house (it's on stilts), a rose-clad Monet-style bridge crosses the mill race, gardens stretch along the river bank, windows drink in the views. Bedrooms reflect the hand of a deluxe designer: French sleigh bed and slipper bath in one; sophisticated aubergine and cream colours with an alcove bath in another. The star has French windows to the garden and a super-duper bathroom. The open-plan living room wants for nothing – fireplace (logs provided), comfy sofas, elegant dining table, soft lamps, soft rugs and a fleet of windows leading to a marble terrace: perfect for suppers overlooking the floodlit garden. Cooking is no hardship in a kitchen where only the best will do. Everything is to hand, from binoculars for birdwatching to tumble-dryer to stocked larder. The charms of the Normandy coast are near, if you can tear yourself away from sybaritic indulgence. *B&B also.*

Price	£1,000–£1,600 per week.
Sleeps	6.
Rooms	3 doubles; 3 bathrooms.
Meals	Restaurants within walking distance.
Closed	Rarely.

David & Lesley Craven
Culey le Patry, Calvados

Tel	+33 (0)2 31 79 19 37
Email	info@chateaulacour.com
Web	www.chateaulacour.com

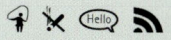

2 impasse de l'Horizon - Three Apartments

This is a striking, brand new building in an ultra-modern design, white-painted outside with black-framed enormous picture windows and a glorious position by the sea wall. Arromanches is reached up wide slate steps and has gorgeous views, a white tiled floor, sliding windows and smart bedrooms. Les Pieds dans l'Eau is at ground floor level with a living room looking over sea, beach, harbours and beyond. Le Bord de Mer is excellent for those less mobile; light floods into the super kitchen, and there is an internal patio with glazed sliding doors, a paved floor and flower borders — very private and sheltered from any sea breezes yet with full views to the sea. All the apartments are spotless and with dashes of bright colours showing off white walls. You need only cross the lawn and the (pedestrians only) coast road to reach the sandy beach for very safe bathing. Visit the landing beaches, the lovely watery inland area of the Marais du Bessin; hurl yourselves into a multitude of sporty pursuits or try a trip in a 1940s Jeep. Asnelles is quiet, with a few small shops; not for ravers! *Small cottage also available.*

Price	€420-€840 per week.
	€60-€165 per day.
Sleeps	9.
Rooms	Cottage: 1 family room for 4;
	1 bathroom.
	Apartment 1: 1 family room for 3;
	1 bathroom.
	Apartment 2: 1 double; 1 bathroom.
	Apartment 3: 1 double, 1 twin;
	1 shower room.
Closed	Never.

Isabelle Sileghem
Asnelles, Calvados

Tel	+33 (0)2 31 22 21 73
Email	ranconniere@wanadoo.fr
Web	www.gites-en-normandie.eu

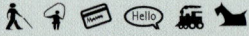

Le Clos St Bernard - Les Camélias & Les Fuchsias

The very first farmhouse built in this Normandy village – well placed for countryside and coast – has been transformed into two neat, spotless gîtes and sits in the walled courtyard opposite the owner's house. Les Camélias has a living/kitchen room on its ground floor with exposed stone and beams, cane armchairs, floral drapes, sofabed and dining table; the equipment in the well-supplied kitchen stretches to a raclette machine and an electric mixer. An open-tread stair leads to carpeted blue and white bedrooms, the double with a fitted pine wardrobe and original stone sink and spout, now a display unit. Visitors can drive in to unload, then park safely outside; gates are securely locked at night. Les Fuchsias, on the first floor, is reached via a stone stair. It has a charmingly beamed kitchen/sitting room with pretty tiles and curtains and a white tiled floor. It, too, is well-equipped: try the fondue set! A corner of the gravelled courtyard has been set aside for both gîtes, each with loungers, parasol, table, chairs and barbecue. *Sawday B&B.*

Price	Camélias €270–€450.
	Fuchsias €250–€400. Prices per week.
	Linen & electricity not included.
Sleeps	6.
Rooms	Camélias: 1 double, 1 twin;
	1 shower room.
	Fuchsias: 1 twin, sofabed; 1 bathroom.
Meals	Restaurants 3km.
Closed	December–January.

Nicole Vandon
Reviers, Calvados

Tel	+33 (0)2 31 37 87 82
Email	leclosbernard@wanadoo.fr
Web	www.leclosbernard.com

Manoir de la Rivière

Isolated at the end of the manor's walled garden, this little gem is the cosiest lovers' retreat. Built into the high walls around the old manor, it was once the watchtower for the fortified farm and was probably also used by customs officers fighting the smuggling along this coast. All you'll spy today are the Leharivels' 80-odd dairy cows mowing the lush pastures of the Cotentin peninsula. Arrive in winter and Isabelle will have lit a fire for you in the wood-burner; come in summer and you have a sun-drenched terrace to lounge on. Pale stone walls and pretty toile de Jouy create a mood of light and calm for the bedroom, with its corner shower cubicle. A steep staircase leads down to the tiny beamed living room: darkly atmospheric, it's just big enough to squeeze in a sofa, a drop-leaf table and a corner kitchenette. The beach is a stroll away; restaurants and shops are a short drive. And you can visit the D-day landing beaches, including Pointe du Hoc on Omaha Beach where you'll still see German bunkers and shell-holes in the cliffs. *Sawday B&B. Second gîte for 4 in manor house.*

Price	€280–€420 per week. Linen hire available.
Sleeps	2.
Rooms	1 double; 1 shower room, separate wc.
Meals	Dinner, with wine, €25. Restaurant 3km. Breakfast on request.
Closed	Never.

Gérard & Isabelle Leharivel
Géfosse Fontenay, Calvados

Tel	+33 (0)2 31 22 64 45
Mobile	+33 (0)6 81 58 25 21
Email	leharivel@wanadoo.fr
Web	www.lemanoirdelariviere.net

Gîte Margency

Set in one of the loveliest parts of the Cherbourg peninsula, four miles from the sea, this atmospheric 19th-century manor is a thoroughly old-fashioned French family retreat. Sturdy and imposing on the outside, with green shutters and doors, inside reveals solid old features, gleaming boards and an unpretentious charm. Big formal bedrooms with handsome furniture may conjure up times past but mattresses and duvets are comfortably 21st-century. You share one modern shower room, spotless with two basins, and get a separate loo on each floor. The living/dining room, heavily beamed, is brightened by yellow walls and curtains, and warmed by a wood-burning stove in its fireplace; a leather sofa and chairs occupy one end, an antique dining table the other. You can also eat in the light, happy kitchen, or knock up a barbecue outside. The huge unmanicured garden is perfect for boisterous games of football, while adjoining outbuildings conceal a garage and ping-pong. The countryside is green and lush, all narrow lanes winding between fields of dairy cows and market gardens. Magnifique!

Price	€270–€700 per week.
Sleeps	8.
Rooms	3 doubles, 1 twin; 1 shower room, 2 separate wcs.
Meals	Restaurant 4km.
Closed	Mid-December to end December.

Christiane & Jacques Allix-Desfauteaux
Tamerville, Manche

Tel	+33 (0)2 33 40 10 62
Email	margency@wanadoo.fr
Web	www.bellauney.com

Normandy

Les Sources

Peaceful narrow lanes between high banks and hedges bring you to Les Sources. Hydrangeas and old-fashioned roses surround the early 19th-century *longère* – restored, traditionally furnished and nicely equipped by Roger and Sandra. They used to own an award-winning hotel and restaurant in Wales so the kitchen brims over with every culinary aid you could want, from Le Creuset pots to seafood pans. Rooms are beamed, spotless and comfortable; in winter, curl up with books, games, puzzles before a crackling fire – logs are provided for the big granite fireplace. Open-tread stairs (with safety gate) lead to three carpeted bedrooms with sloping ceilings, roof windows, coordinated bedding, bedside lamps and pictures. The bathroom is on the ground floor. Such a lovely setting – nearly an acre of lawns, trees and shrubs and a stream to one side. There's a herb garden, too, and an orchard full of rich fruit-bearing trees. All around are fields and the sea is less than two miles, with deserted sandy beaches and a view of Jersey. *Babysitting available.*

Price	£275–£595 per week.
Sleeps	5.
Rooms	2 doubles, 1 single; 1 bathroom, separate wc. Extra single bed.
Meals	Restaurants 4km.
Closed	Never.

Roger & Sandra Bates
Pierreville, Manche

Mobile	+44 (0)844 232 7487
Web	www.ourgites.net

La Ferme des Grèves - Jersey Gîte

Forty minutes from Cherbourg, walking distance from sea and sand, the position is plumb-perfect. Stroll into Barneville for market-fresh lobsters, oysters and mussels; the cheeses will tempt you, a bottle of calvados wouldn't go amiss. Spend a happy afternoon at the beaches, or cycle to the pretty port of Portbail. James and Pascale (he English, she French) have a hotel catering background and a sympathetic eye for restoration. Now they offer one gîte for guests, the neat and dapper Jersey, once part of the stable block across the courtyard from their farmhouse; the original shutters and the handsome brick and grey stone façade remain. Step in to an open-plan ground floor, light and simple with pale tiles, walls of stone or white plaster, a country table and a bright sofabed. The kitchen is modern and well thought-through; the wooden floored bedrooms are pretty with low windows and colourful bedspreads. A slim strip of grass runs the length of the cottage, edged by a low breeze-block wall, with views over flat marshland. The front looks onto the gravelled drive and the houses down the lane.

Price	€300–€610 per week. €50 for 2, €70 for 4 per day in low season.
Sleeps	4.
Rooms	1 double, 1 twin, sofabed; 1 bathroom.
Meals	Restaurant 1km.
Closed	Never.

James & Pascale Boekee
Barneville Carteret, Manche

Tel	+33 (0)2 33 93 16 48
Email	james.boekee@wanadoo.fr
Web	www.ahouseinnormandy.co.uk

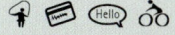

La Merise

Another pretty little cottage with rambling pink roses by the front door. It basks on the sunny side of Mont Castre, an island of stone in a sea of green. You are marvellously quiet and private in a national park: marshland, coastal dunes and woods burst with all sorts of birds; wild flowers flourish. Back at the ranch French Chris and English Suzanne have brought a colourful organic garden to life; you have your own piece of it, with barbecue, for outdoor dining. This tiny gîte, attached to the owners' home, is encased within 300-year-old walls: simple, cosy, good value for two. The front door opens to a sunny kitchen/living room and a dear little mezzanine bedroom, reached via a steepish stair. There are books and bicycles to borrow and old railway lines to cycle along. In summer, grab the boogie boards and head for the beach. You will find a local market for each day of the week, or try the fisherman's cooperatives for oysters, mussels, lobster, crab. Lessay with its abbey is well worth a visit; its September festival has been going for over 900 years – the oldest country fair in Europe.

Price	€260–€340 per week.
Sleeps	2.
Rooms	1 double; 1 shower room.
Meals	Restaurant 5km.
Closed	Never.

Chris & Suzanne Souillac
Gerville la Forêt, Manche
Mobile   +33 (0)6 37 41 30 22
Email   la.merise.et.la.grande.merise@gmail.com

La Germainière

Find bucolic bliss at this grand old farmhouse behind high hedgerows. Past orchards and fields of quiet cows, down a private half-mile drive, the 300-year-old stone façade comes into view. This is a house that feels solid, loved and lived in – three floors of robust stone walls, characterful beams, tiled floors and a huge Normandy fireplace. The big modern kitchen – beech units and all the equipment – leads into a dining room with massive table and dresser. In the warm, beamed lounge, cocoon yourself before the fire on the occasional rainy day in velvet and leather sofas. Bedrooms are big, carpeted, personal: a 1920's poster here, silk flowers there, the odd friendly antique. One twin room is a vision in shocking pink, there are yellows and golds in the master room and calming lavender and blue elsewhere. Outside, a vine-shaded veranda for leisurely meals, lovely views over the tree-fringed valley, glimpses of the fine big swimming pool, a lawn and hidden orchard to keep the children happy. There are five old bikes for free: you can be at the village bistro in five minutes. Peace, comfort and charm.

Price	£750–£2,250 per week. Short breaks available. Linen £18 p.p.
Sleeps	12.
Rooms	2 doubles, 4 twins; 1 bathroom, 2 shower rooms.
Meals	Restaurant 1.5km.
Closed	Never.

Brian & Sue Smart
Guéhébert, Manche

Tel	+44 (0)1747 812019
Mobile	+44 (0)7970 000680
Email	hambye@hartgrovefarm.co.uk
Web	www.normandyfarmhouses.co.uk

Normandy

Le Mesnil Gonfroy

Loads of bedrooms and bathrooms, masses of character and a garden you can lose the kids in. Find honey-coloured heaven in this old Normandy farmhouse with its acre of well-tended, fenced garden, apple orchard and heated pool. The house is almost two in one: one front door, two ground floors – on one side, a pretty room adapted for wheelchair users, nicely private, on the other, kitchen, dining room and sitting room. Bedrooms are upstairs – traditional, friendly, with solid sober furniture and the odd surprise: a massive mirror, a stunning French dresser, a tiny stained-glass window. The largest, with its ancient crossbeam and single beds, was tailor-made for midnight feasts! One bathroom, with 'wooden' boards, has a nautical air. Blue and white tiles brighten the kitchen, deep sofas and Normandy fireplace warm the sitting room, French windows fling open to a south-facing terrace and the breakfast room is charmingly rustic. Amble down to the pool on the lower lawn, with its glorious views of forested hills. Table tennis and boules here, sandy beaches a 20-minute drive. *Logs provided.*

Price	£850–£2,675 per week. Short breaks available. Linen £18 p.p.
Sleeps	14.
Rooms	2 doubles, 3 twins, 1 quadruple; 3 bathrooms, 1 shower room.
Meals	Restaurants 2.5km.
Closed	Never.

Brian & Sue Smart
Hambye, Manche

Tel	+44 (0)1747 812019
Mobile	+44 (0)7970 000680
Email	hambye@hartgrovefarm.co.uk
Web	www.normandyfarmhouses.co.uk

Maison Normande

A perfectly restored little farmhouse, its old stones carefully pointed inside and out, its beams sand-blasted and proud, new honey-coloured timber floors for bedroom warmth and modern fittings where we need them, set among green pastures and hedgerows. The owners, who have done B&B for decades about 15km away, have thought of everything and will be here to settle you in. The wood-burner takes the chill off any damp evening, the contemporary French leather sofa contrasts with the fine oak interior shutters and the country antiques – table and chairs, an old dresser with pretty plates. There's even a high chair in the utility room. The good-sized bedrooms are just as comfortable, each in its own colour scheme of printed cotton quilts, the landing sports large bouquets of colourful artificial flowers to remind us we are in rural France and a small garden is in the making. Mont St Michel and the coast – Cancale for oysters, St Malo for pirates, and fascinating medieval Dinan – are half an hour away, there are many country markets nearby, great walks from the front door. *Sawday B&B.*

Price	€320–€570 per week. Linen not included.
Sleeps	8.
Rooms	1 double, 3 twins; 1 bathroom, 1 shower room, separate wc.
Closed	Never.

François & Catherine Tiffaine
Tirepied, Manche

Tel	+33 (0)2 33 48 31 86
Email	ctiffaine@hotmail.fr
Web	www.tiffaine.com

La Cahudière - Coquelicot & Bleuet

The lane runs out at La Cahudière — into the peace and quiet of rolling folds and deep country. A family venture, this 100-year-old stone farmhouse with hay barn has been converted into two immaculate gîtes. Window boxes brim with colour, butterflies come for the peach trees, you may gather the fruit. There are white walls and new pine, shuttered windows, pastel fabrics and tiled floors. Wood-burners give winter warmth, thick walls keep you cool in summer, pretty bedrooms are spotless and have check curtains, cane furniture, good beds. There are big double rooms for adults and twin and bunk rooms for children. Sit out in front and watch the cattle graze; spot deer in the woods. It's great for families: a new pool with decked area (all yours if you book both gîtes), tennis and fishing nearby, satellite TV and a video/DVD library for cosy nights in. Children have masses of space to run around in safely and there's a private patio for each gîte. The village, a mile away, has good little shops and a restaurant for lunch. Mont St Michel is within striking distance; Cancale, a pretty coastal town, is known for its oysters. *Shared laundry & pool.*

Price	£350-£1,495 per week. See website for details. Linen not included.
Sleeps	19.
Rooms	Coquelicot: 1 double, 1 triple with bunks, sofabed; 1 bathroom. Bleuet: 3 doubles, 2 twins, 1 room with adult bunks, 1 room with children's bunks; 2 bathrooms, 1 shower room.
Meals	Restaurants 1.5km.
Closed	Never.

Margaret Atherton
Saint Martin de Landelles, Manche

Tel	+33 (0)2 33 49 30 45
Mobile	+44 (0)7973 817338
Email	enquiries@lacahudiere.co.uk
Web	www.lacahudiere.co.uk

Les Chouettes, Les Alouettes & Les Hirondelles

To stay or to go? So much to do here, and so much to discover beyond! In rolling fields-and-woodland countryside, these cottages are perfectly placed for families. Breton beaches, adventure park, zoo, aquarium and Mont Saint Michel are all within driving distance; and there are free bikes and walks from the door. In two acres of lawned gardens, with trampoline, swings and slides, football and boules *and* fabulous heated pool, this sprawling row of farm buildings goes right back to the 17th century. Inside you have the best of country cottage living: thick walls, exposed beams, steep wooden stairs (in very old Les Hirondelles), cosy rugs on tiled floors. Bedrooms (upstairs and down) have fresh colours and simple wooden furniture; bathrooms are practical and spacious. A joy are the open-plan living areas where everyone can do their thing — cook, read, play. It's home-from-home comfy with kitchens that are functional and well equipped. Chouettes has a wood-burner; Alouettes an open fire; rustic Hirondelles is the most compact. Susan loves children and is endlessly helpful. Come for a weekend — or longer.

Price	€335–€2,300 per week.
Sleeps	24.
Rooms	Chouettes: 3 doubles, 1 room with bunks, 2 twins; 1 bathroom, 2 shower rooms. Alouettes: 2 doubles, 1 quadruple; 1 bathroom, 1 shower room. Hirondelles: 1 double, 1 room with bunks; 1 shower room.
Meals	Restaurant 4km.
Closed	Never.

Susan Hazelwood
Tremblay, Ille-et-Vilaine

Tel	+33 (0)2 99 97 74 20
Email	susan.hazelwood@gmail.com
Web	www.brittany-cottages.co.uk

Le Bois Coudrais - Bakery, Granary, Mills One & Two

Claire and Philippe manage the impossible: their little hamlet feels miles from anywhere yet there's masses going on. A campsite, pool, play areas, bicycles, café/bar, animals to feed – among private patios and shady trees. Beyond lie woodland walks and countryside. The four gîtes – converted farm outbuildings, three linked, one detached – are prettily grouped near the pool, close enough for the children to make friends but distant enough for privacy. Cosy, characterful and homely, with beams, exposed stonework and granite fireplaces, the open-plan living areas have simple furniture, earthy coloured rugs on tiled floors, companionable wood-burning stoves, and new compact kitchens suitable for holiday meals. Whitewashed walls and pretty fabrics make the most of the small, slopey-ceiling bedrooms. The Yberts are charming, enterprising people and will steer you towards the many historic towns, castles, zoos, aquariums, markets and, of course, Emerald Coast beaches – all within a half-hour drive. This place is about having fun, making friends and relaxing out of doors. *Shared pool.*

Price	€270–€660 (£225–£525 sterling) per week.
Sleeps	17.
Rooms	Bakery, Mill Two & Granary: each 1 double, 1 twin; 1 shower room. Mill One: 1 double, 1 triple; 1 shower room.
Meals	Light meals available in summer.
Closed	Never.

Claire & Philippe Ybert
Cuguen, Ille-et-Vilaine

Tel	+33 (0)2 99 73 27 45
Email	cpybert@orange.fr
Web	www.vacancebretagne.com

Le Bois Glaume

Rustic and romantic, this very pretty late 17th-century limestone château has tall windows and doors, fish-scale slates and a bucolic feel. On a south-facing slope above a beautiful wooded valley, you enter through wrought-iron gates with stout stone pillars and a crumbling pigeonnier; a courtyard is formed by a delightful chapel and a restored stable block. Find plenty of space downstairs, with three salons to choose from, one with walls of books, fine blue and white china and a wonderful, largely Russian, art collection with some modern oils; a grey-panelled room has a table for breakfasts and a marble fireplace. Clean and simple bedrooms vary hugely, from old French iron beds with soft blue and cream furnishings, to a 1930s extravaganza with pink bed covers, busts and pictures, some with places to sit, others smaller. All have lovely views and everywhere there is eclectic artwork. Bathrooms are a bit dated but that is part of the charm, as is Daniel who cooks for you if you want to stay in. A large untamed area of trees and rough pasture has a lake with pottering geese. A place for artists and nature lovers.

Price	B&B €95–€130 for 2. €1,500–€2,000 per week.
Sleeps	11.
Rooms	2 doubles, 1 twin, 2 suites for 2; 4 bathrooms.
Meals	Dinner €25–€35.
Closed	Never.

M & Mme Bertheleme
Poligne, Ille-et-Vilaine

Tel	+33 (0)2 99 43 83 05
Email	lbe@hipra.com
Web	www.e-monsite.com/chateau-du-bois-glaume

Château du Quengo - Le Petit Quengo

This place oozes authenticity — and peace. Four centuries old, the gîte at Quengo takes up two floors of the old coach house and feeds into the stables — now a games room — complete with original wood panelling and wrought-iron hayracks. The upstairs was used for drying hemp... you can still see the holes for the hanging poles in the trusses. Step into an open-plan living space with fantastic beams above and sofas and easy chairs below, an old trunk for a coffee table, a piano to play, horse prints on the walls, small lamps for atmosphere, a cupboard on the landing for books and games. Even the fire is laid ready for you, and the logs are on the house. Up the stairs are patterned duvets on comfy beds and wooden floors warmed by big rugs, masses of storage, big bathrooms and two sloping ceilings. Families will adore the outdoor space and the swings, the friendly Leonberg mountain dog, the organic potager, the restaurant you can walk to and the owners who greet you like long lost friends. A deeply eco-friendly place, and with a lovely garden. *Sawday B&B. Unfenced water. English & German spoken.*

Price	€420-€770 per week. Linen & heating not included. Short breaks available.
Sleeps	11.
Rooms	2 doubles, 1 triple, 1 quadruple; 2 bathrooms.
Meals	Restaurant 1.2km.
Closed	Never

Anne & Alfred du Crest de Lorgerie
Irodouër, Ille-et-Vilaine

Tel	+33 (0)2 99 39 81 47
Email	lequengo@hotmail.com
Web	www.chateauduquengo.com

La Julerie - Four Gîtes

Down a winding country lane, a sunny, tranquil hideaway. Converted from a Breton *longère*, the gîtes are close yet there's a feeling of space. Step outside to your private patio, relax by the pool (a barn conversion with sliding doors), leave the children to play (table tennis, ball games, sandpit, boules and swings). The Normans sourced original materials during the renovation, son Tim did all the conservation work, and the result is a blend of modern comfort and characterful rusticity. Open-plan living areas are cosy with beams, cottagey dressers, flowery sofas – easy spaces where you can chat with the cook or gather round the farmhouse table – La Vieille Ferme seats up to 22! Three have dishwashers, two have wood-burning stoves, bedrooms sport simple cottage or Breton-style furnishings, wooden floors and colourful bedcovers. The luxurious Grenier has a generous bedroom in the loft; Les Écuries is wheelchair friendly; take all four and have a party. Tim and his French-born wife Lydiane are lovely and live here, the owls will hoot you to sleep, the beaches are a 20-minute drive. *Pool unheated New Year to Easter.*

Price	€435–€1,290 per week.
Sleeps	20.
Rooms	VF: 1 double, 1 twin, 1 room with bunks, sofabed; 1 bathroom, 1 shower room. G: 2 doubles, 1 twin & sofabed; 3 bathrooms. LE: 1 double, 1 twin; 1 bathroom, 1 shower room. Extra bed. Étables: 1 double, 1 twin; 1 bathroom, 1 shower room.
Meals	Restaurants within walking distance.
Closed	Never.

Ethical Collection: Environment.
See page 370 for details

Robert Norman
Corseul, Côtes–d'Armor

Tel	+44 (0)1373 471983
Email	robdnorman@hotmail.com
Web	www.lajulerie-gites.com

Manoir de Langourian

If it weren't for the framed wattle-and-daub patch of wall on the stairs you'd never guess this attractive manor house started in the 14th century: such sophistication and elegance, from the modern art collection to the jacuzzi and spa. Madame, a journalist and former Director of the Franz Kafka centre in Prague, offers B&B in the manor itself but the two self-catering homes are set privately in the courtyard, perfect for families. The smaller Ker Oliver has a colourful kitchen and living room alive with huge modern seascapes; upstairs, the children's bedroom comes complete with beach toys, games, paper and crayons. For larger groups choose the newly renovated Relais du Chevalier, which sleeps nine in rustic comfort. Outside, in the lovely garden, children can frolic freely around the delightful wooden playhouse with toys and bikes while adults enjoy an evening aperitif; you can arrange tours and tastings in the little stone wine cellar too. Beyond the estate's open parkland and high walls, Brittany's countryside calls out to walkers and golfers, its unspoilt coastline just three kilometres away. *B&B also.*

Price	Ker Oliver €1,000.
	Relais du Chevalier €2,200.
	Prices per week.
Sleeps	10.
Rooms	Ker Oliver: 1 double, 1 twin;
	2 bathrooms.
	Relais du Chevalier: 3 doubles;
	3 bathrooms.
Meals	Restaurant 1km.
Closed	November–February.

Joël & Marta Davouze
Erquy, Côtes-d'Armor

Tel	+33 (0)2 96 63 61 95
Mobile	+33 (0)6 82 03 71 43
Email	marta.davouze@wanadoo.fr
Web	www.langourian.com

Château de Bonabry

This little gem used to house the archives of the château (built by the Vicomte's ancestors in 1373): the family discovered piles of musty parchment documents when they restored it. With the sea at the end of the drive, your own rose-and shrub-filled walled garden to spill out into in the summer, and two lively, loveable hosts who do B&B in the château, this is a wonderful place for a small family to stay. Downstairs rooms have stone vaulted ceilings, crimson-washed walls and age-old terracotta floors, a new sofa and a striped fauteuil; while the kitchen is fitted and white, with a round table and yellow chairs. Beamy bedrooms are beautiful: in the twin, a stripped floor and pink toile de Jouy; in the double, deep yellow fabric-clad walls — an enthusastic redecoration by the Vicomtesse. If they aren't out hunting, your hosts will be on hand to help, and the Vicomte may well bring offerings from his personal vegetable garden. Your 'English' garden is furnished with parasol, barbecue and wooden loungers. This is a dear little place in which to unwind. *Sawday B&B.*

Price	€400–€900 per week. Linen not included.
Sleeps	4.
Rooms	1 double, 1 twin; 1 shower room.
Closed	Never.

	Vicomtesse du Fou de Kerdaniel Hillion, Côtes-d'Armor
Tel	+33 (0)2 96 32 21 06
Email	bonabry@wanadoo.fr
Web	bonabry.fr.st

Brittany

Manoir de Kervingant

The garden has it all: a fenced pond with a little waterfall, a furnished deck outside the kitchen door, a smaller deck with a swing seat, a big splash pool, a sandy play arena (ex lunging paddock), badminton, barbecue, boules, bouncy lawns and plenty of flowers… It's brilliant for families. The Manoir itself is sturdy, enchanting, built of mellow yellow granite with decorative touches, 600 years old and heavily timbered inside. The English owners, totally unobtrusive but helpful and charming, live in a small wing. You get a huge sitting room on the first floor and a TV room downstairs, a cosy be-rugged dining hall with a refectory table and a tip-top kitchen. Bedrooms are a good size and newly furnished, some up in the eaves (shower in the tower!), the water is piping hot, and bed linen is provided but not towels. Buzzards soar over the forested valleys where no other property can be seen, yet you are a short drive from fishing harbours, farmers' markets and unspoilt sands. You can even walk, past châteaux and pretty villages, to Plestin les Gréves. Wonderful. *Stabling provided.*

Price	€2,000–€2,500 per week. Towels not included.
Sleeps	14.
Rooms	4 doubles, 1 family room, 1 family suite; 6 bathrooms.
Meals	Restaurant 5-minute drive.
Closed	Rarely.

Paul & Winsome Riddle
Tremel, Côtes-d'Armor

Tel	+33 (0)2 96 35 16 22
Email	info@manoirdekervingant.com
Web	www.manoirdekervingant.com

Villa Germiny - 1BR & 2BR Gîtes

On a small side road that winds along the coastline, surrounded by huge old cypresses and pines, the villa faces west overlooking the lovely Sables Blancs beach: just a five-minute walk and perfect at low tide. The garden is more English than French, the climate is warm – roses, lilies and lavender grow in profusion. On the lower ground floor, the gîtes have French doors opening onto private terraces and the ever-changing moods of a vast Breton sea panorama. Walls are freshly painted, the brown leather sofas are comfortable, the tiled floors are great for sandy feet back from the beach. Bedrooms are simple, with pale-painted panelling, no shortage of storage space, firmly comfortable mattresses, lace curtains for privacy. Bathrooms are plain and fresh, good new kitchens have cheerful, pretty china; modern comforts include central heating and WiFi. In the villa above live the owners, friendly, well-travelled and happy to advise you. The charming seaside village rejoices in an excellent brasserie as well as several restaurants, a weekly market and concerts in the local church. *Ask about long winter lets.*

Price	€460–€780 per week.
Sleeps	6.
Rooms	1BR: 1 double, single sofabed; 1 bathroom. 2BR: 1 double, 1 twin, single sofabed; 1 bathroom.
Meals	Restaurant 800m.
Closed	October–April long lets only.

Comte & Comtesse Hubert de Germiny
Locquirec, Finistère

Tel	+33 (0)2 98 67 47 11
Email	villagerminy@hotmail.com
Web	www.villagerminy.com

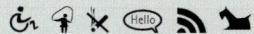

L'Écurie - Manoir de Coat Amour

In twelve lush acres of ancient oak, lime trees, sequoia, maple and orchard, this could be a country estate. But no, Morlaix' bustling port and medieval streets are a five-minute drive, the only clue a distant hum. The former stables of a 19th-century manor, all one level, wheelchair friendly and eminently adaptable for one, two or three bedrooms, promise country-style living; the soft, sober colours, space and light lend a low-key luxury. In the beamed, open-plan living area are oriental rugs on tiled floors, cream leather sofas, antique pine, a polished table, a winter fire. The new, well-fitted kitchen peers over the bar. Airy, sunny bedrooms with pleasing fabrics and big windows onto the grounds underline the reassuring comfort; one room has French doors to a terrace. One of the traditional bathrooms is equipped for disabled guests. Explore the fishing ports, the beaches, the nature reserves, and Brest. Then back off the busy road and up the steep drive to read under a tree, dip in the pool, stroll in a green paradise. *Sawday B&B. Shared pool.*

Price	€700–€1,400 per week.
Sleeps	7.
Rooms	1 double, 1 twin, 1 triple (bunks & single); 1 bathroom, 1 shower room (disabled fittings), separate wc.
Meals	Table d'hôtes, with wine, from €32. On request. Restaurant 1km.
Closed	Rarely.

Stafford & Jenny Taylor
Morlaix, Finistère

Tel	+33 (0)2 98 88 57 02
Email	stafford.taylor@wanadoo.fr
Web	www.gites-morlaix.com

La Maison du Jardinier - Manoir de Coat Amour

The old gardener's cottage was used as a guard post during World War II; aircraft drawings still fly in the bedroom. Your newly renovated, upside-down gîte (salon upstairs, luxurious bedroom down) comes with a modern glass extension and views over 12 acres filled with rare trees. It's a successful blend of old and new – a 'boutique gîte', a doll's house for two, a bit of a gem. Up the steps, enter a small elegant living room with soft green walls and gardener-green checks, a wood-burner for a winter stay, an antique table and a dresser in walnut, a sleek grey-green kitchen with every modern thing. It would be a delight to cook here but there's also table d'hôtes in the main house – the owners are charming – and even a local company to deliver fresh meals to the door. You have your own secluded terrace with barbecue, and landscaped grounds and summer pool to share. There's croquet on the lawn, a decorated chapel for reflection, restaurants, shops and market in beautiful Morlaix (within strolling distance) and beaches and oyster farms a short drive away. *Sawday B&B. Shared pool.*

Price	€425–€765 per week.
Sleeps	2.
Rooms	1 double; 1 shower room.
Meals	Table d'hôtes, with aperitif & wine, from €32. On request. Restaurant 15-minute walk.
Closed	Rarely.

Stafford & Jenny Taylor
Morlaix, Finistère

Tel +33 (0)2 98 88 57 02
Email stafford.taylor@wanadoo.fr
Web www.gites-morlaix.com

Entry 71 Map 2

Ty Bois

Leaving tiny hamlets behind, you're on the track leading down to the river; then a very steep climb up, through a lovely garden lined with agapanthus flowers. The wooden chalet at the summit, modestly fringed by forest trees that conceal a tennis court, sits on the last remaining river plot in the Parc Régional d'Armorique. No wonder the window in the main bedroom is huge! Minimalist bedrooms are decorated with panache: deep purple blushes against neutral tones, piles of large linen pillows on French brocante beds, glimpses of baroque fabric. Big bathrooms downstairs exude a luxurious simplicity. The sociable ground floor also embraces kitchen, dining area and salon in alpine fashion, with splashes of funkiness in artwork and pouffes. The compact, perfectly equipped kitchen has grey-painted cupboards and trim zinc surfaces. Claire and Andrew provide a welcome pack as exceptional as the rest, live nearby and are on hand whenever you need them. The Crozon peninsula is worth exploring; leave the car behind and take the kayak out instead. Fabulous.

Price	€900–€1,650 per week.
Sleeps	5.
Rooms	2 doubles, 1 single; 2 bathrooms.
Meals	Restaurant 3km.
Closed	Never.

Ethical Collection: Environment.
See page 370 for details

Claire Bernard
Rosnoen, Finistère

Tel	+33 (0)2 98 55 29 26
Mobile	+33 (0)6 33 07 22 85
Email	frenchberry@orange.fr
Web	www.frenchberry.com

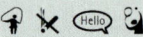

Ty Traez

Even within the masterly seclusion of high stone garden walls, at 300 paces you can smell the sea. Trust Claire to find this family *maison de maître*, tucked into a Breton hamlet with open views of sea-fields; the inside is equally impressive. Slip into the languid ease of long draping linen and voile curtains brushing against neutral walls and natural matting. Venerable beds – one with re-formed shutters for a headboard – are too good to resist. Local artisans made blush-red shelves for the zinc and wood kitchen, and brought similar genius to bathrooms. Modern sofas dance with antique bergère armchairs on quarry-tiled floors, to the amusement of stately armoires; seashells are piled high in glass vases and there's a lovely log fire for the winter. Send fidgeting children to the converted attic with table tennis and huge cushions. And as the nightly ocean breeze tickles candles in their mounts, old sea prints jostle with younger pictures – do they know Pointe du Raz is the most westerly point on the European mainland? All this, and delicious seafood in a pretty Audierne restaurant.

Price	€1,000–€2,000 per week.
Sleeps	8.
Rooms	3 doubles, 2 singles; 3 bathrooms.
Meals	Restaurant 1km.
Closed	Rarely.

Claire Bernard
Primelin, Finistère

Tel	+33 (0)2 98 55 29 26
Mobile	+33 (0)6 33 07 22 85
Email	frenchberry@orange.fr
Web	www.frenchberry.fr

The Gatehouse - Kistinic

The art of good living is no book title, it's this charming stone cottage gatehouse in the heart of Brittany. Built in the 19th century to serve the fairytale château of Kistinic, the cottage's young interior belies its history. A luxurious minimalism is on display here, with a good dose of joie de vivre thrown in. Emerging from indulgent bedding and stepping onto polished wooden floors is a fine way to start the day, as is discovering a spacious bathroom with natural stone flooring. Claire and Andrew love it when families stay — and this cottage is made for easy living, with its uncluttered, glass-chandeliered sitting and dining area and its smartly equipped kitchen. Wonder, too, at the setting… No surprise to learn that Claire once researched locations for television productions. Run reckless through the rhododendrons — as the azaleas and camellias do — growing among enough woodland and lawns to cause delusions of grandeur from your bedroom window. Swim in the infinity pool, explore historic Quimper, follow the winding trails through the woods. C'est magique! *Whole château available (sleeps 12).*

Price	€750–€1,400 per week.
Sleeps	5.
Rooms	2 doubles, 1 twin; 2 bathrooms.
Meals	Restaurant 3km.
Closed	Rarely.

Claire Bernard
Quimper, Finistère

Tel	+33 (0)2 98 55 29 26
Mobile	+33 (0)6 33 07 22 85
Email	frenchberry@orange.fr
Web	www.frenchberry.fr

Guillec Vihan

In a wooded valley deep in the Breton countryside is a cluster of farm buildings, a lazy river winding through the fields below. Robbie and Fiona's children and grandchildren are often around, plus six cats, two dogs and an assortment of horses: it's a lively, family-orientated set up with bags of humour and charm. Close by the Rainbirds' house is another house, while a further property is rented to musicians – there's always something going on. The cottage has traditional stone doorways and oak window frames; in the kitchen/dining room, rush-seated chairs pull up around an oil-clothed table. The dormer-windowed bedrooms are originally decorated with Fiona's artistic and colourful eye; the ground-floor double, ideal for the less mobile, has a huge canopied bed, an old armoire and a hand-painted mural. On one side of the cottage is a gravelled terrace, on the other a big lawn; everywhere, climbing roses and clematis... Fiona loves her garden. One of Robbie's passions is tractors (you'll hear the odd rumble), another is restoring old cars. A place of fun, music and laughter.

Price	€450–€650 per week. Reductions for two people. Towels not included.
Sleeps	6.
Rooms	1 double, 2 twins; 2 bathrooms.
Closed	Never.

	Robbie & Fiona Rainbird
	Collorec, Finistère
Tel	+33 (0)2 98 73 93 60
Email	relaxing-breaks@rainbird-gites.com
Web	www.rainbird-gites.com

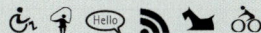

Le Manoir de Prévasy

You enter through tall oak doors onto flagstones and gaze up the wonderful old staircase, timeworn and creaky. This stunningly renovated 16th-century manor is clearly a house of character, not too grand or precious, with huge fireplaces and curtains that show off the stone. The new kitchen/dining room is a revelation, light streams in from three tall windows and the feeling of space, the potential for convivial evenings around the enormous Morbihan chopping block, make you want to linger. Sam has repainted and started refurbishing the good old bedrooms, the slightly dated bathrooms were revamped in 2008. It feels like a large country house – antiques, gilt, silks, old polished floors, coffee-table books – with touches of glamour such as the huge fawn modern sofas round the fire and the balled glass lamps. A rural idyll laden with history: wherever you look are remains of old terraces and fortified walls – what a story these stones could tell. The chapel is in ruins, badminton is played in the old graveyard, a secret passage is rumoured. Fascinating, fun, and perfect for large groups.

Price	£600–£1,700 per week.
Sleeps	16.
Rooms	House: 2 doubles, 2 twins, 1 family room for 6; 4 bathrooms, 1 shower room, separate wc. Cottage: 1 twin; 1 shower room.
Meals	Restaurants within walking distance.
Closed	Never.

Sam Sudderth
Carhaix Plouguer, Finistère

Tel	+1 305 915 9025
Email	samsudds@gmail.com
Web	www.prevasy.com

Kerpoence

Pretend it's a doll's house: a one-up, one-down cottage in a tiny village lane, this is an entrancing place that doesn't feel in the least cramped, and every inch of space has been used to simple, stylish effect. Ceramic tiles cover the open-plan ground floor, a Moroccan rug and bright armchairs add colour; diminutive windows are hung with cream cotton tatting done by Julie's great aunt; a tiny, perfect kitchen is tucked under the steep stairs. Bedroom and bathroom are up under the rafters where Julie's paintings decorate the walls and the low bed, flanked by niche lights, is covered with gingham: curl up here with a book or a DVD. Admire Jez's expert carpentry on the bath panelling (but don't expect to lie full stretch in the bath: it's three-quarter size). You'll like Julie and Jez. They're ex-teachers and live five minutes away. If you want to avoid going in search of restaurants in nearby Gouarec, you may book a vegetarian meal with them. A terrific place for a couple – though not if you're at all creaky. Listen to the church bells and enjoy the lavender in the garden. *Sawday B&B.*

Price	£200-£300 sterling per week. €60 per day. Towels not included.
Sleeps	2.
Rooms	1 double; 1 bathroom.
Meals	Meals on request. Restaurants within walking distance.
Closed	Never.

Julie & Jez Rooke
Laniscat, Côtes-d'Armor

Tel	+33 (0)2 96 36 98 34
Mobile	+33 (0)6 88 57 75 31
Email	jezrooke@hotmail.com
Web	www.phoneinsick.co.uk

Brittany

Le Gohic

Chocolate-box pretty, this private hamlet is too good to be true. A cluster of deep-roofed stone cottages, wrapped around with plants and flowering shrubs, it will be found down a lane in the lush Blavet valley. Secluded and generous, it would be brilliant for family get-togethers with its heated pool, playground and teenage den full of games, as well as bicycles and grassy woodland for pottering around in. Or you'll come to make friends with other guests in this cosy set-up: the five cottages sleep a total of 30 and l'Écurie's huge sitting/dining room even seats 30 for dinner. Open-plan living areas are cottage-pretty with oak beams, deep fireplaces, plaster and stone walls, welcoming sofas and rustic Breton pieces. Nothing fussy, nothing precious, parents can rest easy. Kitchens and bathrooms are neat and functional while bedrooms are simple and quaint. Some cottages have French windows, all have terraces and small gardens. Shops are a five-minute drive and Robin and Sheila are brimming with ideas for walks, markets, beaches. Why not explore the coast in their skippered boat?

Price	Cidre £355-£825. Puits £365-£895. Principale £445-£1,195. Écurie £455-£1,295. Mairie £565-£1,575. Whole hamlet £2,165-£5,785. Prices per week.
Sleeps	30.
Rooms	Cidre: 1 double, 1 twin; 1 bathroom. Puits, Écurie, Principale: each 1 double, 2 twins; 1 bathroom, separate wc. Mairie: 2 doubles, 2 twins; 2 bathrooms.
Meals	Restaurants within 1km.
Closed	Never.

Robin & Sheila Berwick
Quistinic, Morbihan

Tel	+33 (0)2 97 39 76 28
Mobile	+33 (0)6 75 33 96 68
Email	robin.berwick@wanadoo.fr
Web	www.cottagesofbrittany.com

Le Rhun - Four Gîtes

Your children will tumble out of the car and head for the sandpit, swings and small pool, or volleyball, basketball and boules. For grown-ups, there are shady hammocks and a sauna. Family-friendly, easy-going, this lovely German couple have done a high-class renovation job on their cluster of Breton outbuildings – and with two B&B rooms as well as four gîtes, the farmstead becomes a lively place in the holidays. Rooms are simply furnished, colours light and fresh, kitchens modern and well-equipped and everyone gets a terrace and a garden. The ground floors are open-plan; the cooking areas are tucked into a corner or quite separate. You have tiled floors, white walls and beamed ceilings, perhaps an old armoire, a stone table or a drawing by Jurgen's cousin to add an individual touch. Bedrooms feel Scandinavian – pale, uncluttered spaces with shots of colour from curtain or headboard; bathrooms are clean and functional. Cows graze next door, the little lake attracts birds and there are five acres to explore. Beyond: beaches, the castle at Pontivy and canoeing on the river Blavet. *Sawday B&B.*

Price	€270–€575 per week. Linen not included.
Sleeps	16.
Rooms	Gîtes One & Two: each 2 doubles; 1 shower room. Gîte Three: 1 double; 1 shower room. Gîte Four: 3 doubles; 1 bathroom, 1 shower room.
Meals	Restaurant 3.5km.
Closed	October–April.

Eva & Jürgen Lincke
Pluméliau, Morbihan

Tel	+33 (0)2 97 51 83 48
Mobile	+33 (0)6 08 07 40 13
Email	eva.lincke@web.de
Web	www.lerhun.de

Western Loire • Loire Valley

Château de Vaux

Wide mown verges, spreading horse chestnuts and beeches – breathe in the peace of the Sarthe. This pretty 16th-century outbuilding survived the Revolution (the original château was destroyed) and is now a luxurious hideaway. The character has been exquisitely kept: rough beams, parquet floors and a wow-factor staircase of ancient oak blocks that owners Isabelle and Christophe felt must be preserved. A high-ceilinged, deep-windowed living space has chic contemporary fittings and an impressively equipped kitchen; granite steps lead to a lounging barbecue terrace. On the ground floor, a big double bedroom with Louis XV-style chairs, its bath and dressing area tucked behind a screening wall. Upstairs, a double and a twin ideal for children; both light, but with their windows up high: this was once a cider store. These simple rooms are vibrant with Isabelle's hand-dyed linens: aubergine, hazelnut, lime green. Beyond the rose-clambered gate are wildflower meadows, a millpond and 20 acres. Pick vegetables and flowers from the organic potager; book a shiatsu massage or a children's cookery course. *Tennis in village, 1km.*

Price	€780–€1,200 per week. €460–€570 per weekend.
Sleeps	6.
Rooms	2 doubles, 1 twin; 2 bathrooms, 2 separate wcs. Extra bed.
Meals	Breakfast €12. Restaurants 8-10km. Basket of fresh food from market €32.50 p.p.
Closed	Never.

Christophe & Isabelle Jeanson
Gesnes le Gandelin, Sarthe

Mobile	+33 (0)6 85 83 89 16
Email	contact@chateau-de-vaux.fr
Web	www.chateau-de-vaux.fr

Château de La Barre - Les Glycines & Les Lilas

This delightful cottage (probably an old farm building) sits comfortably within the grounds of the splendid château that came into the family in 1404. Downstairs, Les Glycines is snug with thick walls, chunky beams and old oak shutters at windows with views onto parkland and sheep. You walk straight into the bedroom: original tiled floors, seagrass rugs, an enormous comfortable bed dressed in crisp linen and a modern shower room with a marble basin. The kitchen is tiny and gorgeous with a stable door looking onto the gardens, which you are free to roam. Les Lilas is reached up outside stairs; the smell of wood burning wafts comfortingly over you as you enter the sitting room, which bursts with antique furniture and character. Your little kitchen has all you need to cook; a very pretty bedroom with green bamboo design curtains and duvet covers is reached up an old oak staircase (not for the less than nimble). The snazzy bathroom has oriental wall lights and a triangular jacuzzi bath; the feeling is of being in an immaculate treehouse. There are acres of grounds to scamper in and you are close to the Loire valley.

Price	Glycines €390. Cleaning €45. Lilas €590. Cleaning €75. Prices per week.
Sleeps	6.
Rooms	Glycines: 1 double. Lilas: 1 double, 1 twin.
Meals	Restaurants 3km & 12km.
Closed	Mid-January to mid-February.

Comte & Comtesse de Vanssay
Conflans sur Anille, Sarthe

Tel	+33 (0)2 43 35 00 17
Email	info@chateaudelabarre.com
Web	www.chateaudelabarre.com/GB/cottage.htm

Entry 81   Map 4

Manoir de Saint Frambault

A handsome, high-class farmhouse restored to the manner to which it had been accustomed – beautiful, clean and plush – then furnished with weathered leather armchairs, antique bookcases bearing antique books and the atmosphere of a country gent's residence. The ground-floor bedroom carries hints of Asian gold and modern abstract art beside silk prints of exotic water fowl. The attic room is gorgeously cosy and stylish with embroidered butterflies and a heavenly many-timbered bathroom whose window gives a birdseye view of park and lake. The three other bedrooms are equally individual and subtle and just as unspoilt by cupboards or wardrobes. Downstairs, the big living room, grandly gilt-framed and mahogany, welcomes guests to its myriad chairs. You'd happily be lords of the manor here – and utilities leave nothing to be desired; rustle up delicious meals in your own oak kitchen. There are no fewer than five lakes in the 800-acre estate, no-kill fishing can be organised, the pool is heated, the shoot takes over on some weekends and the river Sarthe is perfect for boating. And don't miss old Le Mans.

Price	€1,600–€2,150 per week.
Sleeps	18.
Rooms	3 twins/doubles, 2 family suites for 3; 3 bath/shower rooms, 2 shower rooms. Annexe: 1 double, 1 children's quadruple; 1 shower room. 2 separate wcs.
Meals	Restaurants 5–8km.
Closed	Never.

Emmanuel de Goulaine
Roeze sur Sarthe, Sarthe

Tel	+33 (0)2 43 77 21 40
Email	franbaldus@wanadoo.fr
Web	www.manoir-saint-frambault.fr

Le Moulin de la Diversière - Martin Pêcheur & Pic Épeiche

Deep in the Loire Valley, on a tree-fringed bend in the river, this 300-year-old mill exudes contentment and calm. Willow-fringed paths lead to honey-coloured outbuildings skilfully converted by eco-conscious Anne and Jean Marc. Gîte Martin-Pecheur's open-plan family bedroom sits snugly in the eaves, while single storey Pic-Epeiche has its bedrooms on the ground floor; smooth pebble floors massage tired feet in stylish shower rooms. Traditional pink terracotta tommettes, limewashed walls and beams treated with milk-based bio-paint keep living areas bright and airy, while winter warmth is assured: you get wood-burners and stacks of logs. Neat little kitchens have all mod cons, but for sheer indulgence you can have breakfast delivered — and later join Anne in the millhouse for delicious family dinners with home-grown veg. In the large, sloping grounds are ponds and streams teeming with wildlife (look out for the resident kingfisher), bloom-laden borders, shady arbours, a playground and a child-friendly swimming pool. *B&B available.*

Price	Pic Épeiche €450–€615. Martin Pêcheur €350–€530. Prices per week.
Sleeps	8.
Rooms	Martin Pêcheur: 1 triple (double & single); 1 bathroom. Pic Épeiche: 1 double, 1 triple (single & bunks); 1 bathroom.
Meals	Dinner, with wine, €23 (€12 for children under 16). Restaurant 9km.
Closed	Never.

Anne & Jean-Marc Le Foulgocq
Savigné sous le Lude, Sarthe

Tel	+33 (0)2 43 48 09 16
Mobile	+33 (0)6 77 44 79 95
Email	contact@moulin-de-la-diversiere.com
Web	www.moulin-de-la-diversiere.com

La Besnardière

Scuttling chickens, ducks on the pond, goats, a donkey: a wholesome feeling of being 'down on the farm'. Close to Baugé yet with acres of woodland and fields, it's ideal for free-ranging children, and there are swings for little ones. Delightful Joyce has turned the farmhouse into a B&B and the stable into a super gîte – a bright, sunny space of exposed beams and terracotta. Roof windows flood the upper rooms with light, bedrooms are jolly affairs with colourful covers and rugs, simple wooden furniture and little lamps; shower rooms are neat and spotless. Relax in the sitting room or a sunny spot on the landing with its reading seats. The kitchen is quirky with the original wooden hayrack housing a cheerful mix of china, and a handcrafted table: not state-of-the-art but all you need to rustle up a meal. Joyce shares her own organic produce and eggs, when plentiful, or you can book her special vegetarian meal – and eat under the stars. Loire châteaux, local markets, swimming in the lake at La Flèche; perfect for families, heritage lovers and unwinding. *Sawday B&B. Aromatherapy treatments available. WWOOF members.*

Price	€450–€500 per week.
Sleeps	6.
Rooms	1 double, 1 quadruple, sofabed; 3 shower rooms. Cot.
Meals	Meals available at farmhouse, on request.
Closed	January & February.

Joyce Rimell
Fougeré, Maine-et-Loire
Tel   +33 (0)2 41 90 15 20
Email   rimell.joyce@wanadoo.fr
Web   www.holiday-loire.com

Manoir des Rosiers

Charming Maïa, a former tour guide, and Frédéric have escaped from bustling Paris to the peaceful Loire countryside and are already expert at looking after you – they're just next door and always on hand if you need them. Your solid stone house – possibly the original stables – sits in the Manoir's garden. Step into a large and luminous living space with white beams above and rosy tomettes below, stunning stone fireplace and cream stone walls, early 19th-century fauteuils and elegant antique mirrors. The neatly contemporary white and wood kitchen is tucked into one end of the dining room where dove-grey ladderback chairs encircle the dining table, topped by a chandelier. The country-fresh minimalism reaches upstairs, to snowy linen under characterful old beams, whitewashed floors, muslin drapes and baths incorporated into bedrooms – the romantic draped four-poster bed is dreamily luxurious. Outside is your own little knot garden, sweet, safe, secluded and furnished with twirly French chairs. A tranquil pool for a swim or lovely days out: browse the brocantes of La Roche Posay.

Price	€490–€1,120 per week.
Sleeps	4.
Rooms	1 double, 1 twin, sofabed; 2 bathrooms, 1 shower room.
Meals	Dinner, with wine, €35.
Closed	Rarely.

Maïa & Frédéric Moreaux
Noyant la Plaine, Maine-et-Loire

Mobile	+33 (0)6 12 17 17 00
Email	mamoreaux@yahoo.fr
Web	www.manoirdesrosiers.com

La Maison Aubelle - Tour, Gaudrez & Jardin

A 16th-century nobleman's house in an old country town, Aubelle stands in secluded gardens flanked by high stone walls, renovated by craftsmen and thoughtfully equipped by Peter and Sally. The original apartments are Tour, Jardin and Gaudrez. Tour – in the tower, as you'd expect – is one flight up a spiralling stone stair; it has a beamed living room/kitchen below with trim red sofas and wraparound views. The garden apartment, with terrace, is as neat as a new pin. White-walled Gaudrez has a 16th-century window, discovered during restoration. The feel is airy, relaxing, comfortable; crisp linen, central heating and daily cleaning are included and the quality is superb. There's a terrace and games room for all and an appropriately large pool. If you can't face cooking, let the Smiths do it for you: they whisk up delicious meals five times a week, cheerfully served in the dining room in winter, on the terrace in summer. Peter and Sally are also on hand to advise, translate or leave you in peace. And they run French courses. *Children over 12 welcome. Shared pool & laundry.*

Price	Tour & Gaudrez €975-€1,250 each. Jardin €875-€1,000. Prices per week. Apartments may be rented together. Minimum stay 3 days.
Sleeps	10.
Rooms	Tour: 2 doubles; 2 shower rooms. Gaudrez: 2 doubles; 2 shower rooms. Jardin: 1 double; 1 bathroom, separate wc.
Meals	Dinner €30, on request. Restaurants 200m.
Closed	Rarely.

Peter & Sally Smith
Montreuil Bellay, Maine-et-Loire

Tel	+33 (0)2 41 52 36 39
Email	maison.aubelle@aubelle.com
Web	www.aubelle.com

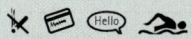

La Maison Aubelle - Coach House & Stable

No sooner had the Smiths finished one renovation than they turned their hands to the old stable and coach house. And with aplomb – the exterior and interior are impeccable. Walls are whitewashed or exposed stone, some ceilings slant, there are lovely old beams and attractive new windows. In the old stable the original hayrack graces the sitting room. You'll find the odd country chest, good sofas, heating beneath terracotta floors (winter warmth is guaranteed). In summer, play chess in the lovely, garden, dine on the terrace, meet fellow guests round the pool. There's daily cleaning, fitted kitchens are packed with all mod cons and linen is provided; all you need do is turn up. Venture beyond the walls to discover the last remaining walled town in the region; the three-minute stroll to the château is rewarded by gorgeous watery views of the Thouet. Stretch out a little further and explore Fontevraud Abbey: Eleanor of Aquitaine and Richard the Lion Heart are buried here. *Coach House & Stable can interconnect for same-party bookings. Children over 12 welcome. Shared pool & laundry.*

Price	Coach house €1,100-€1,250. Stable €975-€1,150. Prices per week. Minimum 3 days.
Sleeps	6.
Rooms	Coach House: 2 doubles; 2 shower rooms. Stable: 1 double; 1 bathroom, 1 separate wc.
Meals	Dinner €30, on request. Restaurants within 200m.
Closed	Rarely.

Peter & Sally Smith
Montreuil Bellay, Maine-et-Loire

Tel	+33 (0)2 41 52 36 39
Email	maison.aubelle@aubelle.com
Web	www.aubelle.com

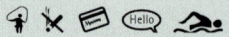

Château de Salvert - La Brosse & Le Pressoir

Quel château! It's a neo-Gothic masterpiece and these little houses lie deep within its parkland. Handsome, comfortable and a delight to spend time in, both were restored by the indefatigable owners, with deft combinations of old and new. La Brosse is a 14th-century farmhouse, modest but dignified, all stone walls and great oak beams upstairs and down. Old the bedsteads may be, on floors of wood or tomettes, but the mattresses are new, the mats are seagrass and the mood is unexpectedly luxurious. Bathrooms are very 21st-century, some tiled imaginatively with old terracotta, all with old beams and tiny windows, kitchens are big, authentic and well-equipped, furniture is classically French. The swimming pool is a four-minute stroll through the grounds and each house has a private, enclosed garden but you can join forces with your neighbours should you wish. Monsieur is jovial and welcoming, his wife friendly and impressively energetic. This is a fine address in an area which is impossibly rich in culture, starting with France's largest Romanesque church in nearby Cunault. *Sawday hotel. Shared pool.*

Price	Brosse €750-€1,600. Pressoir €800-€1,750. Prices per week.
Sleeps	14.
Rooms	Brosse: 1 double, 2 twins; 1 bathroom, 1 shower room. Pressoir: 1 double, 1 twin, 1 triple, 1 single; 1 bathroom, 1 shower room.
Meals	Dinner €44. Restaurants 3-10km.
Closed	January.

Monica Le Pelletier de Glatigny
Neuillé, Maine-et-Loire

Tel	+33 (0)2 41 52 55 89
Mobile	+33 (0)6 15 12 03 11
Email	info@salvert.com
Web	www.chateau-de-salvert.fr

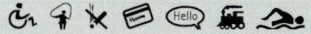

Manoir de Champfreau & Maison Louis Richard

In spite of imposing dimensions and character, there's a soft luminosity to the ancient manoir. History oozes from every crevice: ancestral portraits and tapestries hang on thick stone walls, solid antique furniture and coats-of-arms recall grand inhabitants. With its black tiles, dishwasher and every modern aid (even 200 recipe books), the kitchen is a dream. Smallish sumptuous bedrooms – velvet-draped four-poster, claw-footed bath; a baronial cosy salon – deep sofas before a blazing fire, CDs, books and flowers, and central heating. Views are of the three walled acres and the topiary courtyard. Maison Louis Richard, a fabulously decorated, elegantly luxurious retreat for two, has paintings, objets d'art and kitchen perfection. Bruce, a former chef, is generous with cooking advice. Full of local knowledge, he and Steven live next door and are delightful yet discreet. Set in 50 private acres, it is brilliantly placed for some of the finest châteaux, there's a fish pond, bikes to borrow and cookery courses. A heavenly place. *Pool for Manoir occupants only.*

Price	Manoir €1,200-€1,700.
	Maison Louis Richard €800-€900.
	Prices per week, including firewood.
Sleeps	8.
Rooms	Manoir: 3 doubles; 2 bathrooms.
	Maison Louis Richard: 1 double;
	1 shower room. Extra single room.
Meals	Meals on request.
Closed	Never.

Steven Guderian & Bruce Riedner
Varennes sur Loire, Maine-et-Loire

Tel	+33 (0)2 41 38 40 41
Mobile	+33 (0)6 79 33 68 82
Email	stevenguderian@aol.com
Web	www.saumurfrancemanor.com

Écrin de Vendée

No wonder they call it a jewel case (*écrin*): the farmhouse sits like a gem among lush green fields and a tracery of trees. Two pretty, single-storey outbuildings have been renovated in the traditional manner and painted, like the house, bright white with blue shutters. Inside, they are sparklingly modern: pale walls, white-painted rafters, good prints, comfortable furniture. Les Toucandines, close to the main house, has an open-plan living area, an L-shaped, light-filled bedroom and a small second bedroom that squeezes in bunks and a single bed. Les Florentines, tucked away at the bottom of the garden, has a little double bedroom and a sofabed in the living room. Kitchens are small – in Les Toucandines you'll need to breathe in to pass the narrow door! – but fully equipped. Private decking and lawn make good places to sit and watch the horses graze – on the other side of the electric fences; the pool is planted with lavender and olives and in the orchard are swings, slide and a climbing frame. This is marsh land with navigable water channels, so why not try punting in a yole?

Price	Toucandines €490-€1,050. Florentines €390-€800. Prices per week.
Sleeps	9.
Rooms	Toucandines: 1 double, 1 triple (bunks & single); 1 bathroom. Florentines: 1 double, sofabed; 1 shower room.
Meals	Restaurants within walking distance.
Closed	Rarely.

Frédérique & Frédéric Stoll
Sallertaine, Vendée

Tel	+33 (0)2 51 35 30 73
Mobile	+33 (0)6 83 16 11 96
Email	contact@ecrin-vendee.com
Web	www.location-gite-ecrin-vendee.com

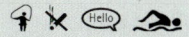

Château de la Flocellière - The Keep & The Pavilion

The Vicomtesse has exacting standards and she oversees every detail of her vast dominion, from the topiary to the maids' attire. All is opulence and beauty and wafting beeswax. There are superb rooms in the château and two historic buildings for rent in the grounds – a medieval Keep and a Louis XIII Pavilion. Impossible to choose between them, the one sturdy 11th century, the other classically graceful 17th century. Both are architectural gems, both have all you might need, both feel exceedingly grand. The Renaissance fireplace in the Keep's double room is monumental and roars with logs in winter beneath the splendidly painted and domed ceiling. Equally refined, the Pavilion has a gracious, immaculate feel and a brand new kitchen. This is living at its most sedate, children are welcome providing they behave impeccably, snacks are no-go in the pool area: "a terrace, not a beach." You also have your own secluded garden with barbecue. Weddings and receptions are not limited to weekends; the setting is sensational. Historic, magnificent, hospitable. *Sawday hotel. Shared pool.*

Price	Keep €1,000–€2,000 for 10. Pavilion €1,000–€1,900 for 11. Prices per week. Pets extra.
Sleeps	21.
Rooms	Keep: 1 double, 2 suites for 4; 3 bathrooms, 3 separate wcs. Pavilion: 2 doubles, 1 double & sofabed, 1 quadruple & sofabed, 1 single; 1 bathroom, 2 shower rooms, 2 separate wcs.
Meals	Meals on request. Restaurants 5-minute walk.
Closed	Never.

Vicomte & Vicomtesse Vignial
La Flocellière, Vendée

Tel	+33 (0)2 51 57 22 03
Email	flocelliere.chateau@wanadoo.fr
Web	www.chateaudelaflocelliere.com

Massay Gîtes & Chambres d'Hôtes

Set round a big courtyard, an unusual 1930s village house and its outbuildings converted to gîtes; beyond the gates, a village street with little family shops; on either side, genuine rural life and characters, all in that heartland of deep France that is the old royal province of Berry. Gîte occupants, the open friendly owners and their children share the courtyard, its fine lime trees and the field behind where two sheep graze. The children's play area is safe and fun. The cottages are well converted, contemporary-cosy inside – red plush and fat cushions, white beds (king-size doubles), ethnic rugs and interesting works of art, modern kitchens and shiny new bathrooms. In the village, the magnificent abbey is a must-see, as are the nearby farms and markets: here you will stock up with artisan cheeses, fresh-off-the-stalk tomatoes, delicious raw milk and myriad other natural delights. Alice, who was in public relations, and writer-photographer Damian, are expert advisors. Beyond are incomparable Bourges, luscious Sancerre, deep forest walks, Loire châteaux and fine gardens. *B&B also. Photography courses.*

Price	€175–€370 per week. Linen not included.
Sleeps	6.
Rooms	Cottage for 2-4: 1 double, 2 single sofabeds; 1 bathroom. Barn for 2-3: 1 double, 1 single in living room; 1 bathroom. Apartment for 2: 1 double; 1 bathroom.
Meals	Restaurant in village.
Closed	Never.

Alice & Damian Bird
Massay, Cher

Tel	+33 (0)2 36 55 61 50
Mobile	+33 (0)6 80 64 47 02
Email	massaygites@yahoo.co.uk
Web	www.massaygites.com

Loire Valley

Domaine de l'Hérissaudière

The château was Diane de Poitiers' hunting lodge. Your pleasant quarters are in the long, low *longère*, once the tack room for the horses. It's a one-storey building, one-room deep, light and appealing. Bedrooms are on your right and the living area on your left: a blue sofabed before a small open fire (and central heating on chilly days), blue curtains, a tablecloth on a round table. Walls are white, beams dark and low; a rug adds warmth to tiles, country furniture adds personality. The kitchen, separated by a breakfast bar, is new and well-designed with matching blue and white crockery. The double bedroom is a good size, crisp and cool, with a large painted wardrobe (again blue!); the twin is a lot smaller. Outside, the best of both worlds: the privacy of your own walled and treed garden, with barbecue, swing and slide, and the lovely grounds to share, with tennis court to hire. The pool is for B&B guests only but there's a good public pool 10km away. A peaceful place for a family to stay – and an excellent restaurant five minutes away, recommended by hospitable Madame. *Sawday hotel. Tennis €10 per hour.*

Price	€500–€800 per week.
Sleeps	4.
Rooms	1 double & child's bed, 1 twin, sofabed in sitting room; 2 shower rooms, separate wc. Cot.
Meals	Restaurant 3km.
Closed	Never.

Claudine Detilleux
Pernay, Indre-et-Loire

Tel	+33 (0)2 47 55 95 28
Mobile	+33 (0)6 03 22 34 45
Email	lherissaudiere@aol.com
Web	www.herissaudiere.com

La Cornillière

A lovely place with delightful owners. Monsieur, an antique dealer with artistic inklings, studied art in Tours 40 years ago, met Madame – and here they are in their elegant house. Beside it, the dear little 18th-century vine-workers' cottage has been decorated with restraint in charming traditional style. Inside, it is as warm and relaxing as your hosts. The furniture is country antique, the walls are plain, the old tiles gleam. From the mantel above the sitting room fire, great-great grandparents look down on cosy armchairs and pretty rugs; bedrooms are two up, one down. There's antique crockery in the kitchen/dining room, antique garden furniture and deckchairs in the garden. Madame is lucky, her husband is also a passionate gardener and happily digs and delves, bringing peace to the outside as well; his mini-Villandry is a marvel; the woods hold box trees once harvested for regimental buttons. Beyond the stone walls of the grounds is the Loire valley with its vineyards and châteaux and the classy city of Tours with shops, opera and great restaurants (simpler auberges lie nearby).

Price	€550–€770 per week.
Sleeps	5.
Rooms	1 double, 1 twin, 1 single; 2 shower rooms, 2 separate wcs.
Meals	Meals on request. Restaurant 4km.
Closed	Never.

Catherine Espinassou
Tours, Indre-et-Loire

Tel	+33 (0)2 47 51 12 69
Mobile	+33 (0)6 03 13 66 12
Email	catherine@lacornilliere.com.fr
Web	www.lacornilliere.com.fr

La Coquetière

Christophe has cleverly restored this farm building next to the family's 16th-century manor using rescued stones and beams to create an authentic house: the staircase of old railway sleepers is a joy. The airy open-plan living area, with grand fireplace, is traditionally beamed and terracotta-tiled, furnished with country antiques and Claudine's paintings (she's a talented amateur). There's a small, well-equipped kitchen and useful utility room. No tantrums over choosing the bedrooms: all are stylish. One has a lofty cathedral-timbered ceiling, two have high chunky antique beds behind beautiful curtains, and there's a pretty children's room; all overlook the Vienne valley or the garden. There are three acres of deer-filled woodland, water, and scented and medieval gardens to explore; you also have a private terrace and pool and can take your pick from the vegetable patch. The owners are delightful, happy to share their love of nature and and tell you about walks, bike trails, rides (stables nearby), weekly markets and the summer cheese festival. It's a lovely walk through the woods to the village restaurant.

Price	€480–€1,640 per week. Towels not included.
Sleeps	10.
Rooms	3 doubles, 1 quadruple; 1 bathroom, 2 shower rooms, 2 separate wcs.
Meals	Restaurants within 1km.
Closed	Never.

	Christophe Leroux & **Claudine Leprince** Ports sur Vienne, Indre-et-Loire
Tel	+33 (0)2 47 65 15 88
Email	leprince2leroux@aol.com
Web	www.lacoquetiere.com

l'Île de Tours

You are perched on an island here in the middle of the river in a wooden annexe to an old blue-shuttered house, owned by charming, artistic Marion. This is a one-roomed bed studio with simple whitewashed walls, some good pictures and a tiled floor with rugs: from comfortable armchairs and an old oak table at the 'living room end' there are super views across the water to the town. A small but well-equipped kitchen sits neatly in an alcove and can be screened off if you don't want to look at it. The sleeping end has a good-sized double bed with a pretty cover and a plain, white-tiled bathroom with a cabin shower. A delightful secluded garden is yours to wander through: find an exuberant squash clambering up a wall, a wisteria-clad loggia, and steps down to the river – ideal for fishing, or simply a gorgeous place to sit with a shockingly cold glass of Chinon in your hand (you are surrounded by some of the best vineyards in the Loire valley). Views from here are to the newly restored castle high up the cliff on the opposite bank; explore the old town, hire a canoe and take to the water, or cycle your socks off.

Price	€250–€330 per week. Short breaks available.
Sleeps	2.
Rooms	1 double; 1 shower room.
Meals	Restaurants 300m.
Closed	Rarely.

Marion Krebs
Chinon, Indre-et-Loire

Tel +33 (0)2 47 93 25 64

Loire Valley

Le Pigeonnier

No artificial pool here but a safe river with sand and a rock-ringed lagoon — swim where fish jump, coypu nest, and kingfishers, terns and herons fish. There are three gîtes on site of which Le Pigeonnier is one, plus an annexe. Reached through lush water meadows, Le Pigeonnier is detached with views up and downstream. Only the frogs disturb the peace of the grassy garden whence a path leads down to the magical riverside with seating and barbecues for each gîte. Le Pigeonnier is an inviting little two-storey house for four. The pretty main bedroom, up chunky open-tread stairs, is in the pigeon loft, complete with nesting holes; across the landing, the second bedroom has a garden view; the bathroom is small, its bath tucked behind a beam. The ground floor is open plan, with a step up from the kitchen/dining area to the cosy sitting room with an open fire. An excellent spot for châteaux lovers, cyclists, gourmets, twitchers and those wishing to mess about in boats — a punt, rowing boat and small sailing boat are all available. There is good fishing — particularly for carp — and permits are available. *Shared laundry.*

Price	Pigeonnier £425-£695. With Annexe £525-£870. Annexe only from £175. Prices per week.
Sleeps	6.
Rooms	1 double, 1 twin, sofabed; 1 bathroom. Annexe: 1 double; 1 bathroom.
Meals	Restaurant 1km.
Closed	End October to March.

Janis Baker
Cravant les Côteaux, Chinon,
Indre-et-Loire

Tel	+44 (0)1763 848755
Mobile	+44 (0)7860 807311
Email	bookings@pigeonnier.co.uk
Web	www.pigeonnier.co.uk

Domaine de Beauséjour

Dug into the hillside with the forest behind and a panorama of vines in front, this wine-grower's manor successfully pretends it was built in the 1800s. In fact, it is 30 years old; Gérard was an architect before he inherited the winery. The gîte is on the lower ground floor, its living room reached directly from the garden. You may be below stairs but the sunlight streams in through your French windows and you have long views of vineyards and valley. The big living room, with exposed stone walls and large patterned rugs, has its dining area at one end, its kitchenette in the corner (sink, double hob, small oven), and its sitting space beyond, round a corner. Divan style beds, ideal for children, are sprinkled with florals; an uncle's pictures grace the walls. The main bedroom is generous; a vast gilt mirror hides the fireplace, bedcovers match curtains and there are great bowls of artificial flowers. The patio is yours, terraces hold the pool, there's wine to taste and buy and exuberant Marie-Claude looks after everyone beautifully. A stunning spot, and the walks are wonderful. *Sawday B&B. Shared pool.*

Price	€550–€650 per week.
Sleeps	7.
Rooms	2 doubles, 1 suite for 3 (double & single); 2 bathrooms, 1 shower room.
Meals	Restaurant 5km.
Closed	Rarely.

Marie-Claude Chauveau
Panzoult,
Indre-et-Loire

Tel	+33 (0)2 47 58 64 64
Email	dom.beausejour@wanadoo.fr
Web	www.domainedebeausejour.fr

Le Clos de Fontenay

Holiday in a vineyard? What could be better! The gîtes here are in the grounds of a traditionally designed, 'modern' château near Tours. You are sitting in 12 acres of red, white and rosé, mixed with formal gardens and woodland with foraging deer. La Closeraie, no longer the wash house, has been transformed into a smart ground-floor apartment; the comfortable salon has an open fireplace for chillier days. Cooks will be happy chatting to diners in the compact kitchen; you can eat in, or take it all out into the garden for a candle-and-star-lit supper. At the end of the smart gravelled drive find the handsome gatehouse with its pale beech and steel staircase. The winery is owned by a friend of the Carlis, who makes sweet white chenins and fizzy Rosière among others; buy some to take home with you. Bléré is the home of one of France's best cheesemakers so take yourselves off on a tour; at local farms you can buy meat, eggs and vegetables 'at the gate'. The Cher river, a tributary of the Loire, winds lazily through the old old town; heavenly Amboise is four miles away, and Chenonceau, Azay, Blois not much further.

Price	La Closeraie €700–€1,030. Le Jardin €580–€890. Prices per week.
Sleeps	8.
Rooms	La Closeraie: 1 twin/double, 1 double, sofabed; 1 bathroom. Le Jardin: 2 twins/doubles, sofabed; 1 bathroom.
Meals	Restaurants 2km.
Closed	Rarely.

Nathalie Carli
Bléré, Indre-et-Loire

Tel	+33 (0)2 47 57 12 74
Mobile	+33 (0)6 07 34 48 32
Email	leclosdefontenay@orange.fr
Web	www.leclosdefontenay.com

Moulin de la Follaine

A tranquil place that feels as old as the hills. The mill workers who worked opposite lived in this house; ask Danie to show you the old Azay flour sacks. Your charming young hosts run a B&B in the medieval mill house but gîte guests have their own patio, barbecue and cottage garden (colourful flowers, immaculate lawn) so there's privacy and peace. The dining/sitting room is pleasingly decorated with a mix of modern and antique country pieces, the stone fireplace is stacked with logs for low-season stays. Bedrooms are similarly uncluttered, white walls sport friezes and the kitchen has every mod con. All is spotless, everything matches – Danie is a stickler for detail – and baguettes are delivered for breakfast. There's masses to do right here, from pétanque to ping-pong to fishing (tackle supplied) and gardens to enjoy, their trickling waterways and the lake dotted with ornamental ducks. Don't miss the weekly markets in Azay and Loches and, when you've had enough of cooking, there's a choice of auberges and traditional restaurants nearby. *Sawday B&B. Unfenced water: unsuitable for young children.*

Price	€480–€600 per week.
Sleeps	4.
Rooms	2 doubles, each with extra single bed; 1 bathroom, separate wc.
Meals	Restaurant 3km.
Closed	Winter.

Danie Lignelet
Azay sur Indre, Indre-et-Loire
Tel   +33 (0)2 47 92 57 91
Email   moulindelafollaine@wanadoo.fr
Web   www.moulindefollaine.com

Loire Valley

Château du Breuil

A leafy drive, a quiet river, lush lawns and dense forests — enter another age. This elegant stone château, handsome with turrets, tall windows and extravagant chimneys, wraps you in its history. Roxanna is an architect and passionate about the building, preserving the original lovelies then furnishing with a light touch. The gîte, in the 15th-century east wing, is spaciously and graciously self-contained and full of little corridors, polished oak floors and solid doors. The oak-panelled sitting room, all squashy sofas and hunting trophies, has French windows to a terrace for sun-drenched mornings and shady evenings. A homely dining room, pretty with old baskets and ancient china, has a kitchenette, traditional and simple. For the swathe of fireplaces there is a cellar stocked with logs. Bedrooms are in country-house style with a light mix of French and English antiques, bathrooms have grand roll tops, one with original fittings. Visit historic Loches, walk the old hunting ground of kings — there are wild flowers in spring, mushrooms in autumn — and return to restful gardens and utter privacy.

Price	€1,000–€1,480 per week.
Sleeps	9.
Rooms	1 double, 1 double & child's single, 1 quadruple; 3 bathrooms, separate wc. Extra bed.
Meals	Restaurants within walking distance.
Closed	Never.

Roxanna McDonald
Chédigny, Indre-et-Loire
Tel   +33 (0)2 47 92 55 88
Email   chateau_du_breuil_37310@orange.fr

La Challerie - La Dépendance

Floor-to-ceiling windows in the main bedroom and a full Touraine view: the restoration is excellent, the setting a balm. In two grassed acres with orchards, close to unrestored farm buildings full of charm, the 15th-century Dépendance has an irresistible appeal for those who love 'la belle France'. Its spacious two storeys have been charmingly furnished with country antiques and the best of brand new: warm red sofas in the salon, beechwood table and chairs in the dining room, an oak bed upstairs. The walls are pale exposed stone or fresh white plaster with natural wood beams, the kitchen is delightful and there's new oak for the stairs. L-shaped bedrooms, a wood-burner (logs provided) and original floor tiles add character. You have a terrace for barbecues under the stars, the orchard's peaches, plums and pears to pluck, honey, goat's and ewe's cheeses produced down the road. Stroll into 11th-century Montrésor for delectable bread and pâtisseries, visit Loches for its twice-weekly market. There's a fabulous pool just for you, a lake at Chemillé, and concerts, châteaux and wines to discover. *Pets by arrangement. Tennis courts nearby.*

Price	£400-£750 per week. Linen £20 p.p.
Sleeps	5.
Rooms	1 double, 1 triple, sofabed on mezzanine; 1 shower room, separate wc.
Meals	Restaurant 2.5km.
Closed	Never.

Henry & Susanne Dixon
Montrésor, Indre-et-Loire

Tel	+44 (0)1824 790254
Email	sue@allthedixons.com
Web	www.ladependance.info

La Maison Rose

With its gorgeous pink roses and creeper-clad stone walls, the private courtyard garden in which this 18th-century farm cottage stands is magical. Take breakfast out to the lavender bushes and absorb the peace of the pretty village on the poplar-lined banks of the Indrois. Inside, it is no less charming, the bohemian furnishings and old oak beams exuding homeliness and relaxed well-being. The English owner is a painter and potter and the walls are hung with his colourful pictures. For the cooler months you have books, games and a wood-burner (logs provided). Bedrooms are traditional with arty touches; the twin, on the landing, leads into one double; the shower is upstairs, the bathroom is down. Artists will celebrate the limpid Touraine light, foodies will love the bakery just over the river (the pains aux raisins are legendary) and everyone will love Loches, its medieval citadel and blue slate roofs, its cobbled streets and its market. Buy a locally reared poussin or a piece of gleaming fish, then bring it back and turn it on the barbecue, discreetly hidden behind an old stone wall.

Price	€490-€790 per week.
Sleeps	6.
Rooms	2 doubles, 1 twin; 1 bathroom, 1 shower room.
Meals	Café in village. Restaurants in Loches, 17km.
Closed	Never.

Flora & James Cockburn
Loché sur Indrois, Indre-et-Loire

Tel	+33 (0)2 47 92 61 79
Email	mrsfscockburn@aol.com
Web	www.lamaisonrose.com

La Basse Lande

A lovely old farmstead in gentle Touraine, where you can walk and cycle for miles. The house sleeps ten, with an extra room in an attractive building outside. And there are plenty of corners in the garden in which to find solitude and shade. Downstairs are two double bedrooms furnished in neat country style, with good French wardrobes and peaceful views, and a light and tranquil living room that opens to the garden. Floors are fine old terracotta, subtle lighting reveals the beauty of the 200-year-old beams and the fireplace guards a wood-burner – logs provided. Upstairs are three big bedrooms that lead one into the other (plus a small snooker table) – fun for children. The partly open garden has fruit trees and grass and a big level space that's just asking for a good old English game of rounders. The pretty village, a short drive, sits in the valley of the Indrois, with a 12th-century church and one baker… not to be confused with medieval Loches, famous for its culture, its citadel and its squares that burst into life when the cheese makers, wine producers and market gardeners come to town.

Price	€630–€1,120 per week.
Sleeps	10.
Rooms	5 doubles; 2 shower rooms.
	Extra double in separate building.
Meals	Restaurant 1.5km.
Closed	Never.

Sally Markowski
Loché sur Indrois, Indre-et-Loire

Tel	+44 (0)20 8998 6851
Mobile	+44 (0)7760 366653
Email	sjm@latymer-upper.org
Web	www.holidaygitefrance.co.uk

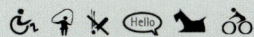

The Cottage

The cottage is set back from the little road, its pretty old stone walls tucked around with swathes of wisteria, its shutters a Provençal blue. The views are stunning and it's a haven for wildlife, including rare birds and butterflies. Step straight into a cosy, rustic sitting room with a beamed ceiling, tiled floor, comfortable leather chairs and a wood-burning stove. The bright, sunny kitchen is perfect for a meal but on summer nights you'll be eating outside on the pergola terrace, surrounded by herbs and lavender. The (larger) double bedroom is perfect for lovers and has roof timbers, exposed stone walls and marble-topped tables; the smaller twin room is neat as a pin. You can soak up the sunshine in the walled and flower-trellised garden, play boules or table tennis in the courtyard – or pop across the lane for croquet, badminton, tennis and a saltwater swimming pool with loungers. Friendly and helpful, Anton knows the best walks, bike rides, châteaux and wine cellars, and Irene can offer Pilates, yoga and dance in the next door studio. A quiet, simple place for families – and plenty of activities. *B&B also.*

Price	£300-£650 per week.
Sleeps	4.
Rooms	1 double, 1 twin; 1 shower room.
Meals	Meals on request. Restaurant 4km.
Closed	Never.

Anton Paget & Irène Ermelli
Barrou, Indre-et-Loire

Tel	+33 (0)2 47 94 90 75
Email	ireneermelli@hotmail.com
Web	www.gitetreat.co.uk

La Chemolière

Tomatoes, peppers, peas, strawberries, melons are yours for the asking, from the family's vegetable plot. Organic, too. Your warm and friendly hosts have done a fine restoration on these old farm buildings just outside the little village (one shop, one café-bar). Relax in the shade of an ancient pear tree, repair to your vine-clad pergola for a barbecue warmed by a wood-burner on cool nights. Inside, the huge stone-floored living room is a timbered delight, its thick walls keeping you warm in winter, cool in summer, its aged character married with modern comforts: a floral three-piece suite, a wood-burning stove, books, games and videos aplenty. The kitchen, with limed units, country tiles and olive trim, has every conceivable appliance to tempt one to cook, the dining area is rustically stone-walled. Up the old oak staircase to two bedrooms and their bathrooms under the eaves; roof windows open to the sky and there's space for a coffee table and a French sofa. Soak in the raised plunge pool, take to the lawns for outside games or potter in the 25 peaceful acres of pasture and wood.

Price	£195–£595 per week.
Sleeps	4.
Rooms	1 double, 1 twin/double; 1 bathroom, 2 shower rooms.
Meals	Dinner, 4 courses with wine, €22.50. Restaurant 500m.
Closed	Never.

Nick & Bev Bull
Cléré du Bois, Indre

Tel	+33 (0)2 54 38 86 32
Mobile	+33 (0)6 24 53 66 96
Email	la_chemoliere@yahoo.co.uk
Web	lachemoliere.co.uk

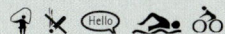

Château de la Motte

Stark against the skyline is a pearly grey, turreted, medieval castle, dominating the village as if plucked from a fairytale. And there, sheltering in the lee of its walls, is your farmhouse home. Its views stretch serenely over Usseau and down a long, soft valley — stunning. Wisely, the interior does not try to compete, it just has that rustic elegance of simple but attractive furniture set against polished parquet, dark-red, beautifully worn quarry tiles and exposed stone walls. There are two good-sized bedrooms in fresh colours — more views — and a cosy room under the eaves that peeps over the garden. The Bardins' paintings are everywhere and there's a butterfly stencil in the shining bathroom. The light-filled living room has doors to the garden — you may barbecue from the old bread oven — and a brand-new kitchen. This is easy living: close to the Loire, restaurants in Châtellerault, a pool shared with the castle's B&B guests. The Bardins are full of energy — creating a monastic garden, running art courses, intelligently filling you in about the area. Great hospitality. *Sawday B&B. Shared pool.*

Price	€450–€600 per week.
Sleeps	6.
Rooms	2 doubles, 1 twin; 2 bathrooms, 1 shower room, 3 separate wcs.
Closed	Rarely.

Jean-Marie & Marie-Andrée Bardin
Usseau, Vienne

Tel	+33 (0)5 49 85 88 25
Email	chateau.delamotte@wanadoo.fr
Web	www.chateau-de-la-motte.net

Entry 107   Map 9

La Grande Métairie - The Cottage

The stuff of dreams! Rose was bewitched by La Grande Métairie which she thought looked like an Arthur Rackham illustration. Fourteen years on, this ancient farm cottage with views over the Creuse valley has kept its enchantment. The stone farm buildings with their unusually angled roofs surround a courtyard shaded by fruit trees; under one stands a life-size effigy of your opera-singer host Richard. This fun and cultured couple do B&B next door and are often around to help if needed. The inside of the cottage will cast its spell over you too: friendly old armchairs round a wood-burner in the cool kitchen/living room, wonderful gnarled beams. Upstairs there are ancient iron bedsteads (with modern mattresses) and thoroughly beamed ceilings. Have a game of tennis on the private court, dine out on your terrace in the large dreamy garden, slip into the shared, enclosed pool, landscaped with shrubs and 200 rose bushes beyond. The well-named Rose runs rose-pruning days in season and makes splendid jams. *B&B also. Shared pool. Can be let with adjoining studio. Babysitting available.*

Price	€465–€715 (£420–£650 sterling) per week.
Sleeps	4.
Rooms	1 double, 1 twin, 1 single on landing; 1 bathroom.
Meals	Restaurant 10-minute drive.
Closed	Never.

Richard & Rose Angas
Leugny, Vienne

Tel	+44 (0)20 8743 1745
Mobile	+44 (0)7966 041744
Email	rose.angas@me.com
Web	www.lagrande-metairie.com

La Grande Métairie - The Studio

There's wood everywhere in this jewel-among-the-rafters in the old farm stables. Stripped age-worn beams bear the sloping ceilings and there are hefty old boards on the floor. A large iron-framed double bed is screened from the living area and kitchen corner by pretty Indian-print curtains; similar fabrics cover the sofabed. You look onto the grassy courtyard on one side and onto the Creuse valley on the other – glorious. A tennis court and a lovely, enclosed pool are shared with the owners and the occasional B&B guest but you get your own space too: stone steps lead up to your front door and down to a private terrace and patch of garden. Come to enjoy the company – out of season – of your interesting hosts, Rose and Richard, and to discover this unspoiled area of France. Once you've explored the farmstead's three acres of gardens and woodland there are châteaux to visit, restaurants and wines to sample and pleasant walks and cycle rides. A baker delivers daily and you can walk to the local farm to buy fresh eggs, ducks and chickens to roast! *B&B also. Shared pool. Can be let with adjoining cottage. Babysitting available.*

Price	€355-€495 (£320-£450 sterling) per week.
Sleeps	2.
Rooms	1 double, single sofabed; 1 shower room.
Meals	Restaurant 10-minute drive.
Closed	Never.

Richard & Rose Angas
Leugny, Vienne

Tel	+33 (0)5 49 85 97 02
Mobile	+44 (0)7966 041744
Email	rose.angas@me.com
Web	www.lagrande-metairie.com

Entry 109   Map 9

La Roseraie

Freshly baked croissants for breakfast? It's a two-minute walk to the bakery in town but you could be in deepest Poitou. These vast and child-friendly grounds embrace a big orchard, a vegetable garden, vines and a heated, salt-treated pool. Behind the 19th-century house – where B&B guests are elegantly housed in one wing – one end of a stone outhouse has been converted into two gîtes overlooking a courtyard. They have quiet style and comfort with a double and a triple bedroom apiece. Each has its own diminutive patio with barbecue, table and chairs; everyone shares the run of the grounds. (Just as well there are four acres: in high summer, there could be up to 20 guests here at a time.) The Lavenders, delightful people with a brace of lively Jack Russell terriers in tow, are English, though Heather was brought up in Zimbabwe. You can watch walnut oil being made down the road and the town has a big weekly market. Hire bikes and spread your wings further: the flat landscape makes for easy cycling and there's masses to visit within an easy drive. A super spot for two families. *B&B also. Shared pool.*

Price	€525-€985 per week.
Sleeps	10.
Rooms	Marguerite: 1 double, 1 triple; 1 shower room, 1 bathroom, separate wc. Atelier: 1 double, 1 triple; 2 shower rooms, 2 separate wcs.
Meals	Dinner, with wine, €28. Children €18.
Closed	Rarely.

Michael & Heather Lavender
Neuville de Poitou, Vienne

Tel	+33 (0)5 49 54 16 72
Email	heather@laroseraiefrance.fr
Web	www.laroseraiefrance.fr

Bois Bourdet - Farmhouse, La Bergerie & La Petite Maison

The couple who own Bois Bourdet are warm, charming and gregarious, and have a little girl; they discovered the tumbledown old place before she was born. What you find now, at the end of the long, bumpy, winding lane, is a beautiful 18th-century farmhouse with barns around, fringed by a horse chestnut and a lime tree from which a swing hangs. It's as pretty as a picture and as stylish as can be. There are flowers on window ledges, box trees in pots and chickens strutting; pure 'France profonde'. The Farmhouse is in a private wing of the main building, the Bergerie is a lofty, one-storey barn and the Petite Maison, with the old bread oven, is a hideaway for two. All have been sympathetically restored to reveal original rafters, beams and creamy stone walls; the Nicholsons then added chunky terracotta floors, charming kitchens, white bathrooms and fresh furnishings. Sheer relaxing delight – plus heated pool, potager, patios, playhouse and treasure hunts. Not forgetting warm eggs from those hens and freshest veg straight from the garden. *B&B also. Shared pool. Aga cookery courses Sept-May.*

Price	Farmhouse £395–£1,075. Bergerie £395–£975. Petite Maison £345–£545 per week.
Sleeps	13
Rooms	Farmhouse: 1 double, 1 twin; 2 bathrooms. Extra family room for 3 & cots on request. Bergerie: 1 double, 1 twin & single bed on mezzanine; 1 bath, separate wc. Petite Maison: 1 double; 1 shower.
Meals	Dinner, 4 courses with aperitif & wine, €35. On request. Restaurant 5km.
Closed	Rarely.

Les & Louise Nicholson
Souvigné, Deux Sèvres

Tel	+33 (0)5 49 76 35 39
Email	info@boisbourdet.com
Web	www.boisbourdet.com

Ethical Collection: Environment; Food.
See page 370 for details

Entry 111   Map 9

Le Clos des Jardins - Le Four du Boulanger & Les Écuries

This is great for families. With its sunflower fields, honey stone walls and carthorses, the tiny village of Mandegault is a reminder of how rural France used to be. Life slows to a tranquil trot, a pace which owners Alison and Francis have been delighted to adopt at their 18th-century farmstead. Hens and ducks potter in the courtyard (children may collect the eggs at feeding time) and you are well supplied with fresh organic vegetables. In both cottages natural colours and fabrics predominate, and rooms keep their honey-coloured open-stone walls and oak beams. Spotless bedrooms are small and simple yet elegant, with scrubbed wooden floorboards and iron or wooden beds. Gardens are secluded and pretty, with herbs, fig trees, lawns and teak loungers, and they can interconnect if two families rent the cottages together. There's a raised wooden pool for children to share, bikes to borrow and a shared games area with a small raised pool. Chef Boutonne, the nearest town, has a fairytale château, fascinating old washhouses and a Saturday market: don't miss the Charentais melons. *Shared pool.*

Price	Le Four du Boulanger €365-€645. Les Écuries €320-€550. Prices per week. Linen not included.
Sleeps	8.
Rooms	Le Four du Boulanger: 1 double, 1 twin, sofabed in living room; 1 bathroom. Les Écuries: 1 double, 1 twin; 1 shower room.
Meals	Dinner €20 (children under 10 free), on request. Restaurant 3km.
Closed	Rarely. November-April long lets only.

Francis & Alison Hudson
Mandegault, Deux Sèvres

Tel	+33 (0)5 49 29 65 31
Email	mandegault@aol.com
Web	www.ruralretreats.org

Le Logis de Bellevue - Le Pigeonnier & La Colomberie

You are five minutes from the prettiest riverside village of the Marais Poitevin; drive straight in to a walled garden with lawns, cedars and acacias. There are two gîtes – perfect for large family get-togethers or groups of friends, converted from a long barn, each with their own entrance and both with a contemporary feel. La Colomberie has views over the pool, a cosy wood-burning stove in the sitting room and an antique dresser crammed with books; Le Pigeonnier is south-facing with a large dining room and a cool, tiled floor. Both have large, hugely functional kitchens with plenty of space, and a bright, sunny feel. Bedrooms have a nautical or farmhouse bent with shell pictures, white wooden walls, wooden floors and neat new rain showers; beds are dressed in cool cottons. The pool is shared with B&B guests, but there are plenty of private spaces – and good seating – in the garden. And there is simply tons to do in the magical 'Green Venice': explore miles of waterways for super walking, cycling, punting and birdwatching, visit La Rochelle's old port, or stroll around Eleanor of Aquitaine's Abbey. *B&B also.*

Price	£950–£1,300 per week.
	£400 per weekend in low season.
Sleeps	16.
Rooms	Le Pigeonnier & La Colomberie: each with 2 family rooms (double & 2 singles); 2 shower rooms.
Meals	Restaurants 400m.
Closed	Rarely.

Marylyn & Anthony Kusmirek
Coulon, Deux Sèvres

Tel	+33 (0)5 49 76 75 45
Email	kusmirek@orange.fr
Web	www.lelogisdebellevue.com

Blacksmith's Cottage

What a pretty stone cottage, this former village blacksmith's house. His forge is next door and Elspeth and Graham have breathed new life into reclaimed timbers and old stones. The dapper exterior hides a snug indoors and the full architectural works: beamed ceilings, stone walls, fine wooden floors. The style is artistic, rustic and easy on the eye. The downstairs bedroom has French windows that open to a pretty terrace and private garden where a walnut tree looms. The kitchen/living room, its flagged floors drenched in golden morning light, has an unusual wooden staircase made by monks that spirals up to the other rooms, one of which has a Goldilocks feel – fun for little ones. The kitchen holds all you need. The charming walled garden comes with a lawn, parasols, barbecue and shade-giving trees, and there's a wild vegetable and fruit garden from where you may harvest whatever is in season; the nearest shops are in Néré, three miles away. The pool is beautifully secluded in its walled and gated garden between the cottage and the owners' house. *Extra room for 2 nearby. Shared pool.*

Price	£375-£500 per week. Linen not included.
Sleeps	4.
Rooms	1 twin, 1 double, 1 children's room; 1 bathroom, separate wc.
Meals	Restaurant 3-minute walk.
Closed	Rarely.

Graham D'Albert & Elspeth Charlton
Romazières, Charente-Maritime

Tel	+33 (0)5 46 33 60 88
Email	elspeth.charlton@hotmail.co.uk

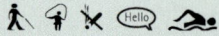

Fisherman's Cottage

Leave the summer throng behind you, wind through the creamy, cobbled backstreets of Saint Martin and discover your peaceful fisherman's cottage. Step from the street straight into the beamy sitting room snug with open fire, comfy sofas and the owner's collection of ceramics. The sitting room blends into the peppermint kitchen and then into a small but perfectly formed garden. It may be teensy but everything is here: walls for privacy, tumbling plants… dine on the terrace, sprawl on the rug-sized lawn, gaze on the buttresses of the medieval abbey that rise majestically above. The twin upstairs comes with portholes that look on to the stairwell; the double has a brass bed, a sloping pine ceiling and a picture window overlooking the garden, the terracotta roofs and the abbey, illuminated at night. If you don't feel like cooking, stroll down into fashionable Saint Martin, pick a harbourside restaurant and watch the bobbing boats. Ré is ideal for family holidays: its lovely white sand beaches are a short walk or bike ride away. *Bike hire close by.*

Price	£400-£600 per week. Linen not included.
Sleeps	4.
Rooms	1 double, 1 twin; 1 bathroom.
Meals	Restaurant 3-minute walk.
Closed	Rarely.

Graham D'Albert & Elspeth Charlton
Saint Martin de Ré, Charente-Maritime

Tel	+33 (0)5 46 33 60 88
Email	elspeth.charlton@hotmail.co.uk

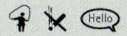

Manoir Souhait - Le Verger

The dining room still has the stone oven where the former inhabitants cooked their pigeons. The birds, a delicacy reserved for the gentry, were reared in the pigeonnier just outside the gates. The house stands in the grounds of the 19th-century manoir where British owners Liz and Will live and do B&B. Camaraderie comes easily to them so you can get to know each other by the fenced and heated pool – a boon for families with its section for children – the sauna or the jacuzzi, and you can arrange to join them at a tempting table d'hôtes dinner in the dining room of the Manoir or on the garden terrace. There's snooker, badminton and table tennis, too. Le Verger used to house farmworkers who made cognac. Inside, it is light and clean and the furniture mostly modern pine, with ancient roof beams to add character. In the pretty town of Cognac, a 20-minute drive, you can tour the distilleries of Rémy Martin, Hennessy and Courvoisier. Try the area's other tipple too, pineau des Charentes, a sweet aperitif. Bikes can be hired locally and there are lovely rides and walks. *B&B also.*

Price	£415–£830 per week.
Sleeps	5.
Rooms	1 twin, 1 family room for 3; 1 bathroom.
Meals	Dinner, with wine, €27. On request.
Closed	Rarely.

Will & Liz Weeks
Gourvillette, Charente-Maritime

Tel	+33 (0)5 46 26 18 41
Mobile	+33 (0)6 08 48 27 34
Email	weeks@manoirsouhait.com
Web	www.manoirsouhait.com

La Maison Cothonneau

Swap four wheels for two on peaceful Île de Ré. The island is criss-crossed with cycle paths and wrapped in 30km of white beaches. In a quiet back street, your cottage is stunningly stylish, beautifully relaxed, full of personal attentions. Eat out in the sunny, flagged, high-walled courtyard dotted with potted palms and an outdoor shower for sluicing sandy children. Downstairs is one large and lovely living space: chunky beams, terracotta, a gentle palette of whites and greys. The smart kitchen can be screened off, a cupboard hides the telly, a Louis XVI fireplace keeps you cosy. Up the 17th-century staircase are three bedrooms pretty with pistachio paintwork, seagrass flooring and flowery throws; the third room is suitably shipshape with a lantern for bedtime reading, cabin-style cupboard doors and a top bunk with a sliding ladder; the bathroom has sparkling new tiles, a 1920s basin, a vintage showerhead. Pop down the road for local oysters and newly landed fish from the bustling harbourside. Welcome gestures include a choice of coffees and leaf teas, fresh flowers, daily croissants… exceptional.

Price	€1,100-€2,150 per week.
Sleeps	6.
Rooms	1 double, 1 twin/double, 1 room with bunks; 1 bathroom, separate wc.
Meals	Restaurants 150m.
Closed	Never.

The Owner
Saint Martin de Ré, Île de Ré,
Charente-Maritime

Mobile	+33 (0)6 10 28 09 14
Email	infos@maison-cothonneau.com
Web	www.maison-cothonneau.com/index_en.html

Le Batiment

You are a short hop away from St Jean D'Angely with its pretty Romanesque architecture and good restaurants, but all is peaceful here, in the rustic village. Inside this converted, ancient building you find a roomy, open-plan living area with a wood-burning stove, muted colours and a fresh, seaside feel, while a galleried landing has brown leather sofas. This is perfect for four grown ups, with two small terraced areas for al fresco dining and staring at grand views, and a simple, sparkling kitchen with all the bits even a serious cook might need. Bedrooms are just off the living area and are light and airy with some good-looking artefacts dotted about and cool stone tiles on the floors; colours are blues and sands. There are two bathrooms — both absolutely gorgeous in mosaic and stone; one with his and hers sinks and a walk-in shower, the other with a deep bath. There's plenty to do locally (the village has a riding school) and you are near to vineyards if wine is your thing; but the lovely coast is only a 40-minute drive — go all cosmopolitan and hit the Chatilaillon plage.

Price	€425– €850 per week.
Sleeps	4.
Rooms	1 double, 1 twin; 2 bathrooms.
Meals	Restaurants 5km.
Closed	Rarely.

Lesley Hanmore
La Benate, Charente-Maritime

Tel	+44 (0)1444 452248
Mobile	+44 (0)7503 040379
Email	lesley@french-house1.co.uk
Web	www.lebatimentfrance.com

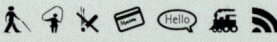

Maison Marennes

What an ideal spot: minutes from the market square (fishmongers, restaurant, boulangerie), and sand and surf a 3km-jog away. As for the house, tucked down a narrow, winding street, surrounded by gardens and smartly walled lawns, it's a treasure, combining French country features — pale blue shutters, beautiful stone winding staircase — with a crisp Scandinavian décor. It would be perfect for two young families or one with grandparents in tow: the downstairs double has its own bathroom and terrace. And you couldn't possibly be stumped for things to do: there's a garden of winding pathways and bursting flowers, a barbecue off the kitchen, several bikes, a kidney-shaped pool, and, in the rare event of the weather being anything other than gorgeous, table tennis, log fire and satellite TV. Décor is a comfortable blend of rough plaster and dusky grey and the open-plan kitchen is the heart of the house. Bedrooms are decorated without fuss but with playful touches — lavender parcels on pillows, giant canvas family photos, a few retro colours. There's even a blackboard so you can plan your excursions! Fabulous.

Price	€450–€1,850 per week.
Sleeps	10.
Rooms	2 doubles, 2 twins, 1 room with bunks; 2 bathrooms, 1 shower room. Cots.
Meals	Restaurants 500m.
Closed	Never.

Joan Groves
Marennes, Charente-Maritime

Tel	+44 (0)28 9188 4216
Email	joangroves@aol.com
Web	www.maisonmarennes.co.uk

Château Mouillepied - La Maison du Vivier

Big French windows overlook the lily-strewn fishpond which gives La Maison its name. A graceful 18th-century cottage, it was once the château's summer house and stands at the edge of the gardens. Now energetic young English owners plan to upgrade its clean-cut but relatively simple décor. Inside, all is open-plan, the entire first floor given over to a big family bedroom; there are exposed beams above and a floor of pale pine. The big sunny living room downstairs has an open fireplace (logs on the house) and a decent kitchen, and those French windows opening to a private patio and lawn. The lovely grounds are shared with the hotel guests (and, sometimes, wedding guests too). Seek out the fine dovecote and the intriguing outhouses, including the bread oven and the decorative *lessiveuses* (washtubs), the original laundry. The owners also plan an English cottage garden to replace the more formal French landscaping. Pick up a fishing licence from the local bakery and stroll along the banks of the Charente to visit the Roman city of Saintes – and the castle said to inspire *Puss in Boots. Sawday hotel.*

Price	€390–€680 per week. Towels not included.
Sleeps	6.
Rooms	2 family rooms for 3, sofabed; 1 bathroom.
Meals	Restaurant 2km.
Closed	Never.

Claire & Patrick Beladina
Port d'Envaux, Charente-Maritime

Tel	+33 (0)5 46 90 49 88
Mobile	+33 (0)6 78 13 93 39
Email	info@chateaumouillepied.com
Web	www.chateaumouillepied.com

Le Logis de Bresdon - Gîte

A secluded 19th-century manor house in deeply peaceful countryside; your stylish gîte was once the cowshed. Now it has a clean, open-plan Gustavian feel with soft blue paintwork, a pretty antique dresser, chocolate-coloured sofas and cool terracotta floors in the living room with its French windows to a private terrace and garden. Bedrooms have seagrass carpets, floral curtains and good views; bathrooms are not huge but are swish and immaculate. The kitchen has everything you need, but you may prefer to pop up to the big house for supper (or even breakfast if you're feeling utterly incapable). Kathy and Chris love to cook so you are free to join the B&B guests for delicious locally sourced dinners, served under the stars in the meditation garden, or in the chic dining room. Acres of well kept gardens have stunning views and an orchard; help yourselves to fruit and nuts. You are in the sunniest region of France: splash in the smart pool, have a game of croquet or table tennis, or hire a bike. The quiet village is three miles away and the Atlantic coast for sandy beaches just over an hour. *Sawday B&B.*

Price	€600–€1,200 per week.
Sleeps	4.
Rooms	1 double, 1 twin; 2 bathrooms.
Meals	Dinner €30. Restaurant 4km.
Closed	Rarely.

Kathy Fortescue
Bresdon, Charente-Maritime

Tel	+33 (0)5 46 25 09 44
Mobile	+33 (0)6 13 82 18 39
Email	kathy.fortescue@orange.fr
Web	www.logis-de-bresdon.com

Maison Brives

A grand 19th-century presbytery in a small Charentais village. It has long pastoral views and is owned by Elisabeth, sculptor, gardener and entrepreneur. Inside, all is elegantly traditional: ochre walls and polished antiques, a downstairs loo with a big antique sink, French windows opening to a 40-foot terrace. The kitchen comes with all mod cons; the charming marble-tiled bathroom has a six-foot Victorian bath; for nights in, there's satellite telly. An elm staircase winds up through shafts of light to bedrooms that exude a gentle stylishness: powder-blue and dusty-pink walls, beautiful fabrics, big comfortable beds. The grounds, impeccably kept and summer-scented, are entirely enclosed and full of shady corners, with a splendid summer saltwater pool. Nearby Saintes exults in an amphitheatre, a summer music festival, a market most days and a *foire* on the first Monday of the month: feast your eyes on Atlantic seafood, artisan cheeses and vegetables still muddy from the earth. And vans deliver croissants, bread and essentials to the village. *Unfenced but alarmed pool. Children over 8 welcome.*

Price	£800–£1,600 per week.
Sleeps	6.
Rooms	2 doubles, 1 twin; 1 bathroom, 2 shower rooms.
Meals	Restaurants 4km
Closed	October–April.

Elisabeth Whittaker
Brives sur Charente,
Charente-Maritime

Tel	+44 (0)20 8995 9255
Mobile	+33 (0)5 46 93 54 77
Email	maison-brives@hotmail.com
Web	www.maison-brives.eu

Moreau - The Farmhouse

Understated elegance and homeliness are skilfully combined in this 18th-century farmhouse; its mood of tranquillity and sophistication beguiles and soothes. Plain yet luxurious, it is decorated throughout with antiques; no surprise to learn that the English owner Marian is an antiques dealer. The house used to be a wealthy farm where the aperitif pineau was made; the chestnut beamed ceilings and stone fireplace have been superbly preserved. The spectacular kitchen – the old distillery – has a huge vaulted ceiling, a wood-burning range and dazzling white walls and floors to set off a sensational display of navy and white china. Enjoy the dreamy views over the fields from the big carpeted bedroom with fabulous antique bed and huge beams. Outside, a private garden with a raised pool. Stock up in Cercoux, or shop at the twice-weekly market at pretty Coutras, a 20-minute drive. Nearby medieval Montguyon holds a folklore festival in July and August; there's also a lake for swimming and a beach area with a little café. Marian is delightful, available yet unobtrusive. Readers are full of praise.

Price	£300-£620 per week.
Sleeps	6.
Rooms	2 family rooms for 3, 1 daybed in sitting room; 1 bathroom, 1 shower room.
Closed	November-March.

Marian Sanders
Cercoux,
Charente-Maritime

Tel	+33 (0)5 46 04 01 66
Email	marianatmoreau@hotmail.com
Web	www.holidayatmoreau.com

Moreau - Le Pressoir

Like the house next door, this fine 18th-century Charentais house is a treasure chest of fascinating antiques and artefacts, all chosen and carefully composed by Marian. The front doors were once French windows from a local château, there's a pitch-pine armoire from a priest's house in Bordeaux and, in the kitchen/dining room, brass chandeliers from Nantes. Marian's great skill, however, is that she's kept furnishings as simple as possible so as to let this lovely stone building speak for itself. Rooms are large, airy and stylish, with pure white walls and original terracotta tiled floors. French windows lead from the kitchen to a big walled terrace, perfect for sunny breakfasts, and a big, private garden with a raised pool beyond. The cool and spacious downstairs double bedrooms are in the old pressoir where grapes were pressed to make pineau de Charentes, the aperitif for which the area is famous. Colours are muted beiges and pinks, beds are handsome brass and views are of the garden. Worth every penny.

Price	£400–£720 per week.
Sleeps	7.
Rooms	2 doubles, 1 triple; 1 bathroom, 2 shower rooms.
Closed	November–March.

Marian Sanders
Cercoux, Charente-Maritime

Tel	+33 (0)5 46 04 01 66
Email	marianatmoreau@hotmail.com
Web	www.holidayatmoreau.com

Les Deux Marronniers - House & Barn

In the soft light of the Charente, far from the summer crowds, one magnificent chestnut tree (*marronnier*) greets you at the entrance, a second shades the peaceful courtyard. The solid stone farmhouse and outbuildings, typically Charentais, are now the owners' family house, which stands on one side of the yard, and the guests' garden and two gîtes on the other. Inside, they are elegantly cool: smart modern sofas on old wooden floors, wrought-iron tables, country chairs, shades of off-white: comfortable, easy living. Both gîtes have central heating, each has its own small terrace and one has an open fire. Pale beamy bedrooms have pretty toile de Jouy or crisp checks and muslin: shades of their former English owners; views roll greenly past. Crunch across the yard through a stone archway to the lovely pool hidden behind high walls, with canvas parasols and a terracotta-roofed lean-to for shade. The essential visits include Romanesque churches, cognac cellars and summer festivals while a spring-fed lake with pedalos and restaurant is a 20-minute drive and the Atlantic just an hour's scenic outing.

Price	Barn €600-€1,250. House €450-€950. Prices per week.
Sleeps	14.
Rooms	Barn: 1 double, 2 twins; 1 bathroom, 1 shower room. House: 1 double, 1 twin; 1 bathroom. Two extra rooms in main house (1 double, 1 twin; 1 bathroom, 1 wc).
Meals	Restaurant 3km.
Closed	Never.

Christophe & Valérie Vuitton
Saint Palais du Né, Charente

Tel	+33 (0)5 45 78 47 25
Mobile	+33 (0)6 22 45 25 60
Email	christophe.vuitton@wanadoo.fr
Web	www.charente-gites.net

Relais de St Preuil

Le Relais de St Paul sits alone at the top of a hill surrounded by vineyards and sky – a fabulous setting. Gentle Madame is from Burgundy, worked in Asia and is now fulfilling a dream: to run a hotel in Poitou-Charentes. The couple were looking for a large 18th-century property and a business adventure, and ended up with a hamlet! Years of hard work and dedication have resulted in a polished holiday complex and some very comfortably dressed rooms. There are three immaculate apartments here, with old stone walls and new cream tiles, leather sofas and neat log fires… perfect for a big group of friends, or for a small, sociable family. And there's so much to do it's impossible to be bored: a tennis court and large pool, a fitness room and sauna, mountain bikes, ping-pong and playground… all has been thought of and more, from in-room massages to generous pool towels. Meet the other guests at table d'hôtes, visit the cognac distilleries – the best vineyards surround you. There's a small supermarket and market in Segonzac, and restaurants and shops in Angoulême and Cognac, both charming towns. *Sawday hotel.*

Price	€400–€1,450 for 4-6 per week.
Sleeps	15.
Rooms	Le Coche: 2 doubles, 1 twin; 2 bathrooms.
	Le Phaéton: 1 double, 1 twin; 1 bathroom.
	La Malle Poste: 1 double, 1 twin, 1 single; 2 bathrooms.
Meals	Breakfast €13. Dinner €40.
Closed	February-March.

Christine Montembault
St Preuil, Charente

Tel	+33 (0)5 45 80 80 08
Email	contact@relais-de-saint-preuil.com
Web	www.relais-de-saint-preuil.com

Fleuret - Main House

The setting of this solid stone 17th-century farmhouse is breathtaking: views of hills and woodland fill every window. This is a sensitive restoration by the architect owner, who lives with wife Gilly and their family in the other half of the building. Walls are thick and space plentiful. The kitchen/dining room is immense with warm wooden flooring, a wood-burner in the ancient hearth, an antique table for family feasts; the sitting room has colourwashed walls, some exposed stone, comfortable sofas – wholly delightful. One double room is downstairs, the other four are in the attic with gabled ceilings, white walls, no clutter. There are books, games, a video library and Tim's photographs on the walls (ask about his courses on landscape photography). On the same site are a separate barn and a cottage – all share farmyard, games room and pool. So, a chance to be sociable, but peace and privacy too. Medieval, hilltop Curemonte, waving to you across the valley, has a market that opens in summer, and there are masses of castles and caves to discover. *Shared pool. Further house for 4 with pool, 8km from Beaulieu.*

Price	€1,190–€1,990 per week. €490 for 3 days in low season.
Sleeps	12.
Rooms	2 doubles, 2 triples, 2 singles; 1 bathroom, 2 shower rooms.
Meals	Lunch/dinner €20 on request. Chef also available on request. Restaurant 3km.
Closed	Never.

Tim & Gilly Mannakee
Curemonte, Corrèze

Tel	+33 (0)5 55 84 06 47
Mobile	+33 (0)6 10 50 47 44
Email	info@fleuretholidays.com
Web	www.fleuretholidays.com

Limousin

Fleuret - The Cottage

The old bread oven adds a rustic note to the big characterful kitchen, its brick surround charred by the ages. It was discovered and restored by Tim and Gilly, who revived the red sandstone farm cottage some years back. Stonework and ancient beams have been preserved and terracotta floors and pine cupboards added; cookery books, strings of garlic and board games add to the informality. The sitting room is charming with cherry-pink sofas and stove; attic bedrooms are simple and cosily carpeted, with small dormer windows to pretty views. French windows let you out of the kitchen into an outdoor barbecue area where you can dine and gaze on fields, woods and never-ending hills. Outside you find a super big walled-off pool, shared with your delightful British hosts next door (who have a bouncy dog), and an amazing barn with a vast oak floor that you may use whenever you like: table tennis, billiards, dancing, grand piano; it can also be hired for weddings. An unfussy home for a family in search of peace and space, in a lovely setting. *Shared pool. Sleeps 18 with Main House.*

Price	€510–€990 per week. From €160 for 2 days in low season.
Sleeps	4.
Rooms	1 double, 1 twin; 1 bathroom.
Meals	Lunch/dinner €20 on request. Chef also available on request. Restaurant 3km.
Closed	Never.

	Tim & Gilly Mannakee Curemonte, Corrèze
Tel	+33 (0)5 55 84 06 47
Mobile	+33 (0)6 10 50 47 44
Email	info@fleuretholidays.com
Web	www.fleuretholidays.com

La Farge

As ideal a hideaway today as it was for refugees during the war, this large Correzian barn overlooks the pastures of the plateau above the Dordogne. English owners Helen and Keith do B&B across the lane, have a wealth of local knowledge and give guests a big welcome; their charming neighbours may stop for a chat, too. Hens potter about the lane, the beautiful Limousin cows occasionally pass by. Inside, there's a fresh feel to the big, terracotta-floored living room, amply furnished with chunky chairs in flowery covers and usefully stocked with books, games and CDs. The kitchen is just as well-fitted. There's a large white bathroom and a cool, blue bedroom with new pine beds, blue-painted furniture and round blue rug. Big blue pots of geraniums surround the barn in summer and 'Le Parc', as it is known by the locals – a large, enclosed area of lawns and trees, with good garden furniture and a barbecue – is all yours. Enjoy the Archibalds' attentive welcome at all times and their sheltered pool in summer. Perfect for those seeking quintessential rural France. *Sawday B&B.*

Price	£230–£345 per week.
	Extra £40 with pool.
Sleeps	2.
Rooms	1 twin; 1 bathroom.
Meals	Dinner, with wine, €32.50. On request.
	Restaurants 15km.
Closed	Rarely.

Keith & Helen Archibald
Monceaux sur Dordogne, Corrèze

Tel	+33 (0)5 55 28 54 52
Email	info@chezarchi.com
Web	www.chezarchi.com

Entry 129   Map 10

Limousin

Le Moulin d'Arnac - Pigeonnier, The Granary, Miller's House

From the motorway to the mill the countryside is gorgeous: dramatic hillsides, ancient woods, lonely hillside villages and many streams hurrying down to the Dordogne. The Miller's House (the most old-fashioned), The Granary and the owner's house straddle the black mill pond; the half-timbered Pigeonnier (no sitting room, just kitchen area) is set to one side. Interiors are simple, with wooden floorboards and pine furniture, bedrooms are not huge but the beds are good and the linen crisp; bathrooms are adequate and clean as a whistle. Each has its own outdoor space and the very pretty garden is big, so you can remain private if you want, but it would be a shame not to use the shared pool – some braver souls swim in the deep pond. Christine is a generous, relaxed soul who scatters industrial quantities of bird seed; there are nuthatches, golden oriels, hoopoes, kingfishers and herons on the pond, not forgetting Pandora the duck. You can fish from the property, there are bikes to borrow, a cheese farm down the road, and if you book all three places you can pitch tents for big family fun. *B&B on request.*

Price	Pigeonnier €400–€500.
	Granary €600–€800.
	Miller's House €600–€850.
	Prices per week. Short breaks available.
Sleeps	12.
Rooms	P: 1 twin on mezzanine; 1 bathroom.
	G: 1 double, 1 twin; 1 bathroom.
	MH: 2 doubles, 1 twin; 1 bathroom.
Meals	Welcome pack on arrival.
	Restaurants 4km.
Closed	Rarely.

Christine Jubb
Nonards, Corrèze

Tel	+33 (0)5 55 91 09 75
Mobile	+33 (0)6 26 17 52 06
Email	chriskenjubb@aol.com
Web	www.moulindarnac.com

L'Abbaye du Palais - Moines

Another graceful restoration by Dutch owners in rural France. In five hectares of forest, meadow and orchard stand a Cistercian abbey, chapel, outbuildings and ruins. Your delightful hosts, with three children and a background in hotel management, have poured hearts and talents into this special place. They live in the 12th-century abbey, do popular B&B and have converted the old monks' bakery into a gîte for eight. A tangle of greenery envelops this generous, two-storey cottage, with its terracotta floors, stone walls, cream drapes, antiques and open fire. The bread oven – still intact – is medieval, the kitchen new. A U-shaped bar separates it from the dining area, there are French windows to a west-facing patio with wooden loungers and barbecue, serenity and light. This is marvellous for robust children: hollow trees to hide in, woods to build dens in, a dressing-up box to raid; bikes, ping-pong, trampoline, pool and games; rabbits, cats, dog and pony – and jolly trailer tractor rides. On Thursdays in summer, great big barbecues are held in the courtyard for (mostly Dutch) guests and friends. *Sawday B&B. Cookery courses.*

Price	€900–€1,600 per week.
Sleeps	8.
Rooms	1 double, 3 twins; 2 bathrooms. Cots.
Meals	Dinner on request. Restaurant 5km.
Closed	January & February.

Martijn & Saskia Zandvliet-Breteler
Bourganeuf, Creuse

Tel	+33 (0)5 55 64 02 64
Email	info@abbayedupalais.com
Web	www.abbayedupalais.com

Raymond - Mandailles St Julien

Walk out of this traditional Auvergnat house into stupendous countryside. You can hear a gurgling stream from your bed and all around are breathtaking views of the cone-shaped *puys*. The 200-year-old house was once two cottages. One half retains the living room where once the family lived, ate and slept: it still has the original wooden beams, long table and inglenook fireplace where you can toast your toes and wind down after a day in the mountains. The other half, a ruin when the Haines found it, feels more modern, extra windows add airiness and light. Bedrooms vary too: ancient, crannied and characterful or light and modern. View the volcanoes from the terrace, visit local cheesemakers to sample Cantal, shower under the waterfall in the river, trawl the market in Aurillac. You can buy yogurt and goat's cheese from the farmer next door and a travelling shop comes three times a week – listen for his horn. There are guided mountain walks, some with donkeys, and adventure sports all summer, mushroom-picking in the autumn, cross-country skiing 1km away in winter. Marvellous.

Price	£250-£350 per week. Linen not included.
Sleeps	6.
Rooms	2 doubles, 1 twin/double; 2 shower rooms, separate wc.
Meals	Restaurants 2km.
Closed	December-Easter.

Ann & Stephen Haine
Aurillac, Cantal

Tel	+44 (0)20 7267 8936
Mobile	+44 (0)7977 307554
Email	annhaine@blueyonder.co.uk
Web	www.auvergne-cottage.com

La Roche

Clinging to a hillside where woods and birds abound and water gushes in the valley below, La Roche stands at the end of the lane in glorious isolation and a blaze of flowers. The delightful, knowledgeable English owners live in the old farmhouse, you are in the remarkably converted barn at the front end of the building. Through the high arched doors a splendid split-level living space ascends to old oak beams. The main floor, lit by that glazed barn door and high windows onto your private patch of wild garden, is where you will cook and eat and gather in unexpectedly urbane 1980s bucket chairs by the wood-burner. The mezzanine has two bottle-green futons, a table and chairs for board games and super photographs of life in old Auvergne. Beyond, two snug bedrooms share a clever little grey-green bathroom where the bath is countersunk to floor level so that you shan't bang your head when showering. The other shower and laundry are in the basement. Nature is queen here and summons you forth whatever the weather; or explore those unspoilt villages and towns. *Book via Gîtes de France: www.gite-laroche.com.*

Price	€320–€450 per week. Linen not included.
Sleeps	4.
Rooms	1 double, 1 twin, 2 double futons on mezzanine; 1 bathroom, 1 shower room, 3 separate wcs.
Meals	Restaurant 8km.
Closed	Mid-November to early February.

Catherine & Michael Slater
Oradour, Cantal

Tel	+33 (0)4 71 23 37 92
Email	catherine@slater-laroche.com
Web	www.gite-laroche.com

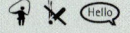

Sweet Little House

Tiny, south-facing and built into the rock, this stone house is described by its owners as "doll's-house pretty". Di and Peter, who moved here from Devon in 1993 to live nearby, hope you will drop in for a glass of wine and a chat. The little house was built a century ago by a hay-rake maker and its slate roof, steeply pitched to fend off the snow, is typical of the Auvergne. Materials are simple – lots of pale pine – and Di has given it style through careful choice of furnishings. Antique china plates decorate the compact, beautifully equipped kitchen; in the bedrooms upstairs are a fine wrought-iron bed with a thoroughly modern base, and country antiques. Rooms are uncluttered and immaculately clean, creating a feeling of light and space. The living room is cosy with its parquet floors and wonderful Godin wood-burner, the original haymaker's tools remind you of olden times. There's a tiny patio for eating out, your gardens are the narcissi-filled meadows, your backdrop, the mountains of the national park. Birdwatchers, walkers, silence-seekers will be in heaven. *Exclusively for non-smokers. Two other houses for 2-4.*

Price	£290–£590 per week.
Sleeps	4.
Rooms	1 double, 1 twin; 1 bathroom.
Meals	Restaurants nearby.
Closed	Rarely.

Di & Peter Scott
Condat, Cantal

Tel	+33 (0)4 71 78 63 57
Email	p.scott@wanadoo.fr
Web	www.auvergneholidaycottage.com

Entry 134   Map 10

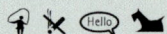

Château de Coisse - Gîte & Studio

After years in tourism and adventure sports, this dynamic couple met a greater challenge: to transform a hotchpotch of rambling ruins (dated 1100s to 1700s: carvings, towers, remnants of former rustic grandeur) where the local lord reigned. The river Dore (for picnics) and 'toy' railway run at the bottom, fields stretch to distant hills, birds flock, dogs rush to greet you. With their own high barn door and great hallway, the two modest gîtes are independent in blue, white and pine with good fittings, kitchen equipment and bedding. The big first-floor flat is fully child-friendly (stair gates, cots, high chair). A vast plateau of a living room, pine-floored, beamed and light, leads out to a private patio-terrace and up to three bedrooms, one blue, one green, one peach, under the sloping roof: simple and pretty, with practical hanging racks and sock baskets. Within immensely thick walls, the small ground-floor flat, without a garden, is cosy and just as well done. Fiona leaves a super welcome quiche. She and Graham are fascinating about their project-of-a-lifetime but you can be as close or distant as you please.

Price	€400-€600. Studio €200-€300. Prices per week. Heating and electricity not included October-April.
Sleeps	8.
Rooms	Gîte: 1 double, 2 twins, sofabed in living room; 1 shower room, separate wc. Studio: 1 twin/double, sofabed in living room; 1 bathroom.
Meals	Dinner, 4 courses, €10. Restaurants 3km.
Closed	Never.

Fiona & Graham Sheldon
Arlanc, Puy-de-Dôme

Tel	+33 (0)4 73 95 00 45
Email	fiandgra@chateaudecoisse.com
Web	www.chateaudecoisse.com

Entry 135   Map 10

Aquitaine

The Beachhouse

It matters not a jot if the children trail sand into the house or bounce beach balls in the bedroom. This pretty 1930s wooden seaside house, five minutes from the beach, is just perfect for families. It's painted green and white and is wholly simple yet very inviting. Jane has bleached the floorboards and painted the smallish bedrooms attractive shades of blue and green. The furniture is 1930s – including the beds, with their firm new mattresses and dazzling white covers – and there are two small galley kitchens. The sitting room isn't huge either; no matter, you'll be spending every spare moment in the cane rocker on the gorgeous covered veranda. This stretches the length of the house and is decorated with floats from old fishing nets; a great place for lunch. The house has its own little garden and is in the centre of town, so expect some noise. There are miles of Atlantic beaches, no shortage of bars and restaurants and a huge daily market in Montalivet. And the fabulous wines of Médoc are just a short drive away. Charming.

Price	€1,200–€4,000. €400 for 4. €800 for 8. Prices per week.
Sleeps	17.
Rooms	4 doubles, 1 family room for 3, 2 children's rooms for 3; 3 bathrooms.
Meals	Restaurants within walking distance.
Closed	Never.

Jane Butler
Vendays Montalivet, Gironde

Tel	+33 (0)5 56 09 32 65
Mobile	+33 (0)6 46 77 55 71
Email	jane.butler@wanadoo.fr
Web	www.medoc-holidays.com

Ethical Collection: Environment.
See page 370 for details.

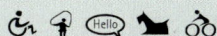

The Country House

A fine 18th-century stone house, Pey au Bruc is a warm, most child-friendly place that has the unmistakable air of being lived in and enjoyed. Jane describes it as 'shabby-chic' and is proud of her collection of antiques. Everywhere has been subtly and thoughtfully restored without in any way being precious. The delightful bedrooms have comfortable antique French beds in original sizes – Napoleonic *lits d'enfants* for the little ones – and the nursery room is packed with old toys, games and dressing-up costumes. Children will also love running with the bunnies free in the garden and discovering the house's secret places, steep stairs and low doors. They have their own sitting room, too, just off the fabulous kitchen. The main salon is gracefully proportioned, with warm stone walls and an open log fire (spiders love it too). Out in the big garden is a lovely stone-edged swimming pool with a good childproof fence and if you prefer the sea, you are six kilometres from the beach. Full of character and quirk, this is not a house for minimalists or health and safety fans.

Price	£2,000–£4,000 per week. Linen not included.
Sleeps	16.
Rooms	5 doubles, 1 double & single, 1 double with 2 children's bed, 1 children's room for 4; 5 bathrooms. Cots.
Closed	Rarely.

Jane Butler
Vendays Montalivet, Gironde

Tel	+33 (0)5 56 09 32 65
Mobile	+33 (0)6 46 77 55 71
Email	jane.butler@wanadoo.fr
Web	www.medoc-holidays.com

Château Coulon Laurensac – Pomerol, Margaux & Sauternes

If you have a passion for wines and want to know more about them, your time here, above the Garonne overlooking Bordeaux, will be delightfully spent. Ronald, knowledgeable and enthusiastic, organises very special tours taking small groups to see the most famous cellars of Médoc or Saint Émilion from the inside – not forgetting a delicious lunch along the way. He and Margaret came to this pretty, compact, 18th-century château with their two young sons and a Jack Russell – aptly named *Bouchon* – a few years ago. They have converted the outbuildings into luxurious guest accommodation: Pomerol was once the cellar master's house; Margaux and Sauternes are in the *chai à barriques*, where wine was aged in gigantic wooden barrels. Pomerol is an exquisite little house spread over two stories, all chunky stone walls, polished tiles, white ceiling beams, black leather sofas. The apartments too have a roomy elegance, and a French style. Kitchens are superbly kitted out, bathrooms are sumptuous, the swimming pool has Roman steps and breakfasts are gourmet. The wines are superb, naturally. *Sawday hotel.*

Price	€750–€1,250 per week.
Sleeps	9.
Rooms	Pomerol: 1 double, 1 twin; 1 bathroom. Margaux: 1 double; 1 bathroom. Sauternes: 1 family room for 3; 1 bathroom.
Closed	Never.

Ronald & Margaret Rens
Latresne, Bordeaux, Gironde

Tel	+33 (0)5 56 20 64 12
Email	coulonlaurensac@wanadoo.fr
Web	www.clbx.com

Entry 138 Map 8

Le Chalard

It is rare indeed to visit an empty house in midwinter and instantly feel a warmth that brings the whole place to life: your cosmopolitan French/Australian hosts have the gift of hospitality tenfold, would welcome you to any family party in the wonderful old barn and want to share their passion for producing organic wine. Jean-Michel's wine knowledge is vast, unpretentious, riveting; Jacqueline can arrange for cookery courses or meals to be prepared on the spot; together they will make your stay unforgettable. Your space is the 400-year-old sunny-ochre pigeon house and pigsties. A glazed door takes you into the stylish yet cosy vaulted and beamed living room with a very effective patterned tile floor, minimal high-quality furniture and original stone walls – a super conversion. The pale bedroom feels fresh and light with all its windows and drapes, the single beds are on the mezzanine. Every summer Castillon gives a re-enactment of the last battle of the 100 Years War; Saint Émilion is nearby, the beaches of Arcachon or the classy boulevards of Bordeaux a little further afield. *Pool occasionally shared.*

Price	€600-€900 per week.
Sleeps	4.
Rooms	1 double, 2 single beds in mezzanine room; 1 shower room, separate wc.
Meals	Restaurants within walking distance.
Closed	Never.

Jacqui & Jean-Michel de Robillard
Flaujagues, Gironde

Tel	+33 (0)5 57 40 15 66
Mobile	+33 (0)6 13 38 26 85
Email	houstonderob@wanadoo.fr
Web	frenchperspectives.com

La Baie du Sureau

Eat, drink and make merry en famille – this rambling farmhouse cries out for it. Young parents Jennifer and Doug have transformed the lovely old blue-shuttered stone house into a great getaway for extended families – or it divides into two smaller, self-contained units. The heart of the Main House is the kitchen with its lapis lazuli tiles and huge table by the fire; there's also a terrace for sun-dappled lunches. The Annexe – reached via the Main House's living room or a separate entrance – is just as well-equipped. In bedrooms, some adjoining, is a mix of quaint raggedy walls, exposed stone and new beds. Ground-floor rooms (better for the less than nimble) open to the garden, where cherries, plums and figs burst with fruit in season; a veg patch is yours for the picking; hens cluck out breakfast eggs. Or have a swing and a splash in the pool; there's a billiards table in the barn, a barbecue on the terrace and a bar for the adults. Ask Jennifer for baby baths, stair gates, babysitting. Even little legs should manage a walk to the fun market town of Monsegur and good beaches and picnic spots are close by.

Price	£1,100–£2,700 per week.
Sleeps	14.
Rooms	4 doubles, 3 twins; 2 bathrooms, 3 shower rooms. 2 cots.
Meals	Restaurants 2km.
Closed	Rarely.

Jenny Moss & Doug Fairbanks
Monségur, Gironde

Tel	+44 (0)844 232 8239
Mobile	+44 (0)7793 797799
Email	jfermoss@live.co.uk
Web	www.feetupinfrance.com

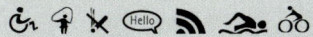

Aquitaine

Les Collines Iduki - Apartments

An attractive holiday complex – 22 gîtes in all, some with one storey, others with two – overlooking one of the prettiest bastide villages of France. A dreamy river sweeps round below, 100-year-old oak trees and fields surround you. Hillside Iduki was designed in Basque style by the architect who built Les Halles in Bayonne and it fits its landscape perfectly. Whitewashed apartments have private terraces with teak furniture and parasols, brightly painted shutters and well-dressed interiors. Small bedrooms have coordinated fabrics, checks and stripes, bathrooms are white, kitchens well-equipped and broadband is throughout. Sitting rooms have stencilled walls, tiled floors, wooden furniture nicely painted. All is comfortable and gently stylish. There are a pool, a play area and organised activities in summer – a treat for sporty couples and active families. The Haramboures run the restaurant by the river and meet you on arrival; the village is a four-minute walk. Come in the last week of July for the fête and three days of carousing in the old village square. *Shared laundry & pool.*

Price	Type A €275-€955. Type B €354-€1,450. Type C €456-€1,850. Prices per week. Half-board €28 p.p. Full-board €47 p.p. HB/FB prices per day extra.
Sleeps	100
Rooms	Type A: 1 double, sofabed; 1 bathroom. Type B: 1 double, 1 twin, sofabed; 1 bathroom, 1 shower room. Apartment C: 1 double, 2 twins, sofabed; 1 bathroom, 2 shower rooms.
Meals	Dinner €24. Restaurant 300m.
Closed	Never.

Marie–Joelle Haramboure
La Bastide Clairence,
Pyrénées-Atlantiques
Tel   +33 (0)5 59 70 20 81
Email   iduki@iduki.net
Web   www.iduki.net

La Conciergerie

In gorgeous, wooded parkland with the fish-filled river Saison gurgling by just a two-minute walk away, this pretty little Béarnais cottage stands next to the 19th-century château, like a 'doll's house' in its own private garden. The new English owners are nurturing roses, oleanders and shrubs: flowering things love it here. Inside, untouched original details include some beautiful, faded terracotta tile work: four floor-to-ceiling windows give an uplifting sense of light streaming into the ground floor from all sides. The sitting/dining room is painted cream and simply furnished in wood and wicker, while colourful Basque fabrics add charm. An attractive narrow wooden staircase takes you up to two smallish bedrooms where more light bounces off the original chestnut floorboards and yellow or pink-and-cream colour schemes. There are birds, butterflies, even otters down at the lovely wild riverside — perfect for a summer dip or picnic. There's fabulous walking in the Pyrenean foothills, skiing higher up in winter, surfing in Biarritz. A great welcome, too.

Price	£350–£575 per week. Short breaks available.
Sleeps	4.
Rooms	2 doubles; 1 shower room.
Meals	Restaurant 20-minute walk.
Closed	Rarely.

Ian & Elizabeth Granville-Miller
Osserain Rivareyte,
Pyrénées-Atlantiques

Tel	+33 (0)5 59 38 51 89
Mobile	+44 (0)7966 279761
Email	elisabeth.granville-miller@orange.fr

Entry 142   Map 13

Aquitaine

The Farmhouse

Families are in clover. The list of child facilities is inspiring, from babysitters (mature English ladies) and baby welcome packs (order ahead) to bicycle seats, balls and sterilisers, toys, buckets and spades. But you get more than comfort and practicalities – there's charm too. The delightful old farmhouse has all the beams, local stonework and 18th-century rusticity you could imagine, and has been studiously, stylishly restored. Floors are of new pale oak or rosy terracotta, bed linens are natural, paint colours harmonious, the kitchen splashback is multi-coloured, the oven range hand-built La Cornue. Sheer pleasure to stay! Well set back from the village road, with contained garden to front and side and fields and Pyrénées beyond, the setting is inviting and the views are spectacular. The owners leave masses of information on what to do and chose the site for its proximity to sand and snow. Biarritz is one hour away, winter sports half an hour, there's white water rafting at Navarrenx and riding and swimming up the road, in unspoilt, idyllic little Gurs. Fabulous all round, and good value.

Price	£595-£995 per week.
Sleeps	6.
Rooms	2 doubles, 1 twin; 1 bathroom, 1 shower room, 2 separate wcs. Extra beds on separate mezzanine area.
Closed	Never.

Samantha Adams
Gurs, Pyrénées-Atlantiques

Tel	+44 (0)1622 747840
Mobile	+44 (0)7905 795784
Email	sam@mountains-2-coast.co.uk
Web	www.mountains-2-coast.co.uk

Clos Mirabel

Welcomed by a couple who live thoughtfully, greet graciously and enjoy the simple pleasures of life, you will feel at ease the moment you arrive. André and Ann fell in love with Clos Mirabel a few years ago, with its sea of vines, parkland and beautiful trees, and its spectacular views – of the entire chain of the Pyrénées Atlantiques, including the Pic du Midi d'Ossau. In the north west part of the manor house, completely independent, your two-storey, two-bedroom, light-filled holiday apartment comes with pristine furniture and fittings, polished granite surfaces and new wood painted pale grey; serene white floorboards and walls add a New England feel. Across the way is the Winery, less contemporary but as immaculate, its dominant colours red and beige, its double doors leading to the shared pool… and those ever-present vineyards and views. The Gatehouse, a third manicured retreat, sits at the entrance to the park, with its own garden. Ride bikes, hike the hills and mountains, surf the Atlantic's waves. Then return to splendid dining in little Jurançon, its famous restaurant blessed with Michelin stars.

Price	Apartment €550–€895. Winery €700–€1395. Gatehouse €550–€795. Prices per week. Linen €16 p.p.
Sleeps	16.
Rooms	Apartment for 4. Winery for 6. Gatehouse for 6.
Meals	Restaurants 2km.
Closed	Never.

Ann Kenny & André Péloquin
Jurançon, Pyrénées-Atlantiques

Tel	+33 (0)5 59 06 32 83
Email	info@closmirabel.com
Web	www.closmirabel.com

Sengresse

Just across the courtyard from the Domaine is the Petite Maison – not so 'petite' but extremely charming. Its white walls tumbled with vines, it has green shutters and an outside stone stair. This solid four-square building was the boulangerie where the bread was baked for the estate, and the old oven and chimney still have pride of place. It was also the *buanderie* (the laundry) and out of season you may rent this, or if you require an extra bedroom take both. The decoration mirrors that of the main house, in which old beams and terracotta tiles form a rustic backdrop to French and English antiques, rich textiles and elegant lights. One bedroom has a rare Chinese carpet in soft aqua, another has a huge kilim. Starck wet rooms are stocked with towels, the kitchen is for cooks. Michèle and Rob will help you get the most out of the area: the biking and hiking, the fishing and riding. Biarritz is a city of style and the Basque villages (Sare, Ascain, Ainhoa) are a delight. Return to three hectares of beautiful grounds for children to wander and a swimming pool shared with the main house. *Shared pool.*

Ethical Collection: Community.
See page 370 for details.

Price	€670–€1,950 per week. From €260 per weekend.
Sleeps	6.
Rooms	La Buanderie: 1 family room for 3; 1 bath & shower room. La Boulangerie: 1 triple; 1 shower room.
Meals	Breakfast €8.50. Dinner, with wine, €25–€35. On request. Restaurant 9km.
Closed	Rarely.

Michèle & Rob McLusky &
Sasha Ibbotson
Souprosse, Landes
Tel   +33 (0)5 58 97 78 34
Email   sengresse@hotmail.fr
Web   www.sengresse.com

La Bergerie - Paguetout

Perfect peace in the middle of the largest forest in Europe. You stay in a lovely old shepherd's house rich with timbers, tucked in total privacy a few yards behind the home of the delightful owner; there's space for all. Step straight into the homely main living area with its big open fireplace, comfy sofas and country furniture; radiating off here are the timber-framed bedrooms with their latched doors, terracotta floors, limed furniture, hand-decorated headboards in wood and wrought iron, pretty linens and French country charm. Only one bathroom, but there's a second loo outside on the terrace that overlooks your own large pool and the beautifully cared-for garden (trees, shrubs, hammock and swing). The galley kitchen is white and duck-egg blue, functional and well-stocked; good restaurants are a short drive. Danièle, who teaches French, is a mine of information about the local area and even knows of sandy beaches that don't get crowded in summer. Great for families, with forest hiking and biking from the door, and aquatic parks not much further. *French courses available.*

Price	£425-£1,495 per week.
Sleeps	8.
Rooms	3 doubles, 1 twin; 1 bathroom, separate wc.
Meals	Restaurant 4km
Closed	Never.

Peter & Tessa Cook
Sabres, Landes

Tel	+44 (0)1727 811414
Mobile	+44 (0)7810 501591
Email	tessa@pecoint.com
Web	www.frenchcountryvillas.com

Entry 146   Map 13

Beaux-Cieux

Colombage, wooden galleries and exposed beams abound, in this unfussily restored *ferme landaise* at the end of a winding road. Around the house is a mowed field; beyond are woods of oak, pine and poplar; a two-minute walk away is a charming, tiny village: just a Mairie, church and school. (The bakery is a five-minute drive.) Nothing amazing about the garden – a few acacia trees for shade – but what it holds is heaven for families: a saltwater pool with a safety roof that slides on and off, a trampoline, a plastic jungle gym, a tree hut, space… and ping-pong on the big veranda. Inside: heaps of books, bright throws on sofas, a piano and logs on the house. Three open-plan spaces run the length of the ground floor, cosily heated underfoot: a sitting room, a hall with a cathedral ceiling and a mezzanine above, a yellow kitchen and a dining area, and a corridor to three simple, spotless bedrooms. Upstairs, under head-ducking eaves, is a bedroom for two children, and, on the landing, room for another two: if you don't mind a gang the house happily takes 13. Ideas for meals, markets and cultural sorties abound.

Price	£440–£1,350 per week.
Sleeps	8.
Rooms	2 doubles, (1 with antique bed), 1 twin, 1 children's twin, sofabed on mezzanine; 2 bathrooms. Extra beds & cots.
Meals	Restaurant 12km.
Closed	Rarely.

Sandrine Hurst
Saint-Julien d'Armagnac, Landes

Tel	+33 (0)1 30 87 06 68
Mobile	+33 (0)6 17 66 26 69
Email	beauxcieux@gmail.com
Web	www.beauxcieux.fr

Les Combes

In rare contrast to the self-conscious chic of so many places, this old bakery has been beautifully and authentically restored. Plaster walls are plain white, floors are of dark glossy wood or old mellow tiles, and, at its heart — which draws you whenever you are indoors — is the irresistible kitchen. Imagine two big farmhouse tables, shelves of interesting china and numerous recesses and unexpected corners. Best of all, the old bread oven is still there and still usable, though you have an Aga and a gas oven as well. Passages wander intriguingly to other rooms, aglow with old country furniture and pieces made by Quentin; the vivid paintings on the beamed walls are by his partner and friends. An open wooden staircase leads you up to delightful bedrooms softly lit by small windows. The lovely old quilt-covered beds are smallish doubles — expect cosy nights! You are surrounded by fields and trees and it's utterly peaceful — just the occasional chug-chug from the tractor next door. No pool but a terrace smothered in vines, and bikes — marginally less old than the house — are on tap. Truly charming.

Price	€750–€850 per week.
Sleeps	7
Rooms	2 doubles, 1 family room for 3; 2 bathrooms.
Closed	Rarely.

Quentin Lowe
Saint Astier de Duras, Lot-et-Garonne

Mobile	+34 650 490646
Email	quentin.lowe@gmail.com
Web	quentin.lowe.googlepages.com

Château de Rodié - L'Appartement

More fortress than château, Rodié comes complete with canon holes, long-drops and tower… wander at will. The story of how Pippa and Paul breathed new life into old stones is inspiring: Paul had a serious accident, they bought the 13th-century ruin and its 135 acres (now their organic farm and a nature reserve) and began the triumphant restoration. In contrast to the tough medieval architecture, they have furnished this excellent big apartment, at a right angle to unshakeable gallery arches, with Empire-period antiques and super metal and wood beds, finishing the rooms with gentle fabrics and rugs that let the old glories glow. Walls are white or pointed stone; atticky windows onto the courtyard and the managed-but-wild nature reserve are small and low with deep sills through the mighty walls. And as it's just been finished, kitchen and bathroom are fully fitted and spanking new. Paul and Pippa farm sheep and run a B&B; Pippa cooks her guests sumptuous organic dinners using much of their own produce: you may arrange to join them. A super-friendly, atmospheric hideaway. *Sawday B&B.*

Price	€250-€400 per week. Short breaks available.
Sleeps	3.
Rooms	1 double, 1 single; bathroom.
Meals	Table d'hôtes on arrival, €20. Meals on request.
Closed	Rarely.

Paul & Pippa Hecquet
Courbiac de Tournon, Lot-et-Garonne
Tel   +33 (0)5 53 40 89 24
Email   mail@chateauderodie.com
Web   www.chateauderodie.com

Entry 149   Map 9

Le Manoir de Monflanquin

In a landscape shimmering with orchards, this fine 1865 manor farmhouse stands in its own park of chestnuts and limes, overlooking summer sunflowers and hilltop Monflanquin. Inside are space, sunshine and an uncluttered, immaculate décor. Up the stone steps to the front door you enter a large hallway off which lie large rooms: a salon with pale plain walls, parquet floor and big windows to the garden; a billiard room with PlayStation and WiFi, perfect for kids; a dining room with two modern tables and a glass chandelier; and a super-duper kitchen with contemporary fittings and masses of light. A wide wood and iron balustrade staircase spirals up to eight bedrooms spread over two floors, all neutral tones, new and pristine, with bathrooms to match. With a south-facing pool lined with loungers and table tennis in the barn, the manoir is an excellent choice for a party of families. What's more, you're a 20-minute walk away from one of "les plus belles villages de France": medieval Monflanquin is full of little shops and restaurants and a vibrant farmers' market in the square on Thursdays.

Price	€3,300-€5,700 per week.
Sleeps	16.
Rooms	5 doubles, 3 twins; 6 bathrooms.
Meals	Restaurant 1km.
Closed	Rarely.

Sarah Gledhill
Monflanquin, Lot-et-Garonne

Mobile	+44 (0)7786 113558
Email	sgledhill47@googlemail.com
Web	www.manoirdemonflanquin.com

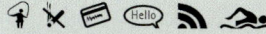

Manoir Serenita

In a woodland clearing at the end of a drive planted with young poplars and willows, smartly floodlit at night, a fine restoration. Up the steps into an immaculate, huge sitting room with tiled floor, fireplace and aged oak beams. Antique stained-glass doors lead to a TV room, and a dining room seating 18 with no trouble. The kitchen is oak-fitted, the French windows open to the heated pool, the tennis court and acres of gardens stretch beyond and the vast games room trumpets table tennis, exercise machines, snooker: everything is on a grand and generous scale. Upstairs are old armoires and period beds, tapestry-style curtains with matching cushions, pictures and plates on ochre walls, fine rugs, brand new mattresses and top-of-the-range linen. Blue or green bathrooms have gleaming fittings and old oak doors. The gardens are fenced to keep out the deer so children may roam to their hearts' content while you play the piano or lounge on the long patio for a starlit barbecue; the local charcutier can deliver. Head out for golf, riding, fishing; and massage and mud baths in nearby Casteljaloux.

Price	£2,595-£4,295 per week.
Sleeps	18.
Rooms	5 doubles, 4 twins; 2 bathrooms, 8 shower rooms, 11 wcs.
Meals	Restaurants 5-8km.
Closed	Mid-October to March, except Christmas & New Year.

Christopher & Louisa Taylor
Fargues sur Ourbise, Lot-et-Garonne

Tel	+33 (0)5 53 20 88 03
Mobile	+33 (0)6 09 96 85 67
Email	louisa.taylor@wanadoo.fr
Web	www.frenchmanoirs.net

La Brugère

A treasure trove of surprises lies behind the sober facade of this 19th-century house, once a hunting lodge. Tapestries and curtains glow in the dining room off a wood-panelled hall, the drawing room, elegant in cream and draped gold, has a stone fireplace, sofas and antiques. Vast French windows open onto two sides of the terrace. There's a panelled library with telly and a fabulous kitchen: two fridges, a large oven, silver cutlery for the dining room, stainless steel for the terrace. Two of the double rooms have four-posters with luscious curtains, chandeliers and polished wooden floors; the master bedroom is reached by its own staircase and the trompe l'œil in its bathroom is fantastic. The twin room has antique sleigh beds. The lavish, even breathtaking, decoration and comfort holds all the way to the parasols round the pool and the delicious towels. Yet the house feels like a home and children will love it; there's badminton and table tennis, three acres of parkland to explore and swimming and fishing in the river Isle. The owners' daughter lives nearby, full of friendly advice. A magnificent place.

Price	£1,500-£2,800 per week.
Sleeps	12.
Rooms	5 doubles, 1 twin; 5 bathrooms.
Closed	Never.

Lisa Grist
Nantheuil de Thiviers, Dordogne

Tel	+44 (0)1438 831239
Email	lisa@tallents.plus.com
Web	www.labrugere.com

Les Taloches - La Grange

Another big, comfortable place to stay in the same grounds as its neighbour La Châtaigne. The airy living space, reaching up to the rafters, has great glass doors across the entrances at either end – a legacy from its past as a drive-through barn. Today a courtyard lies to one side and a large private pool to the other. In the main room is a magnificent fireplace, a long monastery table that could seat two dozen; down a few steps is the kitchen. Also on the ground floor, hidden behind the fireplace, is a large bedroom with its own wisteria-clad patio and a rather grand four-poster. A second sitting area on the mezzanine, filled with a lustrous light, houses the television, DVD and a tempting library of books. Upstairs, beds and walls are patterned or floral, there are two small and dramatically beamed twins and a discreet double, with a private entrance and a balcony terrace. Peaceful, tranquil, secluded, Les Taloches is a lazy walk from the pretty riverside village of Tourtoirac – take a drink in the café/bar, pick up your croissants. The Château of Hautefort and its gardens are near, too. *B&B September-May only.*

Price	B&B €65 for 2. €840-€2,065 per week.
Sleeps	8.
Rooms	2 doubles, 2 twins; 3 bathrooms, separate wc.
Meals	Occasional dinner in summer kitchen.
Closed	Rarely.

Jo & John Sturges
Tourtoirac, Dordogne

Tel	+33 (0)5 53 50 20 26
Mobile	+33 (0)6 30 84 29 05
Email	jsturges@wanadoo.fr
Web	www.les-taloches.com

Les Taloches - La Châtaigne

You're faced with a dilemma here, in 18 lovely hectares of woodland and meadows: which house to choose? Set either side of a courtyard, this one is the old farmhouse, the other its barn. Both are spacious and extremely comfortable, both have their own private gardens and fenced pools. La Châtaigne is beautifully proportioned and full of character with creaky old staircases, twisted beams and bright white walls. The attractive sitting/dining room has a warm stone fireplace at either end and russet floor tiles; the kitchen is super, modern and well-equipped, with a breakfast area overlooking the pool. A double bedroom on the ground floor opens on to the terrace; three more (a twin and a double with a small, bunk-bedded room off) are on the first floor while up in the attic is a vast and delightful family suite — but mind your head in the bathroom! Set well away from both houses are a communal play area and a covered barn with table tennis. There's also an outdoor summer kitchen — a brilliant touch — where Jo will cook meals for guests from time to time. *B&B September-May only.*

Price	B&B €65 for 2. €980–€2,400 per week.
Sleeps	12.
Rooms	2 doubles, 1 twin, 1 room with bunks, 1 family suite for 4; 4 bathrooms, separate wc.
Meals	Occasional dinner in summer kitchen.
Closed	Never.

Jo & John Sturges
Tourtoirac, Dordogne

Tel	+33 (0)5 53 50 20 26
Mobile	+33 (0)6 30 84 29 05
Email	jsturges@wanadoo.fr
Web	www.les-taloches.com

La Maison des Beaux Arts & The Aurora

Space, light, a harmony of colours: clearly an artist's eye created this small, sunny ground-floor flat within a 19th-century townhouse in spirited Nontron. Next to Delia's art studio, downstairs from her B&B rooms, the flat runs through from room to room. First, a well-equipped kitchen with glass-fronted cupboards and drawers built into an old chimney; then the light-flooded living room with oriental soft furnishings and a sofabed for children; and lastly the lovely bedroom at the end, with its antique Indian bed head and armoire; through a large window, a long, green valley of pine and acacias stretches forth. All is quiet, tidy, simple. Hop out through French doors for a barbecue on a private gravel terrace, shaded by a bright yellow parasol, or head to the pretty garden and saltwater pool, which is shared with B&B guests. Delia's enthusiasm for the town and region is well-founded: in the former, famed knife-makers, glass-makers, cabinet-makers, weavers, ceramists, a good choice of restaurants. In the latter, hiking, biking, golf, water sports, caves and fascinating archaeological sites. *Sawday B&B.*

Price	B&B €70–€85 for 2.
	The Aurora €450–€600 per week.
Sleeps	17.
Rooms	5 + 1: 3 doubles, 2 family rooms for 3.
	The Aurora: 1 double, sofabed; shower
	room.
Meals	Restaurants within walking distance.
Closed	Rarely.

Delia Cavers
Nontron, Dordogne

Tel	+33 (0)5 53 56 39 77
Mobile	+33 (0)6 71 09 64 72
Email	delia@deliacavers.co.uk
Web	www.la-maison-des-beaux-arts.com

Forge Basse - The Barn & The Cottage

The Forge Master's House, 1480: how real does that ring on your 21st-century anvil? One of the most atmospheric places possible, the forge once had some 55 iron workers producing cauldrons for the West Indies, cooled by the river that still rushes past the door. Each gîte occupies half a fine stone barn with an extra room in the middle for one or the other. The well-named Barn is all height, beams and open plan. Huge granite blocks from the forge rise again in the door surrounds. The Cottage is cosy with its wood burner in the old fireplace. Both have a talented mix of old furniture and modern style, good quality and simplicity: simple carpeted bedrooms with good lighting and beds, bright bathrooms, open, well-fitted kitchens and lots of light. Each has its own wisteria-clad patio for privacy and barbecues but you all share the super garden, its heated pool, rowing boat and fishing. Nontron's knife factory and art galleries must be seen, lovely Brantôme is a bit further. And your charming knowledgeable hosts hold open house for aperitifs on Mondays. *Shared laundry & pool. Unfenced water.*

Price	£410–£1,240 per week.
Sleeps	14.
Rooms	Barn: 2 doubles, 2 twins; 2 bathrooms, 2 separate wcs. Cottage: 2 doubles, 1 twin; 2 bathrooms; 2 separate wcs.
Meals	Restaurants 5km.
Closed	November–Easter.

Robin Fenton
Nontron, Dordogne

Tel	+33 (0)5 53 56 99 71
Email	robin@forgebasse.com
Web	www.forgebasse.com

Entry 156   Map 9

Aquitaine

Jovelle - La Chartreuse

White walls, pale oak floors, a rolling loft space, peace – city chic in the country. The 19th-century house, on the site of a monastery, has been rigorously renovated by the owners, who live across the courtyard in the main house, to create a modern space alongside original features. The open-plan living area sweeps across the ground floor; quarry tiles, a grand fireplace, antique furnishings, underfloor heating. The shiny-smart kitchen – convivially at one end – is a cook's delight. Bedrooms are bright, uncluttered spaces of oak boards and sandblasted beams. Bring well-behaved friends and you also get the use of the vast attic apartment in the main house: two bedrooms, sloping beamed ceilings, antique furniture and claw-foot baths, and a soaring loft space scattered with rugs and comfy sofas. There's a smallish garden, a terrace for al fresco meals, a saltwater pool with a shower, and you are well-placed for exploring the Dordogne, the vineyards of Saint Émilion and pretty riverside Brantôme. Too tired to rustle up a meal? A Leith-trained cook is to hand – just say when.

Price	£500-£950 per week. Ask about apartment prices and extra rooms in main house. Pool towels included.
Sleeps	8.
Rooms	House: 1 twin, 1 double; 2 bathrooms. Apartment: 2 doubles, 2 bathrooms. Extra rooms in main house.
Meals	Restaurants 4km.
Closed	Christmas.

John & Sally Ridley-Day
Leguillac de Cercles, Dordogne

Tel	+33 (0)5 53 56 51 19
Email	info@lachartreusedordogne.com
Web	www.lachartreusedordogne.com

La Geyrie - Gîte Maison

La Maison is attached to the Dunns' house; across the yard is Le Pigeonnier. This is a working farm with an ancient feel: sheepdogs roam, cats doze, there are hens in the yard and a clutch of Jack Russells; Peter and Louise are busy and committed and everyone may happily muck in. Inside are the classic limewash walls and terracotta floors, chairs are straight-backed, the sofa is small and a 1930s dresser houses the crockery – plain but genuine. Bedrooms and bathroom upstairs feed into each other with a fine-sized bedroom at the front dominated by an old fireplace and a bedroom at the back that is big enough for a growing family. Mattresses are new, cotton sheets are coloured, the bathroom is for everyone and the small kitchen even has a dishwasher! This is an outdoorsy place where free-range families will be happy. Hidden in the woods is the Dunns' new goat barn-cum-milking parlour – all organic and with a rainwater collector, solar panels to heat water and reed beds for effluence. Peter is enthusiastically germinating seed for vegetables and flowers; nuts and fruit are organically grown. *Service wash available.*

Price	£260–£415 per week. Linen not included.
Sleeps	8.
Rooms	1 double, 1 quadruple & bunks; 1 bathroom.
Meals	Restaurant 2km.
Closed	Never.

Louise & Peter Dunn
Verteillac, Dordogne

Tel	+33 (0)5 53 91 15 15
Email	peter.dunn@wanadoo.fr
Web	www.lageyrie.com

Ethical Collection: Environment.
See page 370 for details

La Geyrie - Le Pigeonnier

A pair of nesting owls sometimes takes up residence in the tower of this 15th-century pigeonnier… you might spot roe deer in the woods, too. inside is charming and pleasantly cool, with tiled floors downstairs, floorboards everywhere and heavenly old rafters. Furnishings are basic and well-used – an upright pale green sofa, a set of pine shelves with yellow crockery, a corner kitchen with a new gas cooker. There are rugs scattered on floorboards, 1940s furniture, a fine armoire, pastoral views; the almost-as-big shower room reveals its pigeon holes and a rustically paved floor. You may not be steeped luxury, but the simple pleasures of a farm and a small tribe of animals should more than compensate. Hidden in the woods is an eco-friendly organic goat barn and milking parlour; guests are welcomed with homemade goat's cheese and you can buy more at the local market. Borrow the bikes or bring your own: the nearest shops, market and restaurant are a mile away in La Tour Blanche. Down the road, the wonderful Limousin-Périgord National Park; in the Limodore reserve nearby, rare orchids. *Service wash available.*

Price	£220–£340 per week. Linen not included.
Sleeps	2.
Rooms	1 double; 1 shower room. Two extra single beds.
Meals	Restaurant 2km.
Closed	Never.

Ethical Collection: Environment.
See page 370 for details.

	Louise & Peter Dunn
	Verteillac, Dordogne
Tel	+33 (0)5 53 91 15 15
Email	peter.dunn@wanadoo.fr
Web	www.lageyrie.com

La Meynardie - Kabarole

'Kabarole' is a Ugandan invitation to 'come and see' what this dramatic old barn is about. Discover sweeping terracotta tiles, a striking terrace that runs the length of the building, a pool and barbecue hewn into the hillside. Raids on the vegetable patch begin and end here, dining al fresco on your green-gotten gains. Sheep graze beyond the meadows, in full view of the family's château-manoir home (filled with stone staircases, monumental rooms and, some say, a secret passage to perfect Siorac and its medieval church). All this is rivalled by Kabarole's own offerings. Twin beds are tucked into the attic; downstairs bedrooms reach up to lofty chestnut and oak-beamed ceilings; there are lime-rendered walls and mushroom-pink terracotta floors. With enough room for a celebratory dance around Ugandan chairs, nothing stands in your way to the generous, wood-columned bathroom. The living area arranges itself round a limestone chimneypiece, a relaxed dining area set behind, and a modern white-on-white kitchen to the side. Wonderful spaces, timbers, fittings – and great for families. *Shared pool.*

Price	€660–€1,500 per week.
Sleeps	8.
Rooms	2 doubles, 2 twins; 2 bathrooms. Cot.
Meals	Restaurant 500m.
Closed	Never.

Judith & Nigel Nicholson
Siorac de Ribérac, Dordogne

Tel	+33 (0)5 53 91 84 60
Mobile	+39 0685 585000
Email	meynardie.siorac@wanadoo.fr
Web	www.meynardie.com

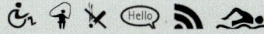

Les Marais

Set quite alone on an old flood plain, the unfussy clean lines of this former cattle barn find echo in the regimented vines that march in perspective away from the garden, the wooded ridge rising towards Saussignac giving relief. Made of local materials, the house has a modern contemporary feel. Walls are stone, the roof terracotta, the wide-open ground floor done in big black slates – a magnificent living space. A floor-to-ceiling window in the centre of the house brings light pouring in, a rafter-hung contemporary chandelier hovers over the solid wood table, the super-comfy sitting area has an open log fire and the generous kitchen is fine oak and stainless steel. Ian and Annabel, the young owners who live nearby, are justly proud of their new renovation (the garden comes next). A staircase takes you up to a gangway that feeds the properly simple plaster and pine bedrooms with soft-toned plain-coloured bed linen, white blinds and a pristine white bathroom each. A great place to do your own thing, taste wines, discover old villages, swing through the trees, crash out – and excellent value.

Price	£350–£700 per week.
Sleeps	4.
Rooms	1 double, 1 twin, sofabed; 2 bathrooms, separate wc.
Closed	Rarely.

Ian & Annabel Hull
Saussignac, Dordogne

Tel	+33 (0)5 53 73 19 03
Email	enquiries@dordognegite.com
Web	www.dordognegite.com

Le Roudier

The 300-year-old hamlet of Le Roudier lies in beautiful, rolling countryside of sunflowers and corn, with 30 acres of bird-rich woodland in which to roam. Converted from farm buildings with letting in mind they are clean, comfortable and perfect for families. What makes this place special is the vast terraced pool that drops away to the meadows. In the old bakehouse is a summer kitchen and games room with table tennis, a paddling pool, slides and swings. Each cottage has its own patio on which you may barbecue and the larger ones have shady, vine-strewn terraces that face the pool but are fenced and secure. Inside, the usual terracotta floors and open-plan kitchen/diners, spotless and excellently equipped. Work out in the gym or flop in front of a huge screen in the media room; the idea is to relax, and the whole enterprise is run by the Smiths, an English/Irish couple with a young family who do all they can to make you happy. Rabbits in the meadows, three golf courses within striking distance, canoes on the Dordogne, vineyards all around and mountain bikes to borrow for energetic cycling. *B&B also.*

Price	£200–£2,000 per week.
Sleeps	30.
Rooms	Maison: 2 doubles, 2 twins; 3 bathrooms. Ferme: 2 doubles, 1 twin, 1 triple; 1 bathroom, 1 shower room. Garenne: 1 double, 1 twin, 1 family room for 3; 1 bathroom, 1 shower room. Chai: 1 double, 1 twin; 1 bathroom. Nid: 1 double; 1 shower room.
Meals	Restaurant 5km.
Closed	Never.

Paul & Dearbhla Smith
Razac d'Eymet, Dordogne

Tel	+33 (0)5 53 24 54 96
Email	leroudier@wanadoo.fr
Web	www.leroudier.com

Les Bigayres

You won't forget the bedrooms of this elegant converted dovecote: one has gnarled beams that grow like trees through the tall pointed ceiling, another has an amazing *Princess and the Pea* bed with the highest mattress ever. Teenagers will go for the third, a sunny bunk bedroom with its own poolside entrance. In 30 acres of grounds belonging to a lovely 17th-century manor, and with its own private drive and terrace, this beautifully furnished cottage is quite a find. You share the pool with the French owners but they use it infrequently so you'll often have it all to yourself. The open-plan kitchen and living area is pure, light and roomy, with white or exposed stone walls, grey-green beams supported by unusual stone columns and prettily patterned red and green curtains. Fine, hexagonally-laid tiles run through the ground floor, there are wooden boards upstairs. Wallow in luxurious sofas by the stone fireplace, stroll out of the French windows to the lawn with its long wooded views. You have everything you need, from dishwasher to barbecue, and charming Bergerac is no distance at all. *Shared pool.*

Price	€600–€1,500 per week.
Sleeps	6.
Rooms	2 doubles, 1 room with bunks, sofabed; 1 bathroom, separate wc.
Meals	Restaurant 1km.
Closed	November–February.

Jane Hanslip
Liorac sur Louyre, Dordogne

Mobile	+44 (0)7768 747610
	+33 (0)6 32 62 43 15
Email	jhanslip@aol.com
Web	www.dordognerental.com

Le Bourdil Blanc

All this could be yours: a fine 18th-century manor with a long, tree-lined avenue, views down to the lake and a super big pool. When you've finished lazing in the huge grounds or being sporty around tennis or croquet balls, retreat to the sitting room, with its lovely old wooden floors, open fire, comfortable sofas. The dining room, magnificent with William-Morris-type fabrics, mirrored fireplace and polished floors, seats 14 on upholstered chairs. Upstairs, a long, light passage leads to the roomy bedrooms and bathrooms; then, in the loft, three bedrooms with brand new shower rooms. The sunny kitchen and the bathrooms are more functional than fabulous, and there's central heating so you're as warm as toast in winter. The Wing is less grand than the main house but has an open fire, tiled floors, warm kilim rugs, some good antiques and a fitted kitchen; the Pigeonnier is charming, with fine furnishings, stunning stone fireplace and private walled garden. So much space indoors and out, and stacks to do in the area. *Babysitting available. Riding & wine-tasting. House & Wing must be let together in July & August.*

Price	House €1,400–€3,000. Wing & Pigeonnier €800 each. House & Wing must be taken together in July & August: €7,000. With Pigeonnier €8,000. Prices per week.
Sleeps	20.
Rooms	House: 3 doubles, 4 twins, 2 sofabeds; 4 bathrooms, 4 shower rooms. Wing: 1 double, 2 sofabeds; 1 bathroom. Pigeonnier: 1 double, 1 twin; 1 bathroom.
Meals	Meals on request. Restaurant 3km.
Closed	Never.

Jane Hanslip
Saint Sauveur de Bergerac, Dordogne

Mobile	+44 (0)7768 747610
	+33 (0)6 32 62 43 15
Email	jhanslip@aol.com
Web	www.dordognerental.com

Aquitaine

La Martigne

This glorious stone *chartreuse* is utterly, incontrovertibly French – it could be nowhere else. It is a pleasing mix of simple yet luxurious, unadorned yet ornate. Splendidly isolated, with magnificent views of the Périgord Noir, the house has been beautifully restored by its French owners who have lived here for generations. Members of the family occasionally use the grounds but otherwise the cascading terraced lawns, the private park and the pool are all yours. Dark antiques and pretty fabrics harmonise with simple bare stone, soft painted walls and aqua-blue doors with their china handles. Polished wooden floors gleam in the two living rooms, comfy sofas and elegant blue and white upholstered Regency chairs invite you; next door is a formal dining room with rich red wallpaper and attractive rugs. There are several open fireplaces, one of them the focus of one of the bedrooms which, huge and light, all open onto the south-facing terrace and the loveliest views. The kitchen is as well fitted out as you would expect and the bathrooms are super. *Pool occasionally shared.*

Price	€1,500–€2,500 per week.
Sleeps	10.
Rooms	2 doubles, 2 twins, 1 family room for 3, 1 single; 1 bathroom, 2 shower rooms, 2 separate wcs.
Meals	Meals on request. Restaurant 3km.
Closed	Never.

Jane Hanslip
Lamonzie Montastruc, Dordogne

Mobile	+44 (0)7768 747610
	+33 (0)6 32 62 43 15
Email	jhanslip@aol.com
Web	www.dordognerental.com

Domaine des Blanches Colombes - Monet & Renoir

The doves are still here; only their cooing ruffles the calm, and the distant hum of the tractor. The Domaine is a 17th-century manor in a hilltop hamlet, built of golden stone, encircled by high walls and run by a friendly and enthusiastic English couple. Two of the cottages stand side by side in the west wing but still manage to feel private. Renoir is creeper-covered, Monet has an array of hanging baskets. They are engaging, comfortable, homely: wooden or tiled floors, open-plan living rooms, blue and white crockery, gay gingham. The furnishings are a mix of old-fashioned and funky modern and the kitchens are brilliantly equipped. Everything is in perfect working order. Give the owners notice and they will rustle up a meal – perhaps bœuf bourguignon, fresh fruit pavlova – deliver it to your table, then clear up afterwards. They can arrange for bread and croissants to be delivered each morning, too, along with a buffet in the fridge on arrival. With a shared games room, garden and pool, the Domaine des Blanches Colombes is a superb spot for families. *Shared pool. Babysitting available.*

Price	Monet €395-€1,200. Renoir €595-€1,400. Prices per week.
Sleeps	10.
Rooms	Monet: 1 double, 1 twin; 2 bathrooms. Renoir: 1 double, 2 twins; 1 bathroom, 1 shower room.
Meals	Meals on request.
Closed	Never.

The Owner
Grand Castang, Dordogne

Tel	+33 (0)5 53 57 30 38
Mobile	+44 (0)7825 160 296
Email	info@quality-gites.co.uk
Web	www.quality-gites.com

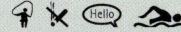

Domaine des Blanches Colombes - Degas & Matisse

Just over the road are two other gîtes, converted from an old village house. Relaxing, friendly, comfortable places to stay, they share a garden and have been recently renovated, each with a brand new kitchen. Degas is diminutive and cosy with a painted double bed, views over rooftops to the rolling hills and a little purple and green bathroom downstairs. Matisse, larger and full of character, has wooden stairs that wind up to two attractive big bedrooms. Both cottages share the many delights of the Domaine; surrounded by trees and shrubs, a fabulous L-shaped pool shelters in the angle of two barns, while another barn has been converted into a games room. If the ball pit, darts and table tennis don't keep the young happy, every cottage has a DVD player and there are board games – just ask. Six miles off is Lalinde, a pretty village with a spectacular Thursday market, while the bustle of Sarlat is 20 minutes upriver – a gorgeous drive. Bergerac is close, as are the caves of Lascaux. Bliss to return to the bucolic Domaine – heaven for families. *Shared pool. Babysitting available.*

Price	Degas £215–£450. Matisse £300–£955. Prices per week.
Sleeps	6.
Rooms	Degas: 1 double; 1 bathroom. Matisse: 1 double, 1 twin; 1 bathroom.
Meals	Meals on request.
Closed	Never.

The Owner
Grand Castang, Dordogne

Tel	+33 (0)5 53 57 30 38
Mobile	+44 (0)7825 160 296
Email	info@quality-gites.co.uk
Web	www.quality-gites.com

Entry 167   Map 9

Le Gers

The views from this hilltop farmhouse, over lovely Limeuil where two rivers meet, are mesmerising. Peaceful, too, yet you are a ten-minute stroll to the shops, craft studios and restaurants of the old walled town. Restored in bold fashion by a previous artist owner, the farmhouse has touches of quirkiness and heaps of space. The soaring living room – exposed stones, high beams, brick walls – is overlooked by a mezzanine sitting area with books, music and TV. Light and brightly furnished, it's a wonderful space to eat, relax, chat. The separate kitchen has a more rustic feel: a working fireplace and all the pans you need. Then up the open staircase to two floors of bedrooms, uncluttered, inviting and stylishly simple. Cream stone walls, wooden floors, colourful rugs, soft lamps: such a friendly feel. Unexpected touches include an innovatively tiled bathroom and a stained glass window. Treat the children to La Bugue, with its aquarium and working farms; return to the pool (it's a walk down from the house) and the views, badminton in the barn and the sunsets over the valley.

Price	€770–€1,900 (£550–£1,750 sterling) per week. Heating extra.
Sleeps	6.
Rooms	2 doubles, 1 twin; 2 bathrooms, separate wc.
Meals	Restaurants 10-minute walk.
Closed	Rarely.

Louise Bonafoux
Alles sur Dordogne, Dordogne

Tel	+44 (0)23 8055 5486
Email	lbonafoux@hotmail.com
Web	www.le-gers.com

Entry 168   Map 9

Le Relais de Lavergne

Easy to fall in love with this place with its cows in the field, tractors in the barn, and a pig called Plonk. This huge, golden 17th-century farmhouse house has three doors to the front, a great pool at the back, a cottage opposite (for the guardien) and a courtyard with outbuildings attached. Inside is inviting, enchanting, charming, from the hand-stencilled doors and country armoires to the colourful towels and dresser with brass rings. One bedroom has wonderful views over the valley, another has a carved stone fireplace and a tapestry, the family room on the ground floor is a touch more pedestrian. The only 'small' room is the kitchen, the rest are big and comfortable, furnished with books, plants, piano, a flowery sofa, a big oval table, a games room with a ping pong table for wet days. You can join Mirabelle, the youngest Pillebout sister, for painting and sculpture classes in the Relais grounds – she exhibits your work there too. There's a bar/tabac/pizzeria at tiny Bayac – perfect for those lazy days; more restaurants at Molières, La Linda and Beaumont, bastide towns all. Walk the forests, fish in the Couze.

Price	€2,300–€2,800 per week. €800 per weekend. Linen €15 p.p B&B €100 per day.
Sleeps	13.
Rooms	2 doubles, 1 twin, 2 family rooms (1 for 4, 1 for 3); 2 bathrooms, 3 shower rooms.
Meals	Cold snack & wine on arrival €15. Restaurant 3km.
Closed	Mid–November to March.

Famille Pillebout
Bayac, Dordogne
Tel   +33 (0)5 53 57 83 16
Email   relaisdelavergne@wanadoo.fr
Web   relaisdelavergne.fr

Manoir des Bernoux

You can walk from the garden to Issegeac – small, medieval and perfectly formed. Visit on a Sunday and the market will be in full flow. As for the gîte, it's in the left wing – the old wine pressoir – of an 18th-century manor house in a six-hectare park and is really quite grand. In the central courtyard is a fountain that plays, in the grounds is a pool overseen by handsome old trees. Inside are a cream-tiled ground floor (cool in summer) containing sitting room, dining room and kitchen, a couple of bedrooms, too; upstairs is warmly oak-floored with rustic pale rafters. Furnishings are classic: upholstered dining chairs, a bluer-than-blue sofa with armchairs to match, decorative antiques in dark heavy wood – more Spanish than French – and a fireplace fronted by a red Persian rug. Bedcovers are flowery, fleur-de-lys or toile de Jouy, bathrooms have big chequerboard tiles. It's spotless and smart, and spacious both inside and out: great for hide and seekers and footie fanatics. Bring the family! Madame lives in a distant wing and helps you plan your forays. *Option to rent ground floor only.*

Price	€1,800–€3,500 per week. Ground floor only €900–€1,250 except July/August.
Sleeps	9.
Rooms	3 doubles, 1 twin, 1 single; 3 bathrooms, 1 shower room.
Meals	Restaurant 3km.
Closed	Never.

Evelyne Lemasson
Montaut d'Issigeac, Dordogne

Tel	+33 (0)5 53 24 91 12
Email	lesbernoux@orange.fr
Web	www.chateaubernoux.com

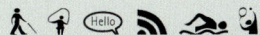

Aquitaine

Domaine de Leygue

This is a pretty pocket of France, peaceful and pleasing on the eye: five acres of grounds insulate you from all but wildlife. And here are four tidy little cottages: two near the courtyard and the owners' house, two (more modern) beyond a pretty grove of walnut trees. All are utterly private and aimed at couples. There are even two pools and, as the sunbeds stay by the cottages, you'll have plenty of private swims. And more: boules, and bikes too for those who wish to pedal round paradise… Graham and Elli are young, flexible and eager to help. Domaine de Leygue was once a small farm and two of the gîtes are conversions, two newly built; all have stone walls and a neatly furnished terrace. All bedrooms are on the ground floor bar those in the Tower cottage, where views stretch over farmland and woods. All is spotless, light, immaculate – checked sofas in one, new cherrywood in another, chestnut beams, Villeroy & Boch china. There's central heating for cool days, fans for warm nights and no TV or children to disturb the peace. Perfection in the heart of the Dordogne.

Price	£470-£720 each per week. From £210 for 3 days.
Sleeps	8.
Rooms	Each cottage: 1 double or twin; 1 bath or shower room.
Meals	Meals for late arrivals on first night only. On request. Restaurant 4km.
Closed	October–March.

Graham & Elli Dixon
Bourniquel, Dordogne

Tel	+44 (0)844 232 3918
Email	info@peacefulfrance.com
Web	www.peacefulfrance.com

Château de Cazenac

This is the lap of luxury, an adjective-defying 17th-century *petit château* that conceals a dazzling classic/contemporary interior. There are black and white marble floors, stone staircases and a grand salon in which multiple French windows flood the room with light and open to a terrace. A terrifically grand place yet not a daunting one; easy to imagine yourself kicking off your shoes. Bedrooms astonish, be it the double with the vaulting timber-framed ceiling, the twin with its view-filled balcony, or the master suite with its big round-tower bathroom. The dining room can seat 20, the kitchen has murals and a cavernous fireplace. Elsewhere: African masks, a grand piano, statues here and there. Step outside and roam through 25 hectares of private grounds. Long, dreamy views stretch over the Dordogne river and there's a secluded swimming pool with a private terrace. The château sleeps up to 24 so its price is not quite as steep as you might think. If you want to splash out on a once-in-a-lifetime treat, you won't be disappointed: a fabulous place for a wedding. And lovely people.

Price	€4,500–€12,000 per week.
Sleeps	30.
Rooms	4 doubles, 3 family rooms for 3, 1 triple, 1 dormitory for 10; 8 bathrooms.
Meals	Restaurants 20-minute walk.
Closed	Never.

Armelle Constant
Le Coux et Bigaroque, Dordogne

Tel	+33 (0)5 53 31 69 31
Email	info@cazenac.fr
Web	www.cazenac.fr

Château de Cazenac - La Maison & La Ferme

The Maison stands high on a steep hill whence dreamy views over the river... there's a simple shop a mile away but you feel beyond the call of the outside world. The interior of this 16th-century Périgord farmhouse is a charming *mélange* of old antique furniture, lime-rendered walls and ancient terracotta. Windows frame sublime views of valley and forest while rooms combine a studied rusticity with a kaleidoscope of colour. Vast bedrooms have vaulted ceilings and exposed beams, bathrooms a Moroccan touch, the open-plan living room's sliding glass doors open to a terrace, then a pool, and the kitchen reveals two pretty dressers. There's a vine-shaded terrace for barbecues and a delightful garden in which to fall asleep to the sounds of the valley. The newly-renovated Ferme sits just outside the château walls in its own private garden with an above-ground pool abutting an old barn wall. Inside: more style, more charm. Chestnut floors are scattered with rugs, beams are exposed, paintings hang on rendered walls. A delectable place, run with great enthusiasm by a new generation of Constants. *Winter truffle breaks are planned.*

Price	€1,000-€2,200 per week.
Sleeps	20.
Rooms	Maison: 1 double, 1 twin, 2 triples; 3 shower rooms, 3 separate wcs. Ferme: 1 double, 2 quadruples; 3 bathrooms, 3 separate wcs. Extra bed.
Meals	Restaurants 20-minute walk.
Closed	Never.

Famille Constant
Le Coux et Bigaroque, Dordogne

Tel	+33 (0)5 53 31 69 31
Email	info@cazenac.fr
Web	www.cazenac.fr

Les Milandes - Manoir, Ancienne Mairie, Maison du Gardien, Arc en Ciel

The view from here must be one of the most ravishing in Europe. Part of the good-looking village that clusters round the château walls and hangs out over the banks of the Dordogne, these houses rejoice in a lord's position above the sweeping river. Their pretty terraced gardens are full of interest. Be your choice the aristocratic manor or one of the former workers' cottages, you will find a well-planned living area with polished wooden floors and good rugs, smart comfortable furnishings – soft-painted beds, ornate bedcovers, floral or Chinese or pastel walls – and, of course, quite a lot of beams, sometimes painted white to give a lighter feel. You may have a fireplace, always a restrained elegance, lots of good crocks in well-fitted kitchens, fine modern shower rooms. Milandes' most famous name is Josephine Baker, the black cabaret artiste who took Paris by storm in the 1920s, adopted France, Milandes and lots of children, and brought them together in the château here. A great jump-off place for all those Dordogne explorations. *Manoir & Mairie have a pool each; Gardien & Arc en Ciel share pool.*

Price	Manoir £2,000–£3,500.
	Mairie £1,000–£1,750.
	Gardien & Arc en Ciel each £600–£975.
	Prices per week.
Sleeps	24.
Rooms	Manoir: 3 doubles, 2 twins, 1 single, 1 child's room; 4 baths.
	Mairie: 1 double, 2 twins; 2 baths, separate wc.
	Gardien: 1 double, 1 twin; 2 baths.
	Arc en Ciel: 1 double, 1 twin; 2 baths.
Meals	Restaurants within walking distance.
Closed	Never.

Christopher & Sarah Chapman
Castelnaud la Chapelle, Dordogne

Tel	+44 (0)1458 252971
Email	info@lesmilandes.com
Web	www.lesmilandes.com

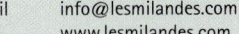

Aquitaine

La Treille Haute

The setting smacks of a fairy tale and five of the Périgord's most spectacular châteaux, clinging to the craggy cliffs of the Dordogne, are a short drive from this converted stone barn. You can even see the floodlit Château de Beynac, awesome and grand, from the comfort of the bed. English owner Felicity lives in the adjoining house: metre-thick walls between the two buildings ensure total privacy and you have your own sweet garden with amazing views. Old exposed stone walls with the vaulted beamed bedroom may have sheltered pilgrims: one stone bears a Templar cross. The modestly furnished open-plan ground-floor living area includes the kitchenette – with a hob, a microwave/oven and a glazed door to the terrace – and also leads to the bathroom. The historic village has a shop with fresh produce and an excellent boucherie/charcuterie. Treat yourself to some of the local specialities and picnic in the wooded hills, or explore the steep, fascinating, stone villages of this understandably popular area. *B&B also. Babies & children over 4 welcome: garden unsuitable for toddlers.*

Price	€310–€590 per week. Extra twin €50 per day. Short breaks €70 per day. Linen not included.
Sleeps	4.
Rooms	1 double, sofabed; 1 bathroom. Extra twin with separate entrance.
Meals	Restaurant 1km.
Closed	August.

Felicity Martindale
Castelnaud la Chapelle, Dordogne

Tel	+33 (0)5 53 29 95 65
Email	f.martindale@gmail.com
Web	martindale.free.fr

Beaux Rêves

Only the honey-coloured stone walls and one window are original but you'd never guess it: this 18th-century barn has been so perfectly restored. Four years ago it was in ruins; now it stands, complete with pigeonnier, under a demure grey roof. Opposite is the main house where Éric and Helen live. She's English, he's French and they juggle B&B with running a five-hectare estate and bringing up two young children. They've given enormous thought, care and money to this new project. The ground floor is one vast room, with tawny floor, stone walls and a wood-burning stove at its very centre. A few steps lead up to the kitchen, arresting in its faultless simplicity and superbly equipped. Lounging on a white leather sofa in the sitting area, enjoy the dazzling view of St Anne's church, spectacularly floodlit at night. Upstairs are three big, white bedrooms, each with vivid rugs, interesting pictures, a fine antique. Bathrooms are big, bright and excellent. You have the gardens to explore, your own private fenced pool, good restaurants and a small pub a stroll away. *B&B also.*

Price	€1,050–€2,250 per week.
Sleeps	8.
Rooms	2 doubles, 1 family room for 4; 1 bathroom, 2 shower rooms.
Meals	Bread & croissants delivered daily.
Closed	Rarely.

Éric & Helen Edgar
Saint Crépin Carlucet, Dordogne

Tel	+33 (0)5 53 31 22 60
Email	lescharmes@carlucet.com
Web	www.carlucet.com

Aquitaine

La Maison Josephine

Sarlat is a place of pilgrimage, a well-preserved medieval town that throngs with tourists (no cars) strolling around gorgeous food shops selling walnut oils and foie gras. Duck down a quiet side street to find a lovely, light, first-floor flat (the stairs are steep) in a 16th-century stone building, with tall windows and high ceilings. The apartment is a homage to Josephine Baker who, in 1947, bought a château nearby: find her picture on every shelf, vintage posters on the walls and a full figure metal sculpture on the little terrace. There are Art Deco decorative mouldings, lovely lamps and some classy antiques in the sitting room with its comfortable bright red sofa and a dining table with white leather chairs. More photos of Josephine crowd the master bedroom walls (there's a further, small bedroom off this room) with its sumptuous bed, large window and silk taffeta Moroccan curtains; this leads to the terrace with a small mosaic table and metal chairs. The very well-equipped kitchen is straight out of a magazine – black floor, black cupboards, smart bar stools – and the compact bathroom is tip-top modern.

Price	€710–€1,045 per week. Cleaning €45.
Sleeps	2.
Rooms	1 double; 1 bathroom. Single bed in alcove.
Meals	Restaurants 100m.
Closed	Never.

Phillipe Lecerf
Sarlat la Caneda, Dordogne

Tel	+33 (0)5 53 29 44 90
Email	pqi@wanadoo.fr
Web	www.in-sarlat.fr

Lavande

Brigitte and Christophe spotted this 18th-century farmhouse and its wooded acres while on holiday. It was love at first sight; several busy years on they run an enchanting B&B and have converted the stone stables into two self-catering cottages. Lavande, with its serene views over wooded hills, is the larger and, although near the other buildings, is peaceful and private. The inside has been thoroughly restored and has a newish feel within old beams and exposed stones. In the living room: sumptuous black leather armchairs and a sofa on an immaculately polished wooden floor; in the dining room: an antique trestle table and chairs. The pièce de résistance, however, is the beamed white and blue bedroom which looks like a piece of Delft china. Gourmets will make a beeline for the restaurant L'Esplanade in Domme – you can glimpse the splendid hilltop town from here. You share the delightful park – and saltwater pool – with other guests; if you like good home cooking, you may share meals, too. Do buy Brigitte's delicious homemade pâtés for your picnic baguettes. *Sawday B&B. Shared pool.*

Price	€490-€1,100 per week. Linen not included.
Sleeps	6.
Rooms	1 double, 1 twin/double, 1 twin on mezzanine, sofabed; 1 bathroom, 1 shower room, separate wc.
Meals	Meals on request.
Closed	November-March.

Brigitte & Christophe Demassougne
Cénac et Saint Julien, Dordogne

Tel	+33 (0)5 53 29 91 97
Email	contact@la-gueriniere-dordogne.com
Web	www.la-gueriniere-dordogne.com

Mas Baronet

Deep in unspoilt wild chestnut country, the strong old farmstead stands firm and golden on its ridge, the hills ebbing and flowing into two little valleys: a form of paradise. Bees and butterflies, boar and deer thrive under Robin's conservationist husbandry, flowers, bushes, trees and veg flourish under Pat's loving, expert hands. She is a whizz with plants - it's her profession, after all; your private garden shimmers with colour and you may be allowed some fine fruits from the orchard and kitchen garden. A vibrant couple who have lived and learned a lot, they enjoy sharing their space and experience. Your ideal family holiday: a week in the lofty old barn with its comfortable bedrooms (big double with bathroom downstairs, two smaller doubles with shower up), large living room (books, DVDs, games), super kitchen. Add myriad marvels in spring, orchids in early summer, mushrooms and truffles in autumn, all the treasures of the Quercy year round: food, drink, walks, rivers, lovely little towns, devastating cave paintings - you can't stay away. *B&B also.*

Price	€425–€1,450 per week.
Sleeps	6.
Rooms	3 doubles; 1 bath & shower room (disabled fittings), 1 shower room, separate wc.
Meals	Dinner, with wine, €25. On request. Restaurant 5km.
Closed	Rarely.

Patricia Shears & Robin Hare
Campagnac les Quercy, Dordogne

Tel	+33 (0)5 53 29 65 71
Mobile	+44 (0)7887 480789
Email	robinghare@gmail.com
Web	www.masbaronet.com

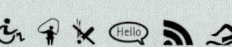

Le Prieuré du Château de Biron - Apartment

The imposing Château de Biron sits on the highest point of the little village, below and behind it the church which gazes over it all, and behind that the charming Prieuré with an enclosed cobblestone courtyard and pretty flowers: at the tower end is your light, high-ceilinged, two-room flat. Walk straight in through a separate entrance to the large bedroom with a powder blue and soft grey colour scheme, exposed stone walls, 16th-century basin, comfortable armchairs and toile de Jouy curtains. Off this is a pleasing, spotless little kitchen which overlooks the garden, then a sitting/dining room on a corner: light comes pouring in from two sides. Space is neatly divided between sitting and dining areas, walls are cream, the sofa and armchairs in off-white linen, the working fireplace is of carved stone, a large ornate mirror decorates the mantelpiece. The bathroom is a good size with a bath tub, smart blue tiles and a separate loo. You are in the heart of the village but there is absolute quiet and there are charming little spaces in the garden to read or dream. *Sawday hotel.*

Price	Apartment €950-€1,130. Entire Prieure €4,700-€5,400. Prices per week.
Sleeps	19
Rooms	Apartment: 1 double, 1 twin in alcove; 1 bathroom. Entire Prieure: 4 doubles, 1 single, 2 triples; 5 bathrooms.
Meals	Restaurant 50m.
Closed	Mid-November to February.

Elisabeth Vedier
Biron, Dordogne

Tel	+33 (0)9 60 47 46 07
Mobile	+33 (0)6 84 31 38 38
Email	leprieurebiron@yahoo.com
Web	www.leprieurebiron.com

Midi – Pyrénées

Le Couvent

This elegant village retreat started life as a convent school for girls: today's sunlit rooms were classrooms and dormitories. Rosalie and Malcolm have renovated in abundant style: original wooden floors, painted furniture, fluttering muslin at shuttered windows, charming antique finds. (One wonderful bed left France for Cairo in 1850, took a detour to Sussex and is now back home.) There's a dreamy sense of country life: old floral linen cushions on a bedroom sofa, light bouncing off colour-washed walls, a chandelier rescued from a barn gracing the salon. The old well stands in the gorgeous three-level garden that leads you up to the woods, so you can chase the sun or retreat to the shade (and the hammock). The dining room and salon are cool and calm and there's a hungry wood-burner in the beautifully fitted country kitchen. The medieval village is listed: a lovely collage of tiled roofs and mellow stone houses, it rests peacefully in a lush valley encircled by the river Vers. Rosalie's warmth and artistry is reflected in every corner. Really special.
Ask about children on booking.

Price	£450-£700 per week.
Sleeps	6.
Rooms	2 doubles, 1 twin; 2 bathrooms.
Meals	Restaurants 10-minute drive.
Closed	November to mid-May.

Rosalie Vicars-Harris
Saint Martin de Vers, Lot

Tel	+44 (0)20 7483 2140
Mobile	+44 (0)7966 799916
Email	rosalievh@yahoo.co.uk
Web	www.lecouvent-lot.com

Le Manoir

A gathering of antiques around a huge old fireplace, faded kilims on terre cuite floors, paintings, books, memories and high rafters… the grand old manoir is easy, friendly and so atmospheric. The original façade has pure lines and fine proportions; the medieval entrance is being restored – along with a stone stairway that sweeps into the park. Flaunting nothing too valuable or precious, this big laid-back family retreat has been taken on by a family of musicians. Now they are tackling the grounds, delightful for children with their spreading acacias and shady maples, run-around lawns and fenced pool. The 70s corner kitchen is darkish but bustles with the necessities; another big sitting/kitchen area is up a spiral stone stair. The largest bedroom is the dreamiest, with 14th-century windows and great planked floor, grand piano (tuned) and books to the ceiling. Another room has a charcoal mural by Toulouse Lautrec as a child. Bread is delivered and there are two restaurants you can walk to. Wonderful Saint Cirq Papopie and Rocamadour are 20 minutes by car.

Price	€1,800–€2,000 per week.
Sleeps	14.
Rooms	4 doubles, 2 twins; 3 shower rooms, 1 bath room. 2 extra beds in library.
Meals	Restaurants in village.
Closed	November–March.

M & Mme le Pichon
Cahors, Lot

Tel	+33 (0)1 42 78 35 64
Mobile	+33 (0)6 60 40 85 69
Email	lepichon@wanadoo.fr

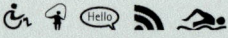

La Théronière

A very pretty 19th-century L-shaped stone building tucked away on a quiet road and secure in its own grounds. The largest room in this much-lived-in house is probably the kitchen which is rather French in style with lots of wood, a dark tiled floor and all the gadgets you need; a good place to eat and socialise. The very light and airy sitting room is also large, with a merry fireplace, comfortable modern furniture and doors leading to a patio. There's a good bedroom on the ground floor for those who prefer not to tackle stairs, and another upstairs with a dressing room (perfect for a child's bed), beautiful white linen and glass doors to a covered balcony; stairs from here lead back down to the garden. There are two other gîtes (small kitchens) in the house, with a connecting door if you want, for family parties or groups of friends. Cosmopolitan Prayssac is a short walk and full of good places to eat, and there are lots of local markets and canoeing on the Lot. Walk and cycle those hills, visit numerous châteaux; there's a tango competition not to be missed in July and a jazz festival at Castel Merle.

Price	€800–€1,600 per week. Pets extra.
Sleeps	8.
Rooms	Main house: 2 doubles; 2 shower rooms. Annexe: 2 doubles; 1 bath & shower room.
Meals	Restaurants 1km.
Closed	Rarely.

Karen Durant-Pritchard
Prayssac, Lot

Tel	+33 (0)5 65 20 15 47
Email	info@theroniere.com
Web	www.theroniere.com

Domaine de Roubignol

Roubignol is an 18th-century winemaster's house. The title impresses, the house even more so. Breathtaking in its scale and architectural peculiarities, it has ancient stone floors, creaking floorboards, hidden alcoves and a beam to duck; three eating places inside, four terraces and, cut into the steep cliffside, an infinity pool, underwater-lit at night. There's even an old bell to summon people to lunch from pool frolics or barn table tennis. The house has five bedrooms, from the tiny single in the pigeonnier to the large Romeo and Juliet room with canopied bed and balcony, of course. The Tower has a twin room, central heating and a sofabed in its top-floor sitting room. Furniture is a happy mix of French antique and modern, the L-shaped sitting room is big enough to waltz in, the antique-dealing owners have an eye for the odd quirk (the semolina cave painting in the loo is by a member of the RA…). You are five minutes from Luzech's shops and market (25 on foot down the valley path) and spoilt for wine-tastings and gastronomic choice. The views sweep and soar… a heavenly place.

Price	Main house €930–€2,150. Tower only available in July/August with main house: €300–€430. Prices per week. Linen included on request.
Sleeps	13.
Rooms	House: 3 doubles, 1 twin, 1 single; 2 bathrooms, 1 shower room. Tower: 1 twin, double sofabed in sitting room; 1 bathroom.
Meals	Chef on request. Restaurant 2.5km.
Closed	Main house: November–March. Tower: Never.

Roger & Jill Bichard
Luzech, Lot

Tel	+44 (0)1225 862789
Email	info@moxhams-antiques.co.uk
Web	www.french-house-roubignol.co.uk

Domaine Lapèze - Cottage & Terrasses

Once a resting place for pilgrims on their way to Santiago de Compostela, this is a place to linger. Those who come find much to recharge city-drained batteries: pool, vineyards, plum orchards, peace. The starkly beautiful collection of old stone buildings is wrapped in 12 acres of blissful rolling country and you can gaze across to an 11th-century tower in Montcuq (charmingly French, with two markets, three bars, four restaurants, shops with all you need). Terracotta tiles keep you cool, white walls soak up the sun and there are warm colours inside. In the Cottage, expect an open-plan living area with comfortable, if dated, lemon sofa and armchairs and a lovely big fire for winter. The Terrasses apartment, nicely private for two or four, has marvellous views from… its terrace; bedrooms are reached from two separate doors on the upper terrace. There's a gorgeous pool (floodlit at night) which you share with B&B guests, lakes to swim in, wine to taste and Romanesque churches to visit. Knud is on hand to help during the week, Caroline appears at weekends, both are delightful. *B&B also. Shared pool.*

Price	Cottage €600-€900. Terrasses €500-€800. Prices per week.
Sleeps	8.
Rooms	Cottage: 1 double, 1 twin; 1 bathroom, separate wc. Terrasses: 1 double, 1 twin; 2 bathrooms. Flexible rental out of season.
Meals	Restaurants 2km
Closed	Rarely.

Caroline & Knud Kristoffersen
Montcuq, Lot

Tel	+33 (0)5 65 24 91 97
Email	lapeze@fastmail.net
Web	www.domainelapeze.com

Entry 185   Map 14

La Chave

Lindy and Tony found a rare jewel here: a farmhouse untouched for over a century. Eight miles from medieval Montcuq (small shops, Sunday market), the mellow stone house has kept many of its original features; the old bread oven, two wells in the garden, and the outbuildings where the tobacco was hung to dry. Lindy has a flair for decoration and has created an unusually delightful place to stay. There's a glorious and well-equipped kitchen, its dresser loaded with bright crocks, a sitting room with a wood-burner to keep you snug all year round, and a long pine table for meals in the shade. Bedrooms in soft creams and greens are furnished with country pieces – a French walnut armoire, an antique quilt – while old wooden floors, topped with kilims, have been polished or painted white. Attic bedrooms are cosy for children… this would be just perfect for two families. Outside: ping-pong, table footie and darts in the open barn, fig trees in the garden, a sandpit for little ones. And, on the lower lawn, a lovely large saltwater pool, safely fenced and with bucolic views.

Price	£500–£1,650 per week. Pool towels not included.
Sleeps	10.
Rooms	3 doubles, 2 twins; 2 bathrooms, 2 shower rooms.
Meals	Restaurants 10-minute drive.
Closed	November-April. Ask about winter lets.

Lindy & Tony Ball
Cézac, Lot

Tel	+44 (0)1725 519529
Mobile	+44 (0)7747 620552
Email	lindy@martindown.co.uk
Web	www.lachave.co.uk

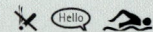

The Pigeonnier at La Taupe

Seekers of peace will be happy here in the middle of nowhere, surrounded by only hills and woods – 'La France profonde' indeed. The Pigeonnier sits on a hill across the courtyard from the main house, but nonchalantly looks the other way. You enter on the middle level straight into the high-ceilinged, cream-walled sitting room, with a working wood-burner, family pictures, lots of books and comfortable armchairs; the smaller, beautifully decorated, bedroom is on this floor and a cool, pale, big bedroom upstairs has great views, vibrant paintings and a working marble washbasin. Downstairs find a small, light and bright dining room with glass doors to the patio and a large kitchen good enough for committed foodies. You have your own terrace and lawn, but the rest of the garden with its fountains, huge mosaic pool and covered terraces is yours to roam. Good markets abound, especially at Prayssac on Fridays; stock up on delicious local meats, cheeses and pastries then burn it off on those hills, either biking or hiking. Your easy-going hosts are on hand should you need them and they kindly offer dinner on the first night.

Price	€1,550–€1,650 per week. €285 per day. Breakfast included.
Sleeps	4.
Rooms	2 doubles; 2 bathrooms.
Meals	Meal on arrival, with wine, €25. On request.
Closed	Rarely.

Ed & Sally Green
Roquecor, Tarn-et-Garonne

Tel	+33 (0)563 95 26 21
Email	la.taupe@mac.com
Web	vacationrentalfrance.net/

Entry 187   Map 14

Roujol

In a beautiful fertile landscape, all vineyards and fields of corn, is a 19th-century barn with 78 acres, airy, immaculate and big enough to sleep ten – in huge comfort. Owners Heather, Chris, their young son, their ponies and horses moved into the *mas* next door, immersed themselves in the community and now take excellent care of their guests; Heather will even take you out riding. The deep veranda with white banquettes and blue cushions sets the tone: Roujol is a good-looking and generous place. Walls, floor tiles and boutis quilts are white, woodwork is hand-crafted. It is also heaven-sent for families, with a fenced terraced pool, a great raftered salon filled with sofas, a second salon for kids, cots, highchairs, and Heather, happy to babysit when you want a night off. She'll cook for you too, up to four meals a week, served on that super veranda. You get four bedrooms on two levels and a small apartment with its own kitchen. Nearby are two villages where you can stock up on provisions; here you have an honesty bar filled with local wines – another welcoming touch.

Price	£1,500-£2,400. Suite £575 for 2. Prices per week.
Sleeps	10.
Rooms	2 doubles, 2 twins, 1 suite with kitchenette; 2 bathrooms, 1 shower room.
Meals	Lunch/dinner €18-€25. Restaurant 5km.
Closed	Rarely.

Ethical Collection: Food.
See page 370 for details.

Heather Galley
Brassac, Tarn-et-Garonne

Tel	+33 (0)5 63 95 76 11
Email	heather@galleys.org
Web	www.roujol.com

Le Moulin de Salazar

Kingfishers, herons, the occasional otter and a couple of terrapins… This magnificent old watermill proved irresistible to Paulette and Bernard when they abandoned the rat race in 2000. The river flows below and the machinery and sluices still work; Bernard knows how to operate them. In the mill room is the original grindstone – a fascinating communal space where guests can meet over drinks – or dine. On the first and second floors, Paulette has created four bright, welcoming apartments. They have glorious views and are superbly equipped, each with its own colour scheme, open-plan living area, sofabed, WiFi. Outside, take your pick of many different and delightful areas in the five acres of grounds. Laze in the vast garden, take a portable barbecue to a secret shingle beach, fish in the well-stocked pool, set off in a small motor boat. There's a swimming pool, too, and bikes, boules and table tennis – Paulette and Bernard have thought of everything and simply couldn't be nicer. Utterly stress-free and relaxing, but leave small children at home – there's that river! *Unfenced water.*

Price	£490–£595 per week. £85–£95 per day.
Sleeps	8.
Rooms	Each apartment: 1 double, sofabed; 1 bathroom.
Meals	Breakfast €7. Dinner €22. All meals on request. Restaurant 3km.
Closed	Rarely.

Paulette Palmer
Lauzerte, Tarn-et-Garonne

Tel	+33 (0)5 63 94 68 01
Mobile	+33 (0)6 31 25 50 15
Email	paulette@salazarholidays.com
Web	www.salazarholidays.com

La Maison Rose

The long, wide salon glows with sunlight and colour, books, flowers and paintings; it is the heart of this family 'manoir'. The valley's woods and cornfields spread out from the limewashed house on the slopes of Miramont de Quercy village, its arms embracing a huge grassy courtyard – perfect for paddling pool and games. From the salon, a wide dining terrace looks down on gardens full of secret paths and shady corners; choose a spot under the old persimmon, by the fountain or on the hammock slung between the chestnut trees. Quietly elegant bedrooms (one four-poster, two canopied) have a well-loved feel. Antique furniture sits on parquet and cool terracotta; fabrics, from Lady Ashburton's own company, are vintage-inspired. Most bedrooms are on the ground floor with French windows to the courtyard; two hide up the pigeonnier's winding staircase. Gather for meals at the big pine kitchen table, or beneath the wisteria-wound pergola (or Nancy can cook for you, from fresh local produce (delicious desserts!). You can brush up your table tennis, try your hand at boules or simply flop into the heated pool.

Price	£1,700–£3,750 per week.
Sleeps	14.
Rooms	7 doubles; 6 bathrooms.
Meals	Catering possible (£15 per hour). Restaurants 400 yds.
Closed	Rarely.

Sally Ashburton
Bourg de Visa, Tarn-et-Garonne

Tel	+33 (0)5 63 95 71 13
Email	lakehouse@clara.co.uk
Web	www.maison-rose.com

La Petite Grange & La Petite Maison

In a delicious setting, these two diminutive gîtes stand at different levels with their backs to the hillside in the Nortons' seven-acre grounds, just outside the hamlet of Tréjouls. Thick stone walls keep you cool and rooms are pleasantly furnished with splashes of colour from cushion and poster. Up a flight of steps, Petite Grange is a stables conversion, its several doors opening onto the lawn: a comfortable, one-storey house with an L-shaped living room/kitchen. Lavender and morning glory edge the patio. The other, open-sided, end of the stables barn provides shade for hot-weather meals near the pretty pool. Petite Maison is smaller, with a long, south-facing terrace. Its bedsitting room has spectacular views; shower and loo have a separate entrance from the terrace. An NGO to reduce environmental damage and improve life for the poorest is based here: John and Claire are a thoughtful and delightful couple with two student children (and two friendly cats who love to visit). In winter, bask in the greater comfort of La Petite Grange, with its household appliances and central heating. Great value. *Shared pool.*

Price	Grange €315–€490.
	Maison €245–€385. Prices per week.
Sleeps	4.
Rooms	Grange: 1 double; 1 bathroom.
	Maison: 1 double; 1 shower room.
Closed	Grange: Never.
	Maison: November–March.

Claire & John Norton
Tréjouls, Tarn-et-Garonne

Tel	+33 (0)5 63 95 82 34
Email	claire@cubertou.com
Web	www.cubertou.com/petite

La Barrière

On the edge of the hamlet, a house of delights. Artist Catherine and builder-designer Des rescued the stunning 17th-century farmhouse and gave it back its character. Beams, terracotta floors, stained glass and nooks and crannies are complemented by Catherine's stencils, paint washes and exotic finds. Relax in the open-plan living area with its deep sofas, rugs, wood-burning stove and kitchen units fashioned from wine barrels. Bedrooms are wonderfully individual: one open to the rafters, another bright in sunburst colours, another cool in blue… and the cosy single is every child's dream. Bathrooms, anything but bland, are dotted with flowers, shells and bowls. Eat on the wisteria-covered balcony, by the pool or on a shaded terrace. There's also a walled garden full of secret sitting places and organic fruit and veg for you to pick. This is the couple's home; they move into an adjoining studio. Calm and smiley people, they will help you with advice or leave you alone. After a day of discovery (medieval villages, markets, the lovely Bonnette valley) it is lovely to return to such peace.

Price	£550-£1,150 per week.
Sleeps	7.
Rooms	2 doubles, 1 twin, 1 single; 3 bathrooms.
Meals	Restaurant 4km.
Closed	November-March.

Catherine Smedley & Des Dornan
Lacapelle Livron, Tarn-et-Garonne

Tel	+33 (0)5 63 24 00 05
Email	catherine.smedley@wanadoo.fr
Web	www.labarriere.iowners.net

La Maison Blanche

Motor up an ear-poppingly steep hill in a deep rural setting to find this supremely family-friendly long house. An old church building on two floors with many large rooms feeding off a long corridor, it has plenty of space and is unfussily decorated so you can unload all the paraphernalia involved in taking children on holiday. Bedrooms are a similar size too, so nobody gets jealous! Colours are predominantly white with flashes of grey and taupe, floors are wooden and covered in seagrass matting, bathrooms are large and tiled in white with smart black slate floors. If you come with children you will prefer to stay in and cook for yourselves in the evenings: the kitchen will not let you down – there's enough china and glass to invite friends and special plastic sets for children. A super sitting area is very large with an open fire, smooth white walls with abstract canvases, four sofas with turquoise cushions and a glass door to the outdoor covered terrace for sunny or candlelit meals; there's another reading area with sofas upstairs. A garden full of shrubs surrounds you and leads to the pool.

Price	€1,145-€2,125 per week.
Sleeps	12.
Rooms	5 double, 1 twin; 3 bathrooms, separate wc.
Meals	Restaurants 10km.
Closed	Never.

Trudi Harris-Dubon
Caylus, Tarn-et-Garonne

Mobile	+33 (0)6 13 73 83 02
Email	trudiharrisdubon@gmail.com
Web	www.la-maison-blanche-farmhouse.com

The Rustic Retreat

Tucked into a green hillside topped by thick wooded tresses, an old shepherd's house brought back to life as a four-room family home. Gardens climb to the tree line, alive with flowers and swooping swallows – views from the kitchen window are so beautiful you will be rooted. Inside, no frills or fanciness: high beamed ceilings, a shaded veranda, Persian rugs on wooden floors, paintings bright against textured white walls. A basic kitchen has colourful crockery for meals around an old French table. The main bedroom, reached through the children's room or via the garden, has deep raspberry linen and a big family bathroom glimmers in gold travertine tiles. The owners, both artists, and their two young children live a simple life; pick organic veg from the garden (and lend a helping hand); feast on freshly laid eggs (if you promise to look after the hens). Explore Sunday markets for local food, or the river winding through the stunning Gorge du Aveyron (canoeing, swimming, picnics). Medieval St Antonin Noble Val is near for restaurants and shops, Toulouse, Cordes-sur-Ciel are further. Rise with the birds.

Ethical Collection: Environment; Food.
See page 370 for details.

Price	£850–£1,100 per week.
Sleeps	4.
Rooms	1 double, 1 twin; 1 bath/shower room.
Meals	Restaurant 15-minute drive.
Closed	November–March.

Sasha & Mark Drummond Lee
St Antonin Noble Val, Tarn-et-Garonne

Tel	+33 (0)5 63 67 05 18
Mobile	+33 (0)6 04 19 88 11
Email	sasha@therusticretreat.co.uk
Web	www.therusticretreat.co.uk

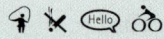

Daramousque

You are surrounded by 14 hectares of mature gardens, rolling hills and stunning views. Sarah and Michael fell in love with this 19th-century farmstead five years ago, already beautifully renovated and restored. It also came with a big open space perfect for children and a saltwater pool. Theirs is the farmhouse, yours is the villa, and its vast open-plan living area is lofty and light. Three French windows lead to a long veranda on whose stylish sofas you will idly sprawl before rising for a lazy dip in the secure shared pool. The furnishings are a pleasing mix of French modern and French antique enhanced by soft golds, ochres and creams, the open-plan kitchen is unquestionably lavish and the two ground-floor bedrooms are spacious and cool, one overlooking a courtyard, the other the garden; the third, a fabulous and spacious double, is upstairs. You are minutes from the shops, restaurants and weekly market of pretty Monclar de Quercy. For the cooler months: log fires and warm-as-toast tiles; these gentle, generous owners want nothing more than for you to be happy. *Shared pool. Cottage for 4 also available.*

Price	€975–€1,500 per week. Reductions for small groups.
Sleeps	6.
Rooms	2 doubles, 1 twin; 1 bathroom, separate wc.
Meals	Restaurants within walking distance.
Closed	November–March.

Michael & Sarah Rule
Monclar de Quercy, Tarn-et-Garonne

Tel	+33 (0)5 63 28 26 17
Email	michael.rule@wanadoo.fr
Web	www.daramousque.com

Domaine Escudes

Big lawns and vast cedars, a pool house with a bar, a tennis court in the orchard, and beds for a dozen or more. This super house, set in a beautifully tended park on the edge of a hamlet midway between the Atlantic and the Med, has just about everything. As the wrought-iron gates open you will note the perfect symmetry of the hunting lodge built 200 years ago, with elegant shutters and a double staircase fanning out from the door. To the side are brick barn buildings, immaculate; behind, a lovely lake-canal sprinkled with ducks; beyond, waving fields of sunflowers and corn. There are two sitting rooms and sofas galore, books, games and satellite TV, and doors that fling open to a deck over the water. You get a kitchen with two vast fridges and utensils to please the most exacting of chefs, a dining room for candlelit dinners, heaps of comfortable beds (mostly twins) dressed in fine linen, numerous bathrooms sporting fluffy white towels. Golf, horse riding, horse racing, Toulouse and Carcassonne – all are near. A friendly young English couple take care of the entire estate. Peace reigns supreme.

Price	€3,500-€4,500 per week. Short breaks €600 per day.
Sleeps	12.
Rooms	1 double, 1 twin/double, 3 twins, 1 room with truckle bed; 1 bath & shower room, 3 bath/shower rooms, 2 shower rooms. Annexe 1 double, 1 twin/double, sofabed; 1 bath/shower room.
Meals	Catering possible (€17 per hour, plus shopping).
Closed	Rarely.

Lucinda Kleinwort
Vigueron, Tarn-et-Garonne

Tel	+44 (0)1444 454181
Email	holidays@escudes.co.uk
Web	web.mac.com/yokehurst/ESCUDES/Welcome.html

Barrau

Bliss for those who wish to leave creature comforts behind and lose themselves in the hills. The main house, where Jennifer lives, is 30 yards away. Secluded on a 15-acre hillside estate with two private sitting-out areas, one filled with lavender and figs, Barrau is perfect for a couple or a solo traveller. And trees, long views and wildlife. Deer and badgers live on the land, 42 species of butterflies have been identified, nightingales sing, the odd salamander scampers by and beehives dot the landscape. Your retreat, a former house for the pigs and hens that goes back to 1890, has been renovated simply. It's rather like camping but without the tent and with a bathroom. You have a pine-floored room with rugs and a plain table, a cupboard, a radio/cassette player, two beds and two easy chairs, a tiny painted-brick shower room and a corridor kitchen. Charming Jennifer lives simply and happily, is passionate about her "wildlife guests" and an expert on the local churches and brocante fairs too. Beneath pollution-free night skies, the tree frogs will sing you to sleep.

Price	€200–€350 per week. Heating not included.
Sleeps	2.
Rooms	1 twin; 1 shower room.
Meals	Dinner, 3 courses, €15. On request. Restaurant 20-minute drive.
Closed	December–March.

Ethical Collection: Environment; Community.
See page 370 for details

Jennifer Boncey
Esparsac, Tarn-et-Garonne

Tel   +33 (0)5 63 26 12 72
Email   boncey@wanadoo.fr
Web   www.haumont.com

Souplassens - Maison Forte

Large spaces, ancient peace – such are the treats in store at this 15th-century stone house in the Avignonet-Lauragais. The defence tower (now a bedroom) is even older: note the gunner holes in the walls. The Renaissance additions include two great fireplaces, one in the dining room, complete with bread oven (logs on the house). It's a charming bolthole for families and the owners live nearby, happy to provide highchair, playpen and child bed; there's even a playroom at the top of the house. As for the décor, the combination of rustic stone and pale wood, tactile textiles, subtle lighting and the odd country antique is nothing short of delicious. Note that three of the bedrooms have tiny windows, including the child-cosy double under the eaves. Bathrooms are big, chic, friendly with real tubs; linen is embroidered cotton. The setting may be nothing extraordinary, on the rich treeless plains around Toulouse, but fruit trees have been planted on site: old-fashioned indigenous varieties. Idle your way down the Canal du Midi, gorge on the regions' cakes and cassoulets, return to a designer lounger by the pool.

Price	€750–€2,000 per week. From €500 per weekend.
Sleeps	10.
Rooms	3 doubles, 2 twins; 2 bathrooms.
Meals	Restaurants 15km.
Closed	Never.

Laure Pagès-Mielly
Avignonet, Haute-Garonne

Tel	+33 (0)5 61 81 59 58
Mobile	+33 (0)6 31 05 20 84
Email	contact@souplassens.fr
Web	www.souplassens.fr

Residence La Guiraude

On its own at the end of a country road, this stylish house has a clean, modern hotel feel. Plenty of space makes it ideal for big family gatherings or groups of friends. Find a large, light, cool complex of indoor spaces and outdoor terraces, fragrant walled gardens and a heated saltwater pool. A spacious hall leads to a sitting room with lofty ceilings and the original fireplace. Chinese rugs soften pale tiles and there's a light-filled mezzanine brimming with leather sofas, books, music and French and English TV. Dining areas have long tables and French windows leading to shady terraces with panoramic views. The kitchen is worthy of a professional, with all the gadgets you could need, the games room sports table tennis, exercise bike and step machine, bedrooms have big beds and cheerful colours, immaculate bathrooms have walk-in showers, bathrobes and fluffy towels. Janine, a wine educator, and Alistair, an excellent cook, are unfazed at the prospect of catering for 20 when a retreat group, wedding party or family takes on the whole fabulous place. Cathar trails, châteaux and vineyards beckon.

Price	€2,200-€5,600 per week. Can be let as 2 separate homes out of season.
Sleeps	20.
Rooms	5 doubles, 3 twins, 1 quadruple; 9 bathrooms.
Meals	Dinner, with wine, €38-€48. Special celebration meals & catering on request. Restaurant 3km.
Closed	November-March. Winter lets on request.

	Janine & Alistair Smith
	Beauteville, Haute-Garonne
Tel	+33 (0)5 34 66 39 20
Mobile	+33 (0)6 20 96 21 02
Email	contact@guiraude.com
Web	www.guiraude.com

La Ferme Plate

The big 19th-century farmhouse, facing south with panoramic views of the Pyrénées, is traditionally constructed of river stone and Toulouse brick, with a wisteria-covered balcony. Let the children loose in this 14-acre heaven of lawns, woods and small lake fed by a natural source where you can sit and watch the resident wildlife – look out for deer and wild boar. For summer there's a big covered terrace with chairs for up to 50, pétanque and a wonderfully private pool, fenced, alarmed and surrounded by stocked borders. Inside has a beautifully fitted open oak kitchen, a multitude of beams, an open fire that warms the soft-couched sitting area, attractive bedrooms and a huge bathroom upstairs. If you want more space, throw open the door to the converted stables next door and take over the huge salon with its massive open fireplace, pool table and more sofas (plus a post-swimming shower). Up above, a superb set of timbers supports the roof over a very big, airy, sun-filled bedroom. The buildings stay cool in summer and warm in winter, making this a cosy holiday house all year. *Large groups welcome by arrangement.*

Price	€1,200–€2,000 per week. Cleaning €120.
Sleeps	16.
Rooms	5 doubles, 1 family room with bunks, double sofabed; 1 bathroom, 2 shower rooms.
Meals	Restaurant 2km.
Closed	Never.

Mark Taylor
La Bastide de Besplas, Ariège

Tel	+33 (0)5 61 69 26 40
Mobile	+33 (0)6 86 60 03 93
Email	mtaylor@orange.fr
Web	www.gite-plavengut.com

Château de Bardies

You'll love the warm intimacy of this family home, lost in the wooded foothills of the Pyrénées. The Vardigans decamp before guests arrive, leaving the house and grounds entirely in your hands. The salon, like all the rambling rooms of this 16th-18th-century château, is brimful of family portraits and mementoes, oriental rugs, books, antique furniture and treasures from the attic. Cook up a storm in the terracotta-tiled kitchen with original pantry, dine grandly in front of the large wood-burner, play a sonata on the library's grand piano. Upstairs are cosy, wonderfully romantic bedrooms full of soft bed linens and period detail, wide floorboards and grand double doors, even a wisteria covered balcony. Large is the master suite, with its dressing room and king-size bed, big shower room and tiny turret for a child's bed. Two century-old lime trees guard the house; beyond, paradise beckons. The lush parkland and old formal gardens with maze will enthrall young explorers, while adults will fall for the sunny terrace, meals under the trees and a pool with heavenly views of the hills and valleys.

Price	£1,800–£3,500 per week.
Sleeps	14.
Rooms	2 doubles, 1 twin, 1 suite for 3, 1 family room for 4; 4 bathrooms, 2 shower rooms.
Meals	Restaurants 10km.
Closed	Never.

Peter & Lola Vardigans
St Girons, Ariège

Mobile	+44 (0)7768 863655
Email	peter@vardigans.net
Web	www.chateaudebardies.net

Les Rosiers

Breathe in the fresh mountain air as you step out of this old farmer's cottage, drink in the High Pyrenean panorama from the controlled-wild garden. Les Rosiers is perched on the edge of Cescau, an ancient stone village facing those breathtaking mountains. The owners, Teresa and Bernard, are artists with a lifelong love of peace and natural beauty who care deeply about the community and organise local concerts. The décor is unpretentious country style, with wooden floors, original beams and an old fireplace that works for those chilly autumn evenings. It's far from tickety-boo but children will enjoy the amazing wooden spiral stair — tread carefully! — up to the twin bedroom under the rafters; its private tiny balcony will only add to their fun. Parents will have a huge bed in the large, downstairs bedroom. While sipping your morning coffee on the tiny porch just off the kitchen you will be inspired by the view over the Pic Long; and if it's a Saturday morning don't miss the picturesque market in St Girons — stock up the larder and return to cook over the old stone barbecue.

Price	€450–€500 per week.
Sleeps	4.
Rooms	1 double, 1 twin; 1 bathroom. Cot.
Meals	Restaurants within walking distance.
Closed	Never.

Teresa & Bernard Richard
Cescau, Ariège

Tel	+33 (0)5 61 96 74 24
Email	tizirichard@yahoo.fr
Web	www.ariege.com/les-rosiers

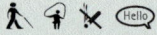

La Petite Écurie

Cross the courtyard from the Furnesses' grand 18th-century townhouse and there is La Petite Écurie, '1758' inscribed over its door. John and Lee-anne have done much of this tiny stables conversion themselves – and made a great job of it. The overall effect is assured, pleasing and comfortable. In the bedrooms you have chestnut wood floors and exposed stone walls to show off the tapestries that hang richly behind the beds; the beamed living room is restful and elegant; the kitchen has every appliance you can think of. This is a quiet corner of town and the garden, with its hammock and saltwater pool, is lovely and secluded, a great place to hide away in. Australians John and Lee-anne came to live here in 1999: she is an accomplished chef and you can book a meal with them in their fine big house where they do B&B. They love living here and know all about the area and its scattering of Cathar castles. Take a picnic hamper (Lee-anne will provide – very well) and go exploring, or spend the day basking on the sunny shores of Lac Montbel. *Sawday B&B.*

Price	€420–€570 per week. €300 per weekend.
Sleeps	4.
Rooms	1 double, 1 twin; 1 bathroom, 1 shower room.
Meals	Dinner €25, on request. Bar/bistro 2-minute walk.
Closed	Rarely.

John & Lee-anne Furness
Leran, Ariège

Tel	+33 (0)5 61 01 50 02
Mobile	+33 (0)6 88 19 49 22
Email	john.furness@wanadoo.fr
Web	www.chezfurness.com

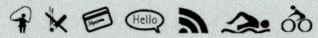

Tresbos Farmhouse

Farmhouse? Manor house, rather, and prosperous in its luxuriant bee-humming garden where even the pool is graciously flowered, furnished and solar-heated. Bedrooms are huge yet cosy, their elegance neither fussy nor overdone – designer touches and country antiques mingle delightfully; their cool sheets feel soft, their polished floors glow in the garden light. And such huge bathrooms, the loveliest marriage of modern and old-fashioned: turn-of-the-century double basins and tubs, a grey-painted armoire, a rattan recliner, vintage taps (with lashings of hot water), cherubs and candles – one could loll happily for days in each. But the super-modern stainless steel kitchen beckons, full of gadgets and charm. Add two sitting rooms, videos, kids' stuff… There are many surprises, all of them good. You can picnic on the lawns or invite your guests to join you at the convivial trestle table in the open-sided barn. It's peaceful, and beautiful. Spain and Toulouse are an hour away, skiing closer, local restaurants offer four-course lunches for €10, dinner is a half-hour drive.

Price	€1,600–€2,310 per week.
Sleeps	8.
Rooms	4 twins/doubles; 2 bathrooms.
Meals	Dinner on request. Restaurant 2km.
Closed	Rarely.

Andy & Vicki Coleman
Puydarrieux, Hautes-Pyrénées

Tel	+44 (0)1621 741126
Email	info@tresbos.co.uk
Web	www.tresbosfarmhouse

Arnauton

Spanning the main farmhouse and the one-storey lodge are bedrooms sleeping 16: Arnauton is the perfect place for a large family holiday in Gascony. The renovation was completed in 2009 and the landscaping is almost there, with a beautiful old lime tree that spreads its shade, and an Italianate garden at the front of the house. Pristine and new are a super big pool with a panoramic view, a games room with ping pong and a tennis court out of sight. The generous downstairs includes a fully fitted kitchen with an American fridge, a dining room with pine tables and chairs, and a high-raftered summer salon – leading to a barbecue space – dominated by a wooden mezzanine from which views sweep over the fields. This well-executed mix of old and new continues into bedrooms in two wings, nicely proportioned, pleasantly unobtrusive. One has armchairs fronting a fireplace, others the original wooden floors; all have white walls, masses of light. There's no excuse not to gourmandize: markets and foie gras abound and Gascony's nectar is Armagnac – more aromatic even than Cognac.

Price	£1,500-£3,500 per week. The House and Lodge must be rented together.
Sleeps	16.
Rooms	House: 2 doubles, 4 twins; 1 shower room, 3 bathrooms. Lodge: 1 double, 1 twin; 2 shower rooms.
Meals	Restaurants 10-minute drive.
Closed	Never.

Tony & Barbara Mackintosh
Condom, Gers

Tel	+33 (0)5 62 68 28 33
Email	anthonymackintosh@yahoo.co.uk
Web	www.arnauton.com/Home.html

Ancien Moulin de Mousque & Écurie

The poplar avenue leading to the wrought-iron gateway is pleasantly private, the five acres are densely wooded and the mill is beautifully restored; these English owners have employed the best people. But what makes this most special is the ever-present water, from the lovely limpid lake-canal to the rushing river and the weir upstream. The mill itself is on an island, totally private; dragonflies and waterfowl abound. Close by is a converted stable with a huge covered area perfect for barbecues, furnished with a wooden table and chairs. Between the two buildings is a fenced pool on a low hillock, and large open areas of lawn that children can happily play on. Bedrooms in both houses are furnished with veneer pine; bathrooms are an airy mix of new tiles and paint. The mill's floors are heated, the living area has a wood-burner, and there's character in ceiling rafters and two huge mill stones last used in the First World War. Close by are the bastide villages of Larressingle, Fourcès, Montréal, while civilisation (shops, markets, restaurants) is ten minutes by car. *Young ones must be scrupulously watched.*

Price	£500–£1,500 per week. The Moulin and The Écurie must be rented together.
Sleeps	8.
Rooms	Moulin: 1 double, 1 twin; 1 shower room. Écurie: 2 twins; 1 bathroom.
Meals	Restaurants 10-minute drive.
Closed	Never.

Tony & Barbara Mackintosh
Condom, Gers

Tel	+33 (0)5 62 68 28 33
Email	anthonymackintosh@yahoo.co.uk
Web	www.moulindemousque.com

Le Vieux Presbytère

This is armagnac country and Richard is happy to organise informal wine tastings. (A wine merchant, he's something of an expert!) He and Jackie have converted a 50-year-old barn in the grounds of their beautiful old timber-frame house into two dormer-windowed gîtes. The rooms may not be huge but they are full of light. Furnished in a mix of French country and English cottage style, all feels crisp, fresh and inviting. Up on a beamed mezzanine with pale walls and gleaming wooden floors, bedrooms in soft green and ivory open onto balconies. La Mouette, has a sitting area upstairs too, a bathroom up and a second bedroom down, and each has a ground-floor shower room, an open-plan sitting/dining area with sofabed, a small kitchen and a barbecue patio. If you want to be thoroughly spoiled one evening, Jackie will prepare dinner and bring it to you. Eat out on the terrace, surrounded by garden, woods and vine-covered hills, with distant views of the Pyrénées. Next door is a church, its spire visible above the trees, its bell plaintively tolling the hours. *B&B also.*

Price	La Mouette €400-€800. L'Hérisson €300-€560. Prices per week.
Sleeps	6.
Rooms	Mouette: 1 double on mezzanine, 1 twin, sofabed; 1 bathroom, 1 shower room. Hérisson: 1 double, sofabed; 1 shower room.
Meals	Table d'hôtes €25, on request.
Closed	Rarely.

Jackie & Richard Wallace-Jones
Noulens, Gers

Tel	+33 (0)5 62 06 48 62
Email	wallacejones@escapetogascony.com
Web	www.escapetogascony.com

Domaine de Peyloubère - Giulietta

Peyloubère is a dreamlike grouping of 300-year-old buildings in acres of gorgeous parkland. There is a river, a lake, a rose garden and langorous walks across the fields. The owners do B&B in the manor house once inhabited by the 20th-century Italian artist Mario Cavaglieri. Your very pretty cottage, on two floors, has basque red shutters and a tiled roof. Walk straight in through French windows from the garden: find cool tiled floors, a beamed ceiling, exposed stone walls, comfortable armchairs and a sofa with bright cushions on a throw. Sleep soundly in upstairs bedrooms with warm wooden floors, one has its own little balcony for gazing at sunsets. The kitchen is modern and light and geared up for good cooks with a smart central island; rustle up a picnic lunch or a candlelit supper and wander outside on warm days. When its raining, or chilly, there are books, games, videos, music and central heating. And – whatever the weather – children will love the woods and the magical waterfall. Even better – a heated pool, table tennis, badminton and a health spa with sauna in the former pig shed. *Sawday B&B. Shared pool.*

Price	€585-€1,650 per week. €1,500 for 2 weeks.
Sleeps	6.
Rooms	1 double, 2 twins; 1 bathroom, 1 shower room, separate wc.
Meals	Restaurant 2km.
Closed	Never.

Ethical Collection: Environment.
See page 370 for details.

Theresa & Ian Martin
Pavie, Gers
Tel   +33 (0)5 62 05 74 97
Email   martin@peyloubere.com
Web   www.peyloubere.com

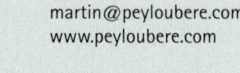

Domaine de Peyloubère - Fermier

Look out for hoopoes by the waterfall, which is fed by the Gers that flows through the estate of this 17th-century manor. With 35 acres of lawns, Italian gardens, woodland and wonderful trees, there's space to roam. You'll scarcely be aware of the guests in the adjoining cottages, or of the delightful English owners. Peyloubère used to be a working farm and Fermier was the farmer's cottage; the beamed inglenook fireplace still warms the living room. Today it is super-cosy with central heating and furnishings crisp and new: light beech furniture, deep-blue sofas, full-length curtains. The state-of-the-art kitchen is painted grey-green and sunflower yellow, with a Saint Hubert dresser and steps to a sunny downstairs double bedroom. French windows take you out to the patio, the large heated pool shared with the other gîtes, and the garden beyond. Gaze over the fields, listen to the birds, identify wild flowers, fish in lake and river – and toast it all with a glass of armagnac after supper, the dry golden brandy for which the area is famous. *Sawday B&B. Shared pool. Health spa with sauna for guests.*

Price	€645–€1,850 per week. €1,700 for 2 weeks.
Sleeps	8.
Rooms	2 doubles, 2 twins; 1 bathroom, 1 shower room, 2 separate wcs.
Meals	Restaurant 2km.
Closed	Never.

Theresa & Ian Martin
Pavie, Gers

Tel	+33 (0)5 62 05 74 97
Email	martin@peyloubere.com
Web	www.peyloubere.com

Ethical Collection: Environment; Community.
See page 370 for details.

Place de l'Église - Two Apartments

A village address in the gently rolling Gers. The car-free village — safe as houses — is a jewel, predating even the lovely bastide towns of the region; the Place de l'Église is a medieval colonnade opposite the church and beside the village green. The old bakery — divided into one apartment for the owners and two for the guests — is at the end of the colonnade. Its sensitive restoration reveals the original colombage, the Toulouse-style brickwork and the lovely tomettes. Each home has two floors — downstairs: light, lofty and open plan, upstairs: cosy. Shower rooms are compact, the small twin bedrooms are ideal for kids, furnishings are plainly traditional: white walls, floral curtains, new sofas, brocante finds. At the back is a little courtyard in which you may barbecue a brochette in summer, then take a table into the colonnade and enjoy it. The helpful couple who live opposite welcome you with an aperitif and before you know it you're immersed in village life. Tillac has a bar/restaurant, a friendly shop (try the yeast-free *campaillou*) and a flower festival in spring.

Price	£230–£350 each per week. Linen not included.
Sleeps	8.
Rooms	Each apartment: 1 double, 1 twin; 1 shower room.
Meals	Restaurant 100m.
Closed	Never.

Ann & Geoff Coombs
Tillac, Gers

Tel	+44 (0)1275 474451
Email	tillac@btinternet.com
Web	www.holidaysintillac.com

La Croix de Fer

The 18th-century barn has it all — stone walls, beamed ceilings, rolling views, ancient peace — but it is the way in which Jacqui and Francis have decorated that makes it shine. Step into a big, light living and kitchen area, with cream tiles, soft green sofa and chairs, a vase of dried flowers. On one side, the palest exposed-stone wall, on the other, white rough plaster; the space spills with light. The twin bedroom is soft lilac and lemon; Jacqui fell in love with the bed throws and linen, then designed the room around them. The double comes in cream and rose, with sofa, beams, wrought-iron bed and windows on two walls that pull in the views. The house stands in ten acres of grass and woodland, the silence broken only by birdsong. There are deckchairs, shady trees and a delicious terrace by the stunning fenced pool. Jacqui has thought of just about everything: fluffy towels in excellent bathrooms, music, books and a wooden kitchen beautifully equipped. Hire bikes in the village, go riding nearby or walk your socks off in the valley of the Aveyron. *Candlelit dinners for special occasions.*

Price	£350-£750 per week.
Sleeps	4.
Rooms	1 double, 1 twin; 1 bathroom, 1 shower room.
Meals	On request.
Closed	November-April.

Jacqui & Francis Suckling
Saint Martin Laguépie, Tarn
Tel   +33 (0)5 63 56 25 20
Email   suckling@wanadoo.fr

Maraval

There's a feeling of remoteness here, although Cordes is no distance at all; only birdsong and the stream flowing beneath the house tickle the peace. Maraval, an ancient mill house in 100 magical acres of woodland, cliffs and pasture, stands at the end of a long, secret country lane. Behind, at the head of the valley, trees cluster steeply round the lawned garden and the lovely pool. The house itself is full of original features – massive beams, uneven floors, a creaky, eccentric staircase – and has white-painted walls and stunning views. Books, pictures, corner sofas and rugs make the split-level sitting room particularly inviting. The kitchen, too, is a delight, with a vast open fireplace (and logs for cool evenings), an ancient farmhouse table, blue and white tiles and an armoire stuffed with crocks and glassware. Outside is a wonderful covered dining terrace. The large, pretty bedrooms are carpeted and furnished with rural antiques and comfortable beds; one bedroom suite is on the ground floor with French windows onto the terrace; the other two are upstairs with the second bathroom.

Price	£650-£995 per week.
Sleeps	6.
Rooms	2 doubles, 1 twin; 2 bathrooms.
Meals	Restaurant 5km.
Closed	Rarely.

Sophie O'Neill Curato
Cordes sur Ciel, Tarn

Tel	+33 (0)5 63 53 81 07
Mobile	+33 (0)6 10 88 03 99
Email	sophy.oneill-curato@wanadoo.fr
Web	www.rent-maraval-house-tarn.com

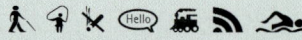

Château de Fourès

Swap stress for bliss at this gem of a cottage in the grounds of a 19th-century château. Come for a beautiful renovation, a tranquil setting in the foothills of Cordes and a secluded tennis court and superb pool which you have almost entirely to yourselves. The charming and hospitable owners live here – Madeleine from Paris and Swiss husband Peter – but are discreet. They also speak excellent English. Inside, the cottage is steeped in charm: furnishings are good quality, furniture is country antique or new pine, there are pictures on open stone walls, vintage lamps suspended from beamed ceilings, cheerful checks and fresh flowers. You eat at a round table in the bright, light corner kitchen that is beautifully equipped, or outside in your own delightful courtyard garden. And the grounds and flowering gardens are yours to share. Relax by the lily ponds, set off for lively Cordes, a mile away, or soak up the peace and the woodland views from your own roof terrace. Unbeatable value and perfect for two or a family with two children.

Price	€650–€950 per week.
Sleeps	2.
Rooms	1 double, 2 pull-out beds in sitting room; 1 shower room.
Closed	November–April.

Madeleine Camenzind–Acory
St Marcel Campes Cordes sur Ciel, Tarn

Tel	+33 (0)5 63 56 13 55
Email	camenzind@wanadoo.fr
Web	www.chateaufoures.com

Château de Labarthe

In a charming hamlet, near the medieval town of Cordes, is this pretty 17th-century house where you have complete independence. Inside there's a cottagey, friendly feel with old beams, exposed stone, a creaky staircase and rustic French furniture (no Ikea here!). Downstairs is totally open-plan and flooded with light. Slump into truly comfy chairs, warm yourself by the open fire on chilly days, treat yourself to something delicious from the market and cook in the modern, well-equipped kitchen; eat inside on an antique table or out in the garden with its loungers and barbecue. Bedrooms are filled with character and charm: antique mirrors, family photos, toile de Jouy curtains and easy chairs; the bathroom is large, flooded with light and has beautiful old tiles. There's a lovely pool to cool off in (shared with the owners) and an Italian-inspired garden filled with lavender, roses and flowering shrubs. Quietly elegant Isabelle is on hand if you need her, Les Cabannes is a five-minute stroll and it's all very romantic: cosy in winter, cool in summer, surrounded by blissful countryside and rolling hills. *Shared pool.*

Price	€460-€1,000 per week.
Sleeps	4.
Rooms	1 double, 1 twin; 1 bathroom.
Meals	Restaurant 4km.
Closed	Never.

	Isabelle Chatelus
	Labarthe Bleys, Tarn
Tel	+33 (0)5 63 56 17 08
Email	isabelle.chatelusdevialar@wanadoo.fr

La Peyre - Maison Bleue

A ten-minute walk from the vibrant village (shops, restaurants, small farmers' market) is a shimmering collection of stone buildings, perfectly restored and sitting pretty in a landscaped garden full of lavender with a floodlit tennis court tucked at the bottom. Maison Bleue has its own large terrace for candlelit dinners and sunny breakfasts, and a private pool for cooling off. Inside find beautiful stonework, exquisite throws on beds, chunky beams, terracotta floors and light pouring in through tall windows. Feel at home on truly comfortable sofas and deep chairs in a stylish sitting room with rugs, books and paintings, and a wood-burner for chilly evenings. Wander to the village for feeding (there are two good restaurants here), or rustle up something delicious in a fully fledged, open-plan kitchen. There are two other gîtes, Rouge and Verte, equally delightful and sharing another pool, making this perfect for large family gatherings or groups of friends. You are half an hour from Albi and its amazing cathedral, there are markets galore, and lots of little local shops to explore. Lovely.

Price	€900-€1,750 per week.
Sleeps	8.
Rooms	2 doubles, 2 twins; 4 bathrooms.
Meals	Restaurants nearby.
Closed	Rarely.

Anthea Pemberton
Cahuzac sur Vère, Tarn

Tel	+44 (0)20 8944 9571
Mobile	+44 (0)7885 656881
Email	stay@lapeyrefrance.com
Web	www.lapeyrefrance.com

Entry 215   Map 15

Château de Mayragues

Superlatives cannot describe this remarkable cottage in its château grounds. It has everything: history, vineyards, atmosphere. The château is 14th-century and, with its overhanging balcony circling the upper storey, is an outstanding example of the region's fortified architecture. Its authentic 20-year restoration won charming Laurence and her husband Alan a national prize. Your home is, improbably, the château's old bakery; it is the prettiest place imaginable and has a south-facing terrace on which to relax with a glass of organic estate wine. It's cosy, light and simply but charmingly furnished – a mix of old and new. There's a living room with a wonderful contemporary kitchen at one end and an open stair to a tiny mezzanine with a single bed. The cool, roomy double has a blue and white theme with pretty checked curtains and new sisal on the floor; the shower room is excellent. Look out onto the 17th-century pigeonnier 'on legs'. Should you tire of being here, there's walking country all around and the medieval hilltop village of Castelnau de Montmiral is well worth a visit. *Sawday B&B.*

Price	€500–€600 per week. Short breaks available in winter.
Sleeps	3.
Rooms	1 double, mezzanine with single bed; 1 bathroom.
Closed	Never.

Laurence & Alan Geddes
Castelnau de Montmiral, Tarn

Tel   +33 (0)5 63 33 94 08
Email geddes@chateau-de-mayragues.com
Web   www.chateau-de-mayragues.com

Les Buis de Saint Martin

Super for a couple. The 19th-century manor, in its park on the banks of the Tarn, has been Jacqueline's home for 30 years; the gîte is in its own wing. How delightful to wander down to the water's edge in this peaceful, special place, where a private pedalo waits to carry you downriver. Inside, a charming minimalism prevails. The ground floor is terracotta, the first floor polished wood; muslin blinds hang at deep-set windows, walls and beams are whiter-than-white. Its contemporary look suits the light and lofty space: wood and wicker, a clean-cut sofa, a big lemon-yellow bed, a few pictures, a simple rug. The galley-style kitchen is well-equipped, the walk-in shower is white and chic, and Jacqueline, who does B&B in the manor, is a dear. Outside, too, is lovely: your own secluded garden by the river, with heated plunge pool and teak loungers. Little Marssac has the basic shops, Albi and hilltop Cordes are close by, the area is filled with good restaurants and the wines of Gaillac, less well-known than the Bordeaux, are one of France's best-kept secrets. Brilliant. *Sawday B&B.*

Price	€400–€650 per week.
Sleeps	2.
Rooms	1 double, sofabed in living room; 1 shower room, separate wc.
Meals	Restaurants 2km.
Closed	Never.

Jacqueline Romanet
Marssac sur Tarn, Tarn

Tel	+33 (0)5 63 55 41 23
Mobile	+33 (0)6 27 86 29 48
Email	jean.romanet@wanadoo.fr
Web	perso.wanadoo.fr/les-buis-de-saint-martin/

Maison Puech Malou - The Cottage

In its own little garden, the prettiest gîte. You step into a very delightful open-plan interior with wood-burning stove, cheerful red sofa, books and easy chairs. The galley kitchen has sun-yellow tiles, dishwasher, hob and oven. The bedroom is cosy and cool – white walls, antique pine, bed linen with towels to match, and shower room en suite. You get your lovely private terrace and garden, with barbecue, at the back and, off the courtyard, reached via an outside stair, an extra bedroom you can rent – ideal for grandparents, older children or anyone wanting independence. Monique is charming, bakes her own bread (which she's happy to sell), keeps her own hens. There's nothing she likes better than to prepare dinner for a big friendly crowd: enjoy table d'hôtes in the big, terraced garden. You're high on a sunny hill (*puech* means 'hilltop' in the regional dialect, *malou* is a type of apple), in a garden lush with lavender, hibiscus and shady corners. Teillet for simple shops is a five-minute drive, Albi and Toulouse are under an hour. *Sawday B&B. Pool may be available by arrangement. Laundry on request.*

Price	€475-€675. With extra room €775-€1,075. Prices per week. Ask about renting The Farmhouse and The Cottage together. Short breaks in low/mid-season. Heating and linen not included.
Sleeps	4.
Rooms	1 double; 1 shower room. Extra double & shower with outside entrance. Farmhouse for 10 also available.
Meals	Meals on request.
Closed	Never.

Monique Moors
Teillet, Tarn

Tel	+33 (0)5 63 55 79 04
Email	info@maisonpuechmalou.com
Web	www.maisonpuechmalou.com

Maison Puech Malou - The Farmhouse

Here is a restoration that is both beautiful and rustic. You arrive at the creeper-clad 19th-century farmhouse by a very pretty back road through wooded country. Inside, a friendly, calming home full of antiques swims in crisp light. Walls are exposed stone or white, the floors are terracotta, the ceilings are beamed in heavy oak: sense the weight of age. The master bedroom has a good big bed and a romantic feel, a couple of bedrooms come with stripped pine boards, another, super-private, is entered by a staircase that rises from the covered courtyard where pots grow colour. You will find two huge open fireplaces in the sitting room, a big rustic dining table beneath more great beams, a generous and delightfully-designed kitchen. Good teak furniture stands on the terrace and the lawn runs down to the pool; there's a vegetable garden you are welcome to plunder and a marked trail that leads from the truly gorgeous garden into the hills. Dutch Monique is friendly, hands-on, bakes her bread daily and is a great cook. Wonderful. *Sawday B&B. Cooking holidays available. Laundry on request.*

Price	€1,500-€2,550.
	Prices per week. Ask about renting The Farmhouse and The Cottage together. Short breaks in low/mid-season. Heating and linen not included.
Sleeps	10.
Rooms	2 doubles, 3 twins; 1 bathroom, 2 shower rooms, separate wc. Cottage for 4 also available.
Meals	Meals on request.
Closed	Never.

Monique Moors
Teillet, Tarn

Tel	+33 (0)5 63 55 79 04
Email	info@maisonpuechmalou.com
Web	www.maisonpuechmalou.com

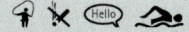

Les Secrets du Bonheur

A triumphant conversion, the 200-year-old barn stands like a medieval lookout on a ridge above the lush Brommes valley and its kaleidoscope skies, a perfect foil in scale and natural solidity for this wild and wonderful region. The architect's renovation is as dramatic as that view: you will revel in the sweep of the split-level living space down to the vast windows, the suspended central hearth, the phalanx of leather sofas, Tony's hefty timber furniture (his hobby, or so he says), a brilliant kitchen area, a brightly clothed futon – all held in by those venerable working stones, all done with much calm taste and very little colour. Up the beautiful new staircase, the best bedroom is more of the same: space and lovely materials, luxurious minimalism and a private balcony over the valley. Below the living floor are the two twin bedrooms with the same excellent bedding and doors onto a little terrace each, the garden – and the view. Superb bathrooms, as you would expect, and generous, enthusiastic owners in the old farmhouse next door who always go the extra mile. *B&B also. Tennis courts 5km.*

Price	€750–€1,050 per week. Short breaks available in low season.
Sleeps	6.
Rooms	1 double, 2 twins, futon; 4 bathrooms.
Meals	Dinner €20, on request.
Closed	Never.

Tony & Hanneke Herbert
Mur de Barrez, Aveyron

Tel	+33 (0)5 65 48 88 31
Mobile	+33 (0)6 72 43 80 53
Email	lessecretsdubonheur@neuf.fr
Web	www.lessecretsdubonheur.com

Languedoc – Roussillon

Can Llouquette - Bergerie & Studio

Birdsong, the rush of water, the rustle of leaves… half-way up Mount Canigou, in the Mediterranean Pyrénées, this lovely old fruit farm in 11 verdant acres has dreamy views of green-cloaked mountains. Immensely restful, it makes the bumpy journey worth it. The sturdy little Bergerie, a former sheepfold, is all soft-coloured stone and eau-de-nil shutters, full of light and simplicity. An open-plan living area – new terracotta, recycled wood – makes the most of the space with modern furnishings: pale elm table, oak chairs, black leather sofa, colourful prints. There's a crisp white kitchen with panoramic windows and doors to a terrace with breathtaking views. Bedrooms are comfortably unfussy in restful neutrals, their bathrooms have walk-in showers, there are no curtains at windows so you could be sleeping under the stars. The Studio is equally charming. Simon and Ashley, warm and friendly, live in the farmhouse and know the best walks, cycle routes, the closest restaurant, café and bar (a 20-minute walk). The coast and Perpignan are under an hour; return for a swim and those heavenly views. *Shared pool.*

Ethical Collection: Environment.
See page 370 for details.

Price	Bergerie £350-£850. Studio £175-£420. Prices per week. Linen €20 p.p.
Sleeps	6.
Rooms	Bergerie: 1 double, 1 twin; 2 bathrooms. Studio: 1 double; 1 shower room.
Meals	Dinner, with wine, €18. Restaurant 3km.
Closed	Rarely.

Simon Williams & Ashley Barrington
Montferrer, Pyrénées-Orientales
Tel   +33 (0)4 68 89 16 64
Email   sa@can-llouquette.com
Web   www.can-llouquette.com

Gîte Cassaigne

The baker toots his horn every morning in sleepy La Cassaigne — no need to go far: croissants and crusty baguettes arrive at your door. The house, built in 1806, sits near the village square and is double-fronted on three levels with a sunny roof terrace on the top floor. It was Araminta's dream to own such a house, and she has added many artistic touches. Behind the beautiful front door is the heart of it all: a farmhouse kitchen with Languedoc tiles, beamed ceilings, an old oak table and a blazing fire. Off here: a large salon with a wood-burner, a huge sofa and plenty of good books. The wooden staircase takes you up to three generous bedrooms with country antiques and there are two bathrooms with power showers and large baths — one on each floor. It's a proper family house for all seasons, cool in summer, cosy in winter; so read, dream or sip a glass of wine on that top terrace and admire sweeping views across the countryside while swifts dance overhead. Carcasonne is near, the medieval arcades of Mirepoix are 20 minutes away; circular Bram, on the Canal du Midi, is even closer.

Price	£675-£1,200 per week.
Sleeps	6.
Rooms	2 doubles, 1 twin/double; 2 bathrooms, 3 separate wcs.
Meals	Restaurant 4km.
Closed	Never.

Araminta Stewart & Hugh Peacock
La Cassaigne, Aude

Tel	+44 (0)1728 832615
Mobile	+44 (0)7979 694779
Email	amintys@aol.com
Web	www.gitecassaigne.com

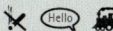

Languedoc - Roussillon

Domaine de Marmiflet

Swathes of wild flowers, wandering deer, fluttering birds and butterflies: Caroline's rustic home, set in a hundred acres of natural woodland and pasture, is a summer haven for 26 native species of orchid, masses of wildlife, artists and families who love peace and the outdoors. The old stone farmhouse is as clean as a whistle and a step back in time with its creaky wooden stairs, ancient beams and wood-burning stove in the sitting room. Gather in the farmhouse kitchen around a long dining table; burst through French doors to a summer kitchen and barbecue by a safely fenced freshwater pool – after lunch on the terrace play table tennis, badminton, lounge in the sun. Bedrooms are light and country-pretty; nights utterly quiet. Several kilometres of grassy paths traverse the property, the Midi-Pyrénées glimmers in the distance; for dinner or shops medieval Mirepoix is a short drive away and Carcassonne's walled La Cité just 35 minutes. For advice or a first-night dinner, ask Caroline, who stays nearby; originally from Wiltshire, her boys flew the nest and she's now happily living out her lifelong dream.

Price	£2,000 per week.
Sleeps	10.
Rooms	4 doubles, 1 twin; 1 bathroom, 3 shower rooms.
Meals	Dinner, 3 courses, €18. Children €9. Restaurant 12km.
Closed	October–May.

Caroline Gorst
Saint Gauderic, Aude

Tel	+33 (0)4 68 24 78 28
Email	caroline.gorst@marmiflet.com
Web	www.marmiflet.com

Yobaba Lounge

This grand, filmic playground of a place is unlike anywhere else. And, on the edge of a Cathar village, fields and stream bounding the natural garden, it's a work in progress; owner Gertrud is restoring the neglected neoclassical manor as a boutique hotel and family getaway. Floor-to-ceiling windows, marble fireplaces, fine wood staircase crowned with a stained-glass lightwell: aristocratic details mix with Gertrud's laid-back colours, thrown rugs on parquet floors and scattering of sofas. Bronze lions greet you in one upstairs suite; in the other, a proud bath sits centrally in a tree-view bathroom. Bed and living-room spaces – two downstairs have working fireplaces – are vast and endlessly flexible. You sleep on high-tech, knee-high 'airbeds' with smooth white linen; furniture is minimal. The big ground-floor kitchen with stainless steel range opens on to the garden. Children can run wild and fish; adults gather for a special occasion. It is quirky, relaxed, dream-like, adventurous. The village, with medieval centre, tree-lined avenues and restaurants, is on the doorstep, the Pyrénées a few miles away. Fabulous.

Price	€950–€1,300 per week. Cleaning €130.
Sleeps	9.
Rooms	1 double, 1 twin, 2 suites (1 for 3, 1 for 2); 2 bathrooms, 1 shower room.
Meals	Restaurants in village.
Closed	Rarely.

Gertrud Keazor
Chalâbre, Aude

Tel	+44 (0)20 7700 0897
Mobile	+44 (0)7834 963000
Email	info@yobabalounge.com
Web	www.yobabalounge.com

11 rue des Deux Ponts - Riverside, Balcony, Market Place

Once upon a time, many centuries ago, there were two houses divided by a cobbled lane. Several centuries later, the cobbled lane was replaced by a steep winding stairwell and a vast sky-lit hallway. Today, this hallway separates three charming apartments. It feels a privilege to stay here, in the medieval ramparts of one of the most historic villages of France, home to a distinguished abbey, a celebrated market square and a major literary festival in summer. And it's wonderful for young children: the small garden at the back of Balcony, shared by first-floor Riverside and Market Place, borders the limpid river so you can paddle in the waters of the pebble beach or wander down to the 11th-century bridge. The apartments are light-filled and lovely, with lofty beamed ceilings and sweeping terracotta floors, pretty bathrooms and modern kitchens, colourful throws on comfy old sofas, quirky brocante finds and good family pieces. The owners, a charming young couple, are passionate about the Corbières and hugely helpful with guests.

Price	Riverside €460–€990. Balcony €450–€1,250. Market Place €360–€700. Prices per week.
Sleeps	15.
Rooms	Riverside: 1 double, 1 triple; 1 bathroom. Balcony: 1 double, 1 triple; 1 bathroom, 1 shower room. Market Place: 1 double, 1 triple; 1 bathroom.
Meals	Can do flexible weekends out of season on a B&B basis.
Closed	Rarely.

Kate & Roger Sampson
Lagrasse, Aude

Tel	+33 (0)4 68 43 19 35
Mobile	+33 (0)6 43 23 64 78
Email	holidays.lagrasse@gmail.com
Web	www.holidays-lagrasse.com

The Courtyard Gîte

Tucked into a sweet courtyard garden, here is a charming bolthole for two. You're in a village yet no-one would know you were here, your little house is so snugly private – that's half the attraction. Step into an open-plan living area with stone and lime-plaster walls, comfy blue sofa, mosaic-topped table and a galley kitchen decked out in yellow and blue. It's spotlessly clean and you have all you need: coffee maker, decent crockery, CD player, good reading lamps. Then it's up the open staircase to the bedroom under the beams. Handsome, quality bedding is set off by a simple pine floor, white walls and prettily exposed stone. A 'Juliet' balcony overlooks the garden; the bathroom, with walk-in shower, dazzles in white and blue. Best of all is the courtyard with its flowered tubs and climbing shrubs, attractive table and chairs and quirky collection of tools and rustic keys. Delightful Sandra lives opposite, on hand to help but respecting your privacy. She'll tell you all about the markets and restaurants, the lake for swimming and the stunning walks.

Price	£280-£360 per week.
Sleeps	2.
Rooms	1 twin/double, sofabed in sitting room; 1 bath & shower room.
Meals	Restaurant 100m.
Closed	November to mid-March.

Sandra Dalgleish
Arques, Aude

Tel	+33 (0)4 68 20 63 69
Email	alanbuckleyindia@hotmail.com

Languedoc - Roussillon

Paradix - Apartment One

The handsome gateway is 19th-century but the interiors are resolutely modern: old and new coexist effortlessly in this collection of four apartments (see next entry). This was once a prosperous wine merchant's house and vines sweep in every direction. The stables and outbuildings have been imaginatively transformed by architect Colin and his Swiss wife, Susanna; they once ran an inn in Tuscany, now they live here. Apartments have two storeys and a small patio garden; the rest – lawns, shady spots, chlorine-free pool – are to share. Inside: a minimalist look with the occasional cushion or Matisse print in colourful contrast to perfect white walls and pale terracotta floors; there's light, space, clean lines. Apartment One, the biggest, sleeping four, has an immaculate kitchen with every mod con, a large sitting/dining room with space in which to sit and read, and views to the lovely jasmine- and oleander-tumbled gardens that keep each apartment private. A yellow spiral staircase leads to luxurious but stylishly simple bedrooms, with beds dressed in fine white linen. *Shared laundry.*

Price	€950–€1,180 per week.
Sleeps	4.
Rooms	2 twins/doubles; 1 shower room.
Meals	Restaurant 200m.
Closed	Never.

Susanna, Colin & Yvonne Glennie
Nissan lez Ensérune, Hérault

Tel	+33 (0)4 67 37 63 28
Email	glennieauparadix@wanadoo.fr
Web	www.glennieauparadix.com

Paradix - Apartments Two, Three, Four

You can tell from the beautiful blue and white kitchens that Colin Glennie was once a professional chef: they're so well equipped that the most reluctant cook will be inspired. All is perfection in these apartments, the interiors a serene symphony of light woods and natural fabrics. Study, read or relax in the large, light sitting/dining rooms; the lighting is excellent and central heating keeps you cosy in winter. In summer, swim in the delicious pool, read under the plane trees, or stroll among the roses and oleander in the communal garden. Or set off for Béziers (don't miss the riotous four-day *feria* in August), the Oppidum d'Ensérune (the nearby site of a 1,600-year-old Gallo-Roman settlement) and the Canal du Midi with its colourful barges. If you want a cheaper option, there's a first-floor studio for two, where striking blues and reds are offset by white walls. Come to Paradix if you're seeking a week of minimalist perfection in discreet and beautiful surroundings and a village you can walk to: Nissan is a lively little place with both market and shops. *Shared laundry.*

Price	€660–€950 each per week.
Sleeps	6.
Rooms	Each apartment: 1 twin/double; 1 shower room.
Meals	Restaurant 200m.
Closed	Never.

Susanna, Colin & Yvonne Glennie
Nissan lez Ensérune, Hérault

Tel	+33 (0)4 67 37 63 28
Email	glennieauparadix@wanadoo.fr
Web	www.glennieauparadix.com

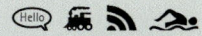

Maison Hirondelles

Former antiques dealers and restaurateurs, Simon and Meg made a brave move to France in 2002 and now Simon will give you his knowledge about wine, and Meg will give you a game of tennis or table tennis. Full of fun, they moved to the pretty wine village of Cazedarnes, turning the 19th-century stone house into a two-bedroom B&B with a gîte on the top floor. With your own entrance you can be as private or as sociable as you like: you may share the pool and verdant garden or retreat to your secluded courtyard with its shady chestnut and Japanese maple. High sloping ceilings, plenty of windows and cool white walls give rooms space and light. The open-plan living area, comfortably but unfussily furnished, has French windows to a veranda with views of vineyards and hills. The kitchen is crisp, modern and in excellent order; the bedrooms have antiques, pretty bedcovers, super bath and shower rooms and lovely views. With maps and bikes to borrow you can explore vineyards, hike in the Canal du Midi, browse markets and visit Carcassonne or the coast (a 40-minute drive). No wonder readers love this place. *B&B also. Shared pool.*

Price	€400-€1,200 per week.
Sleeps	6.
Rooms	1 double, 2 twins/doubles; 1 bathroom, 2 shower rooms.
Meals	Restaurant 3km.
Closed	Never.

	Meg & Simon Charles
	Cazedarnes, Hérault
Tel	+33 (0)4 67 38 21 68
Mobile	+33 (0)6 75 41 95 53
Email	megsimon@mac.com
Web	www.maison-hirondelles.com

Hameau de Cazo - La Vigne

Simple and quietly elegant, this little pink village house will delight all who eschew fuss and clutter. And the views of the vineyards and the red-earthed hills of the Minervois will enchant you. In a small working hamlet, these three storeys have been beautifully restored by Dutch owners Monique and Reinoud, who live in a village nearby. Box trees flank the front door and the garden promises summer shade. Inside, original patterned floor tiles are enhanced by clean white walls and simple furniture. Dine round the farmhouse table or among the almond trees and lavender in the small walled garden. Upstairs are colourful bedspreads and curtains, russet-red tomettes and, in the double, an open fire. It's a charming little house, and a well-equipped one: central heating and two open fires, TV, CDs, DVDs, broadband, coffee-maker, dishwasher, washing machine. Walk in the vine-braided hills and the Mont Caroux, swim in peaceful rivers, drink in simple village life – along with a glass of Saint Chinian – while you watch sheep and goats lazily graze. Perfect, too, for a winter stay. *House for 4-5 available next door.*

Price	€350–€710 per week. Linen not included. Electricity not included in low season.
Sleeps	4.
Rooms	1 double, 1 twin & child's bed; 1 bathroom.
Closed	Never.

Monique & Reinoud Weggelaar–Degenaar
Saint Chinian, Hérault

Tel	+33 (0)4 99 57 03 24
Mobile	+33 (0)6 37 62 98 22
Email	info@midimaison.com
Web	www.midimaison.com

Château de Grézan - Les Meneaux

Enter the battlemented gateway in the 'medieval' castle walls (those turrets are 19th-century follies), cross the cobbled yard and ascend the old stone stairs. Les Meneaux feels big and somehow modern – yards of lovely, wide, original floorboards, high rafters, immaculate white walls and a kitchen that is resolutely 21st-century. The flat is big, light and uncluttered, its paintwork picked out in blue, its sideboard filled with well-chosen china. It has country furnishings, a pretty blue double bedroom, a smaller, spring-flowered twin and two beds up on the mezzanine beneath the roof window. Outside the castle walls is the swimming pool, beautifully protected by palm trees and bamboo, where you can relax and eat; beyond, a sea of vines shimmers beneath the great Languedoc sky. The garden, a superb mixture of wild and formal, has some fascinating native species and you can buy estate Faugères wine. Delightful Madame has a restaurant within the walls and a gîte in the tower, so others share the pool and the grounds. A lovely relaxed place with masses of space. *Sawday B&B.*

Price	€515-€1,200 per week. Linen not included.
Sleeps	6.
Rooms	2 twins/doubles, 2 singles on mezzanine; 1 bathroom.
Meals	Restaurant in grounds. Dinner €20-€25 per person.
Closed	Never.

Marie-France Lanson
Laurens, Hérault

Tel	+33 (0)4 67 90 28 03
Email	chateau-grezan.lanson@wanadoo.fr
Web	www.grezan.com

Entry 231   Map 15

Château de Grézan - La Tour

La Tour is inside the castle gate, its kitchen and bathroom tucked into a circular tower. Oval windows and 'arrow-slits' allow limited light from the outside world of courtyard and restaurant terrace but with great beams, old stones and fresh paintwork this is more atmospheric than gloomy, and blessedly cool in high summer. A sofa and a couple of deep chairs still leave space on the tiled ground floor for a good country table and a great armoire full of crockery. To one side is the double bedroom with a soft-curtained bed and window opening onto the vines. The twin room, behind a curtain on the beamed mezzanine, gets air and light from the entrance hall and faces the old-fashioned bathroom in the tower at the other end of the gallery. The kitchen, off the living area below, is diminutive but fine for holiday cooking. A castle setting, a lovely pool beneath the palms, sloping lawns and massive trees, a little restaurant in the ramparts: it's all most unusual. Madame Lanson, charming, bubbly and deeply interesting, has organised a fascinating wine trail for English speakers. *Sawday B&B.*

Price	€400-€940 per week. Linen not included.
Sleeps	4.
Rooms	1 double, 1 twin on mezzanine; 1 bathroom.
Meals	Restaurant in grounds. Dinner €20-€25 per person.
Closed	Never.

	Marie-France Lanson Laurens, Hérault
Tel	+33 (0)4 67 90 28 03
Email	chateau-grezan.lanson@wanadoo.fr
Web	www.grezan.com

La Roque

The garden slopes down, via several grassed terraces, to the gently flowing river and the private beach. For lunch, your picnic table is in the dappled shade of old trees… the owners provide a rucksack containing plates, glasses and cutlery. Children can play in the shallows, swimmers can float with the current to the bridge, idlers can rest in the hammocks and watch the canoeists pass by. Back at La Roque, two period café doors replace the originals – the entrance to the old wine cellar and stables of the century-old wine grower's house. (The owners, when they come, live upstairs, but all you hear are birdsong and river.) In your very private space you have an open-plan living area with shiny terracotta floors, a wooden kitchen with white crockery and views of old Vieussan clinging to the hills above, a stylish iron sofa painted white with big blue cushions, a round table, a corner for ping-pong. Bedrooms have white walls, new beds, ethnic rugs, mosquito blinds; the open shower is huge. This is a place for lovers of quiet and of walks in the hills – and there's a great restaurant/bar in the village.

Ethical Collection: Environment.
See page 370 for details.

Price	€395–€1,050 per week.
Sleeps	6.
Rooms	1 double, 2 twins/doubles; 1 shower room.
Meals	Restaurant 200m.
Closed	November–February.

Annabel & Martin Shaw
Vieussan, Hérault

Tel	+33 (0)4 67 97 51 69
Email	vieussan@gmail.com
Web	www.vieussan.net

Maison de Garde Barrière

This charming little house, once a crossing keeper's cottage, has been beautifully restored and extended by its English owners. Fling open the pea-green shutters and soak up the views of sun-baked vineyards stretching to the distant dimpled Carroux mountains. The garden is wild and woolly and full of fun; a hammock hangs between pine trees; oleander, mimosa, cypresses and palms stir in the warm breeze. Equipped to feed a biggish family, the brightly tiled kitchen sports a five-ring hob, a bottle of wine awaits in the fridge and the living room is decorated in peachy hues with a corner fireplace for winter nights. Upstairs are pretty bedrooms with white walls, parquet floors and pine furniture; bathrooms are large and clean, new towels plentiful. Outside: a barbecue, a furnished patio and a saltwater pool. So deeply rural is this house (just the sound of an occasional vigneron tractor and the two-carriage trains passing on France's oldest line) that it's not on the grid; energy is solar instead. Simple shops and a Thursday market are a three-minute drive; in Magalas is a supermarket and an exceptional restaurant.

Price	£500–£950 per week.
Sleeps	6.
Rooms	2 doubles, 1 twin; 1 bathroom, 1 shower room.
Meals	Restaurants 10-minute drive.
Closed	Rarely.

Susie Alexander
Laurens, Hérault

Tel	+44 (0)1243 512776
Mobile	+44 (0)7889 469939
Email	susie.a.alexander@googlemail.com

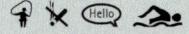

Les Palmiers

The town is one of the oldest in the Languedoc, peaceful but alive with locals – and a sprinkling of tourists in summer. And, right on the market square, a stroll from the river (beach, rock pools, swimming), is this sunny, charming *maîson de maitre*. Sweep into an elegant salon with tall windows and sober chandelier, linen-dressed sofas and white wicker chair, grand marble (working) fireplace and kilim rug on pale floor. The cool downstairs bedroom is restful in soft pink; the kitchen contains everything in cupboards that climb to the ceiling; French windows open to a south-facing, palm-studded garden with a Moroccan mosaic table, shielded from the street by iron railings and high wall. Back inside, stairs curl up to a wide landing and the large luminous bedrooms: white curtains, white mirrors, tall windows, old tomettes, patterned tiles. The Dutch owners live conveniently nearby, while shops, market, cafés and restaurants (just two) are a lazy step away. The Mediterranean is at its best out of season; tempting to book a long stay. *Private garage.*

Price	€350–€710 per week. Linen not included. Electricity not included in low season.
Sleeps	6.
Rooms	2 doubles, 1 twin; 1 bathroom, 1 shower room.
Meals	Restaurants within walking distance in village.
Closed	Never.

Monique & Reinoud
Weggelaar-Degenaar
Cessenon sur Orb, Hérault

Tel	+33 (0)4 99 57 03 24
Mobile	+33 (0)6 37 62 98 22
Email	info@midimaison.com

La Voix du Ruisseau

The end of the sleepy old village opens out into a green and secret valley. Here Jim and Monika have built their dream, a place for peace and rest with a dash of communal living against a rich display of greenery and rocks, lulled by the hurrying stream. A sparky German writer and an American songwriter and guitarist, they have restored an old house with loving care in natural materials only – this is where you drop by for crunchy organic breakfast or meditation – and have built two beautiful yurts on the terraces at the far end of their land, hidden among the oaks and the hazelnut trees. Each is a space with little furniture and a wood stove for chilly evenings, a traditional build using local bamboo and canvas, a central top window and two others for light, a wooden or seagrass floor with rugs: all is simplicity. Wonderful for an easy-going holiday, be you two or half a dozen. The small yurt with its own little terrace is higher up the hill and more private but further from the bathroom and kitchen. Glorious walking straight from the village, myriad things to do and see nearby, and such peace to return to.

Price	€70 B&B for 2. €280-€350. €175-€245 for 1. Prices per week.
Sleeps	6.
Rooms	1 yurt for 5-6. 1 yurt for 2-3. Tent for children. Shower house & compost wc shared by all.
Meals	Breakfast €5-€10. Vegetarian dinner €25, on request. Wine extra. Communal kitchen building. Restaurants 10-minute walk.
Closed	Never.

Jim Benton & Monika Sonntag
Graissessac, Hérault

Tel	+33 (0)9 51 36 50 54
Email	info@voixduruisseau.org
Web	www.voixduruisseau.org

Le Grand Hermitage

Up a country lane, a splendid romantic retreat – or two, on either side of the pretty pool – set against wooded hills and starlit skies (no light pollution, it's a regional park). Richard and Barbara built two fine 'old' barns that sit easily among the Languedoc hills, gave them perfect galley kitchens, old oak floors and English antiques. It is exceedingly comfortable, discreet and welcoming; the luxury is in the service. Barbara's attention to detail goes to bathrobes and handmade soaps, all kitchen basics (oil, vinegar, etc), breakfast stuffs for the first morning, baskets for your shopping. If they have not gone travelling, they will regale you with tales of this ongoing eco-friendly project, all natural materials, lime washes, recycled paper insulation, solar-heated pool: great people. Order a tasty winter casserole or summer salad and invite your friends for candlelit dinner. Or walk through the woods to the nearest (good) restaurant. Then retire to your divinely daring, bronze-balustraded sleeping platform: big, white, soft – and a roll top bath bang opposite the window and the sky. *Not suitable for children.*

Ethical Collection: Environment; Food.
See page 370 for details.

Price	€500-€1,200 per week. Welcome picnic or casserole included. Ask about short breaks. Min. 2 days.
Sleeps	4.
Rooms	Each villa: 1 double; 1 bath/shower room.
Meals	Dinner, with wine, €35. On request.
Closed	Never.

Barbara Simpson-Birks
Clermont l'Hérault, Hérault

Tel	+33 (0)4 67 96 62 31
Mobile	+44 (0)7860 479224
Email	sunfor300days@aol.com
Web	www.legrandhermitage.com

Couvent des Ursulines - Four Apartments

In the heart of old Pézenas, step into a high-walled garden and catch your breath. Before you lie plane trees, palm trees, hammocks and green - children can roar around without fear of damaging anything. Jean-François (French) and Nikki (English) have transformed the graceful 18th-century convent into four strikingly contemporary mezzanine apartments. Arched French windows lead from terraces into open-plan salons: light airy spaces, minimum furnishings, maximum comfort. Sweeping tiled floors and stippled or washed walls make the most of each room's lofty proportions while deep sofas, a wooden dining table and hand-crafted chandelier add a bold edge. A delicate metalwork spiral stair leads to a snug mezzanine sitting room; a neat fitted kitchen is tucked into a corner. Light-filled bedrooms, warm in peach and pink, have a sprinkling of antiques. Take a dip in the pool, pick the garden herbs, visit the coast. Jean-François and Nikki are passionate about their home; they and the convent will charm you and your family. They also run a lively café in town. *Shared fenced pool. French lessons; guided excursions.*

Price	€850–€1,500 each per week.
Sleeps	10.
Rooms	Apartment One: 2 doubles; 3 bathrooms; sofabed on mezzanine. Apartments Two, Three & Four: 2 doubles, sofabed on mezzanine; 2 bathrooms, separate wc.
Closed	Rarely.

Jean-François & Nikki Marques-Quist
Pézenas, Hérault

Tel	+33 (0)4 67 09 49 51
Email	info@pezenas-ursulines.com
Web	www.pezenas-ursulines.com

Domaine du Cayrat - Alicante, Ramonet & Sellerie

It must seem like heaven to the Barys who retired here after stressful careers in Paris. The domaine has been in the family for generations and Jacques and Monique have energetically and carefully transformed their trio of barns into well-equipped gîtes. Each one is fresh, simple and immaculate, with space, finely thought-out detail and views over the surrounding vineyards. The furniture is a good mix of old and new: Monique has obviously enjoyed seeking out the right pieces – a mirror wreathed in vine leaves, the perfect bedside lamp… French windows open from big white living rooms onto private terraces fringed with infant oleanders, each with its own teak furniture and barbecue. Beyond is the grassy shade of the courtyard, dominated by a magnificent, century-old fig tree. Beyond again, hidden behind the courtyard wall, is the pool. This is a great place for families – the Barys' own grandchildren put in an appearance from time to time – and there's masses to do in the area. If you're a Molière fan, elegant Pézenas, one of his favourite towns, is nearby. Fancy having your wedding party here? You can. *B&B also.*

Price	€650
Sleeps	22.
Rooms	Alicante: 1 double, 2 twins; 1 bathroom, 2 shower rooms. Ramonet: 1 double, 2 twins; 3 shower rooms. Sellerie: 1 double, 2 twins; 1 bathroom, 2 shower rooms. Two extra en suite doubles.
Closed	Never.

Monique de Bary
Cazouls d'Hérault, Hérault

Tel	+33 (0)4 67 25 15 44
Email	info@lecayrat.com
Web	www.lecayrat.com

Domaine de Rives Près

Fling open the French windows and scent fills the air: lavender, thyme, rosemary, pine. The ground-floor rooms of this generously restored farmhouse open directly to the perfumed garden. Beyond, the Languedoc vineyards roll into the hazy distance. This is an indoors/outdoors place with cool tiled rooms drifting into terraces, balconies, trees for shade and a secluded swimming pool. Inside, all is space, light and white: stone or plaster walls, beams, vast windows, a series of archways linking the downstairs rooms. Furnishings are uncluttered – white linen sofas, modern paintings, fine bronze sculptures and well-loved family antiques. Plus smart bathrooms, fresh bedrooms with glorious views and a smallish but well-equipped kitchen (and another on the second floor). Toss a coin for the master suite with its balcony and window'd veranda, or the garden bedroom with terrace, ideal for grandparents. Canoeing and sailing nearby, beaches an hour away, shops, restaurants and weekly market walkable – a place of taste that is perfect for large families who love peace, luxury and style.

Price	£750–£1,850 per week.
Sleeps	9.
Rooms	2 doubles, 2 twins, 1 single & folding bed; 4 bathrooms, separate wc.
Closed	Never .

Brenda Kemp
Saint André de Sangonis, Hérault

Tel	+33 (0)4 67 96 61 25
Email	kemp.france@gmail.com
Web	www.rivespres.net

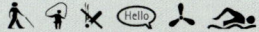

Mas de Villetelle

A simple, rustic hideaway – a joy for those who want to unwind. You are in glorious countryside yet a 15-minute bike ride from Gignac with its restaurants and Saturday market. You stay in a charming converted farm building (the rest are still in ruins) in total privacy with your own shaded patio, hammock, deckchairs and barbecue. Step into an open-plan living space of terracotta floors, white walls, a wood-burner, two comfortable sofas, books. Golden yellow hand-made tiles adorn the kitchen, there are basket drawers for pots and pans, no modern gadgets and a basic four-ring gas hob, but you can walk to a lovely auberge down the road. Bedrooms are up a new ash staircase and are plain, light and pretty with touches of brocante, good mattresses, white cotton sheets. Views are stunning, over vineyards and umbrella pines. A shower room with hand-made tiles sits between the two bedrooms; electricity for lights and music is solar powered. The owners live nearby and leave a bottle of local wine and fresh wild flowers for when you arrive. *Use of owners' pool by arrangement. No washing machine.*

Price	£400 per week.
Sleeps	4.
Rooms	2 doubles; 1 shower room.
Closed	Mid-October to March.

Ethical Collection: Environment.
See page 370 for details.

Terri Andon
Gignac, Hérault

Tel	+33 (0)4 67 86 16 03
Mobile	+33 (0)6 87 28 38 17
Email	terri@languedoc-gite.com
Web	www.languedoc-gite.com

Gîte du Pic Midi

A gentle place to stay beneath the wind-singing umbrella pines, your little holiday home is the ground floor of the owners' house yet you can be as private as you wish with your own pretty terrace and garden, even your own drive for the car. The Mortiers have done a beautiful, simple conversion using soft ochre-limed walls, lamps, tables and rugs from Morocco (they lived there for 30 years), wooden furniture and an excellent big shower room. It is all high quality, there's plenty of storage and no clutter. Cooks will love the battery of equipment in the green and yellow kitchen, the sofabed in the living room hides behind a curtain at bedtime, simple white crockery decks the old farmhouse table and the terrace is perfect for morning shade and sunset vigils. Walk or bicycle out into the quiet countryside where grapes and olives grow, take the children to the nearby 'Ecology' centre or leave the car in Jacou and catch the tram to young and lively Montpellier for a shot of culture or shopping. A perfect marriage of city and country living.

Price	€550–€750 per week. €300 per weekend.
Sleeps	2.
Rooms	1 twin/double, sofabed; 1 shower room.
Meals	Restaurants 3-10km.
Closed	Never.

Yvonne & Patrick Mortier
Prades le Lez, Hérault

Tel	+33 (0)4 67 59 56 37
Email	patrick@mortier.nom.fr
Web	giterural-herault.com

Place Canourgue

The narrow car-free streets of Montpellier's elegant old legal quarter lead to tranquil, tree-lined Place Canourgue where a grand façade, sun-kissed and south-facing, betrays 17th-century origins. The owners of this city getaway are UK-based, so the housekeeper meets and greets, ushering you up a spiral stone staircase to an airy apartment on the second floor. High ceilings, stone floors and large windows keep things cool, while a restrained mix of modern and antique furniture in salon, dining room and hall create an elegant mood. Bedrooms at the back are painted in subtle greys, soft ivory bed linen adds a calm feel, and spotless bathrooms have abundant white towels. The kitchen is beautifully equipped, its welcome basket holding breakfast essentials and wine; just nip to the excellent local boulanger for your croissants. The housekeeper's husband, a professional chef, cooks dinner on request, but neighbourhood restaurants range from simple to five-star and the best of Montpellier laps at your feet. Don't miss the Saturday farmers' market under the Roman aqueduct – marvellous! *Car parks nearby.*

Price	£900 per week.
Sleeps	4.
Rooms	1 double, 1 twin/double, sofabed; 1 bath/shower room, 1 shower room.
Meals	Chef on request.
Closed	Never.

David Roper
Montpellier, Hérault

Tel	+44 (0)20 7494 1000
Email	info@placecanourgue.com
Web	www.placecanourgue.com

Bastide d'Esparon

Two great old houses converted for gentle family living, linked by a terrace outside, doors inside: ideal for one large or two small families. The untouched hamlet is genuine rural France, the eagle's-eye views are amazing, the ancient houses have vaulted ceilings, two of which cover a pair of dark, enfolding bedrooms lifted by pretty stitched bedcovers. Upstairs is lighter, everywhere are lovely kilim rugs and pieces brought back from the owners' travels – fine old wooden chests, antique wardrobes, paintings, books. A well-restored place, much loved by the creative, colour-conscious family who have owned it for 50 years, it has two of everything: sitting rooms with fireplaces, kitchens (one outside), one terrace for privacy and peace, another for joyous gatherings. Inside, history speaks through several levels and thick old walls (some say it was the local Merovingian castle). A most atmospheric, æsthetic retreat from the busy world, cooled by mountain breezes in the blistering summer, with superb walks, rivers for swimming or canoeing down in the valley, unusual excursions galore – and just 9km from all shopping.

Price	Upper house for 5-7: €500-€2,000. Whole house for 10-11: €1,050-€2,500. Whole house with annexe for 14-15: €1,450-€3,000. Prices per week.
Sleeps	15.
Rooms	Main house: 1 suite for 2 with sofabed, 3 twins, 2 singles; 1 bathroom, 2 shower rooms. Annexe: 1 double, 1 family room for 3; 1 shower room.
Closed	Rarely.

Martine Fougeron de Monès
Le Vigan, Gard

Mobile	+1 917 622 8755
Email	info@bastide-esparon.com
Web	www.bastide-esparon.com

Entry 244   Map 15

La Filature - Roquedur le Haut

A stunning and remote mountain area with a fascinating history and a house that marries comfort and style. If you're a nature lover, La Filature, in a hilltop village with a permanent population of 15, has it all. The name, which means 'spinning mill', comes from the period when the silk industry boomed; cocoons were unwound in hot water by the women of this house. The old stone house with its heavenly beams and white painted walls has been well restored and stylishly furnished by its English owner: stunning ethnic chair covers and wall hangings, a gleaming oak dresser, a pretty antique brass bed and a warming wood-burner or open fire for chilly days. Pluck cherries, greengages from the fruit trees, wander through the four-acre Spanish chestnut wood down to a stream, swim in the river Vis, or simply loll on one of the many stone terraces in the large and sloping garden. In autumn look out for truffles, mushrooms and wild boar. The views here on the edge of the Cévennes National Park are memorable. *Children over 5 welcome.*

Price	€470-€595 per week. Linen not included.
Sleeps	6.
Rooms	3 doubles; 1 bathroom, 1 shower room.
Meals	Restaurant 7km.
Closed	Never.

Carmela Pearson
Sumène, Gard

Tel	+44 (0)20 7607 2108
Email	carmela10@btintnernet.com
Web	www.Roquedur-le-Haut.co.uk

Domaine de Bussas - Five Apartments

This is heart-of-Cévennes magic, among rocks, rivers and woodland. After a couple of hairpins you meet the old stone walls, archways and inner courtyard of the ancient domaine. Dating back to 1197, it stands in a secret valley surrounded by 200 acres of nature and pure air. Nothing has changed things over the years, other than the clearing of trees for more light and the careful tending of the garden. Children big and small rejoice in the pool, the huge garden, the games room in the old barn, the river for picnics, adventures and cool plunges. Each apartment has a private terrace and the whole place is a dream for family gatherings. Attractive, comfortable rooms are just right: not over-smart or needing kid gloves. There are antique armoires and colourful fabrics, good modern kitchens and open fireplaces. The caretaker grows organic eggs and veg – just ask. The only sounds are bird calls, sheep bells – and yourselves. With such a variety of spaces to explore and those fabulous views on the spot, you may never get round to the other beauties of the Cévennes. *Option to rent entire château.*

Price	Balcon £600–£1,400. Colombier £360–£815. Source £310–£635. Lucarne £340–£525. Four à pain £255–£550. Whole château £1,600–£3,500. Prices per week.
Sleeps	16
Rooms	B: 2 doubles, 1 twin; 2 bathrooms. C: 1 triple, 1 single, sofabed; bathroom. S: 1 twin, sofabed; 1 bathroom. L: 1 double, single sofabed; bathroom. FP: 1 double; 1 bathroom,1 shower room.
Meals	Caterer available. Restaurants 3-7km.
Closed	Rarely.

Meg Campbell
L'Estréchure, Gard

Tel   +44 (0)20 7229 9754
Email   domainedebussas@btinternet.com
Web   www.bussas.com

La Rouvière

Not for party animals! This secluded place is reached via a long, long winding drive: you arrive and the beauty of the place suffuses your soul. The word *rouvière* comes from the Patois for 'oak' and the hillsides are full of them. No hint of civilisation to be seen: just the slate roofs of an old farmhouse in the valley below. Come in May and June for the wild flowers, in autumn for the trees, in summer for buzzing bees, cicadas and birds. This is almost a *hameau*, with the lovely old house, the barns and the terraces on many levels. Living rooms drift into a terrace, there are two sofas, a fireplace, a round dining table, a polished floor; easy to make this one's home. The kitchen with grey-painted cupboards is well set-up; bedrooms have pine bedsteads and beams (a secret double room lies beyond the terrace). There's a spring-fed pool with spa jets and a hammock under a fig tree: gaze on vast views and dream. The owners live next door, leave you a basket of local apple juice, goat's cheese and honey and create walking paths for exploring; the wonderful Saturday market in Les Vans is close by.

Price	€500–€900 per week.
Sleeps	5.
Rooms	2 doubles, 1 single; 1 bathroom, 2 separate wcs.
Meals	Dinner, with wine, €15. On request. Restaurants 12km.
Closed	November–March.

Ethical Collection: Environment; Community. See page 370 for details.

Claude & Annette Jost
Bonnevaux, Gard

Tel	+33 (0)4 66 61 18 17
Mobile	+33 (0)6 84 09 06 11
Email	claudejost@free.fr
Web	claudejost.free.fr

L'Auzonnet

A magical place. One minute you're in an ordinary village street, the next you enter a cool dark stone tunnel and emerge into a sunlit, secret courtyard. Hydrangeas splash the walls with colour, a stone stairway leads up to the little gîte: it's totally enchanting. The kitchen/living area has painted panelling, pine furniture and brightly coloured crockery. Up on the mezzanine is a Wedgwood-blue and white bedroom – light, pretty and open-plan – and a mosaic shower room. The private terrace overlooks the Auzonnet river but you're also welcome to make the most of the wonderful garden. Cross the courtyard, go through another arch and you find yourself at the top of lovely green terraces dropping down to a small pool and the tranquil river (you may fish). Sit and watch and wait and you may glimpse a heron or the blue flash of a kingfisher – and there will be mimosa in spring. This is the edge of the Cévennes National Park and the village is secluded and peaceful. Lucy and Duncan are on site, happy to give advice on what to see and where to go. *Shared pool. Steep stairs: unsuitable for young children & the less mobile.*

Price	€500–€700 (£350–£500 sterling) per week.
Sleeps	2.
Rooms	1 double, sofabed; 1 shower room.
Meals	Restaurant 10-minute walk.
Closed	December–February.

Lucy & Duncan Marshall
Les Mages, Gard

Tel	+33 (0)4 66 25 39 98
Mobile	+33 (0)6 28 32 86 01
Email	lucy@auzonnet.com
Web	www.auzonnet.com

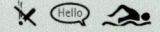

Mas Cagnet

How incredible that a lowly barn has become such a magnificent seven-bedroom house. There is space aplenty for social or solitary pursuits: snooze in the hammock or salute the sun from the activities studio. The bedrooms, with views of vineyards and unspoilt forests, are refined without being too grand. In this well-thought-out family home (the owners used to live here), it's clear the kitchen was designed by someone who truly loves to cook. Golden leather sofas tempt you to cuddle up after meals – the more active can play pool or table football under the covered terrace. Wonderful walks start on the doorstep, and activities abound. Immerse yourself in history at Chartreuse de Valbonne or in nearby Nîmes; comb the Wednesday market in Gougargues. Back at the villa, cool down with a swim; there's a paddling pool for little ones and pretty wicker furniture to flop in. Fire up the barbecue for an al fresco dinner under hanging lights or, for an extravagant evening, nip to the gourmet restaurant down the hill. Perfect for a family reunion (children too!) or a retreat with friends.

Price	€2,400–€3,700 per week.
Sleeps	14.
Rooms	3 doubles, 4 twins; 7 bathrooms.
Meals	Meals on request. Restaurant 2km.
Closed	Never.

	Elliot Godfrey
	Goudargues, Gard
Tel	+33 (0)4 66 82 12 02
Email	elliott@wiredlogic.co.uk
Web	www.mascagnet.com

Mas de la Bousquette - Le Grenier

This lovely mas was once a sheep and cattle farm: ancient stone buildings cluster round an entrancing courtyard, a cypress tree pushes through a gap in a hotchpotch of slanting roofs, goldfish glitter in a pool. It's a place for children: play with the affable dogs, join in with Pippa's cookery courses (parents have a day off and return for the meal), care for the chickens: they get a certificate too! The big garden has a willow tree beside a pond, hammocks and chairs, plenty of shade, a fabulous veg patch. Peg out your washing in the old orchard, with the rare-breed chickens pecking round your feet. The two gîtes, separated by a long covered veranda, are equally fetching. In the old grain store – two storeys in the south-west tower – you eat in a lovely big split-level space: rafters, creamy stone walls, fresh modern décor. Bedrooms have large and comfortable beds, French windows open to a private terrace, there are ceiling fans for summer. The kitchen is perfectly equipped, there are bikes to borrow, good exploring to do, a pool… you'll want to come back; magical. *Shared pool. Extra B&B room for 2 on request.*

Price	€800–€1,680 per week.
Sleeps	4.
Rooms	1 double, 1 twin & sofabed on mezzanine; 2 bathrooms.
Meals	Dinner, with wine, €39.50.
Closed	Never.

Ethical Collection: Environment; Food.
See page 370 for details.

Tim & Pippa Forster
Lussan, Gard

Tel	+33 (0)4 66 72 71 60
Mobile	+33 (0)6 89 72 11 56
Email	masbousquette@free.fr
Web	www.mas-bousquette.com

Mas de la Bousquette - Le Mûrier

The ancient, rose-roofed mas rests at the foot of high-perched, castle-topped Huguenot Lussan. The countryside rolls out before you, the air is pure and the sun is golden – even in winter. In the north-west tower where silkworms were once reared is a charming little gîte, its balcony-terrace tucked beneath a glorious roof. Fresh and clean with inspired touches, it makes a romantic nest for two. Living room and kitchen are beautifully equipped and the bedroom has a delightful simplicity: white walls, terracotta floor, antique iron and brass bed, muslin curtains. Pippa and Tim are warm, generous people and offer you everything: books, games, bicycles, binoculars, fresh fruit, lavender, fresh bread at your door, towels for the heated pool. Pippa loves cooking, gives guests' kids healthy cooking lessons and you a free dinner on arrival, and runs a little shop selling delectable homemade jams and organic eggs. This is southern France at its most peaceful. Within walking distance of an excellent restaurant, near lovely Uzès, not far from Avignon and Nîmes. *Shared pool. Extra B&B room for 2 on request.*

Price	€600-€1,300 per week.
Sleeps	2.
Rooms	1 double, sofabed; 1 bathroom.
Meals	Dinner, with wine, €39.50.
Closed	Never.

Ethical Collection: Environment; Food.
See page 370 for details.

Tim & Pippa Forster
Lussan, Gard

Tel	+33 (0)4 66 72 71 60
Mobile	+33 (0)6 89 72 11 56
Email	masbousquette@free.fr
Web	www.mas-bousquette.com

Maison des Cerises

This village cottage seduces all. Britta is a gifted artist with an eye for light, harmony and spotting the potential in bric-a-brac finds. She has restored the three-storey house with sympathy and skill – walls are stone or limewashed, floors warm terracotta, beams darkly aged, colours pure and natural. The ground-floor bedroom, a creamy space of painted wooden furniture and pretty fabrics, opens to a small, bamboo-edged herb garden scented with lavender, rosemary and thyme. Its bathroom, equally spacious, is *Country-Living* perfect with a claw-foot bath. The romantic top bedroom, with sparkling shower room, is tucked under the eaves. In between is the light-washed living room – elegantly simple with candlesticks, neutral curtains and wine-dark sofa – and, a few steps up, the rustic dining room/kitchen with pine dresser and thick, cream china. The living is easy here: step out to the baker's and the grocer's, basket in hand. Take the children to the water park at Uzès, swim in the river Cèze, hunt for bargains in village markets, then return to your little garden, and feel at peace with the world. Exceptional.

Price	€680–€850 per week.
Sleeps	4.
Rooms	1 double, 1 twin/double; 1 bathroom, 1 shower room.
Meals	Restaurant 5km.
Closed	Never.

Britta Brand
Saint Marcel de Careiret, Gard

Tel	+33 (0)4 66 63 89 40
Mobile	+33 (0)6 75 33 38 19
Email	brittabrand@wanadoo.fr
Web	www.maison-des-cerises.com

L'Hirondelle

Vézénobres caps its hilltop site with a crown of unspoilt medieval stone. Famed for its festival of figs, the village brims with arts, crafts and festivities, and is inhabited all year round. Find the clock tower in the old centre, then climb the townhouse stairs to your charming gîte. At the top, simple, airy and inviting, is L'Hirondelle; steep stairs take you up to the smart bedroom with black iron bedstead and a romantic terrace for stunning sunsets. The open-plan living space has views of vines, hills and woodland, a big open fireplace, books and games for cosy nights, a farmhouse crockery cupboard, a long pine dining table and a small but well-equipped kitchen. Outside is a pretty walled terrace with a plunge pool and pots of bright flowers – eat out in the fig tree's shade. Welcoming owner Julie and her husband live nearby. There's wonderful hiking and biking through spring-flowered countryside, ideal for active, post-buggy children. Return to the village square, beautiful with its historic fountain playing, and plenty of places to eat. *Pool shared with Les Figuiers.*

Price	€395–€595 per week.
	May be rented with Les Figuiers.
Sleeps	2.
Rooms	1 double; 1 bathroom.
Meals	Restaurants 2-minute walk.
Closed	Never.

Julie Aldred
Vézénobres, Gard

Mobile	+33 (0)6 78 84 88 12
Email	info@realsouthfrance.com
Web	www.realsouthfrance.com

Les Figuiers

Oodles of history right here in the unspoilt village where you can dither around the cobbled shady streets and archways, discovering doorways, balconies, stone stairways. One of them leads to a secluded walled terrace with a splash pool, tables and chairs in the shade of a fig tree, and bonny potted flowers. Walk straight in to the middle bit of this stone house set in the hillside; the living room faces south and has huge, rural views from its shuttered windows. An open-plan kitchenette has all you need to conjure up wizard meals and you will sleep soundly in rather smart bedrooms, but you won't be able to resist sitting in the square watching the fountain running and the people passing. There are plenty of restaurants here to choose from, and an annual fig festival to attend, not to mention the world championships for square boules! Further afield there's Uzès with its famous Saturday market, Nîmes, the Pont du Gard, and hiking and biking galore; come in early summer when the countryside is bursting with wild flowers. You will be welcomed by friendly Julie who lives nearby. *Pool shared with L'Hirondelle.*

Price	€395–€595 per week. May be rented with L'Hirondelle.
Sleeps	4.
Rooms	1 double, 1 twin/double; 2 bathrooms, 2 separate wcs.
Meals	Restaurants 200m.
Closed	Never.

	Julie Aldred
	Vézénobres, Gard
Mobile	+33 (0)6 78 84 88 12
Email	info@realsouthfrance.com
Web	www.realsouthfrance.com

Languedoc - Roussillon

2 chemin de la Carcarie

Arlette is the perfect hostess, welcoming but discreet. And cultured: her tortoises have Greek names. You'll meet them in the large wild garden. Her patch is the wonder of the house and Arlette will happily walk you round, passing on the names of the plants and giving you the local gen. Views here take in the pretty village, which has a château. You feel part of local life, yet close to Uzès, one of the most beautiful medieval towns in France (they filmed *Cyrano de Bergerac* there). This 17th-century farmhouse is slightly shabby – all part of the charm – but there are both washing machine and dryer and all linen and towels are included. Upstairs, a big bedroom sleeps four (one very comfy bed, two singles on the mezzanine) so the house is best suited to a couple or a young family – and there's space for football in the garden. Dried garden flowers hang from old beams in the dining room, and you eat on the terrace under a Provençal sun. Arlette lives in part of the house: she is on hand to chat, advise and inform while leaving you all your privacy. No dishwasher, so bring your Marigolds.

Price	€420–€580 per week.
Sleeps	4.
Rooms	1 double & child's bed & twin beds on mezzanine; 1 bathroom.
Meals	Restaurant 800m.
Closed	Never.

Arlette Caccamo-Laniel
Montaren, Gard

Tel	+33 (0)4 66 22 52 14
Email	arlette.laniel@wanadoo.fr

Mas des Vignes

Patchwork fields, copses and the Cévennes mountains: you can't escape the views. Handsome in honey stone and blue shutters, this 19th-century farmhouse revels in its sunny situation. Large, light-filled rooms, comfortably but not fussily furnished, make it ideal for families. There's a welcoming living room, bright with modern sofas and prints, and a fire for chillier months. Teenagers can repair to the games room for table tennis, music, doors to the garden; big families will love it. A rustic-style dining room, with a jolly blue-and-white kitchen tucked to one side, also opens to the outdoors. Bedrooms are restful spaces with their original patterned tiles or old terracotta, and simple mix of antique and country furniture. Linen curtains and cotton bedcovers add a splash; the main bedroom has stunning views and a luxurious bathroom. Follow the sun around the garden and the terraces; drop into the pool, with its backdrop of olive trees. The owners have collated a superb info pack on walks (from the garden), canoeing, vineyards, markets, and restaurants to visit or avoid! History abounds, the coast is close.

Price	£850–£1,800 per week.
Sleeps	8.
Rooms	1 double, 1 twin/double, 2 twins; 2 bathrooms, 1 shower room.
Meals	Restaurant 3-minute walk.
Closed	Never.

Elizabeth Lacey
Aigremont, Gard

Tel	+44 (0)1403 790413
Email	leapinglizzie@hotmail.com
Web	www.masdesvignes.co.uk

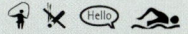

La Terre des Lauriers

The setting – six hectares of bird-filled woodland stretching down nearly to the river – is breathtaking. Let the local canoe-hire folk ferry you up the river, then float back again via that marvel of Roman engineering, the Pont du Gard. These delightful owners are escapees from Paris; Marianick draws, paints and makes sumptuous jams, Gérard has created a botanical trail down towards the water. The 18th-century sheepfold has been restored with simple elegance: the large, lofty, open-plan space, attractive with fine new furniture, plenty of books and games and a yellow and white counter kitchen, is linked by a steep, white metal staircase to mezzanine bedrooms upstairs. You share the huge grounds, pool and garden with B&B guests and those staying in another cottage but have your own small balcony, a terrace for dining and views of the private vineyard. The wild and flowering surroundings are full of pine and olive trees, buzz and flutter, and you will find many fine restaurants nearby too. Magic for families. *Sawday B&B. Shared pool: owners' private use 1.30pm-3pm.*

Price	€800-€1,200 per week. End-of-stay cleaning not included.
Sleeps	4.
Rooms	1 double, 1 twin, sofabed in living room; 1 bathroom, separate wc.
Closed	Never.

Marianick & Gérard Langlois
Remoulins, Gard

Tel	+33 (0)4 66 37 19 45
Email	langlois@laterredeslauriers.com
Web	www.laterredeslauriers.com

Rue Baratier

In lovely old Calvisson, Rue Baratier's three storeys have been restored to reveal old beams, terracotta tiles and honey-coloured stone. The palette is stylish creams, greys and whites, there are linen curtains and period antiques. From the front door a stone staircase invites you up to light, open-plan living, a broad, well-equipped kitchen space, a contemporary dining table with upholstered benches, a salon with a winter-welcome fireplace. And through to an outdoor courtyard with a bubbling water basin, just about big enough to whip up a sociable barbie. Up again to bedrooms: the first with a king-size bed, an antique wardrobe and a chaise longue, the second smaller and intimate; both peaceful. Chic en suite bathrooms have large showers with pebble floors. This is a grown-ups-only house – watch the steepish stairs – and a perfect place for exploring the Gallo-Roman south, the horsey Camargue and the glittering Med, 20 minutes away; wheel a bike out from the garage for some leisurely exploring. Calvisson's Sunday market has flowers and artisanery – and an excellent caterer for no-cooking-please days.

Price	€650–€950 per week.
Sleeps	4.
Rooms	2 doubles; 2 bathrooms.
Meals	Restaurants 500m.
Closed	Never.

Julie Aldred
Calvisson, Gard

Mobile	+33 (0)6 78 84 88 12
Email	info@realsouthfrance.com
Web	www.southfrancevillagehouses.com

Domaine des Clos - Five Apartments

When David and Sandrine returned to their Beaucaire roots, they found a worthy vessel for their creativity in an 18th-century wine estate. All has been authentically and lovingly restored. There are five apartments here, all in the main house, looking out onto vineyards (two from private terraces) or the courtyard lawn. Beyond are exquisite Italianate gardens and the best of Provence – from among the olive trees, jasmine and bougainvillea, shady stone pergolas emerge. Inside, fine antiques, including a Louis XIII table and some venerable farmhouse pieces. Modern touches have been beautifully added in the form of bold colours and exotic wall hangings. Well-organised kitchens fulfil all cooking needs; sweet dining areas are tucked into inviting nooks. Consider an aperitif (or a booked meal) on the terrace of the old stables; in winter, keep warm by the fireplace in the communal salon, delightful with deep fuchsia walls and ceilings hung with handcrafted fixtures. It is hugely original, wonderfully artistic, and the information booklet includes enough markets to keep the lunch bag brimming. *Sawday hotel.*

Price	€500
Sleeps	21.
Rooms	Apartment 1: 1 double; 1 bathroom.
	Apartments 2, 3 & 4: 1 double, 1 twin;
	1 shower room.
	Apartment 5: 1 double, 2 twins,
	1 single; 1 bathroom, 1 shower room.
Meals	Meals on request.
Closed	Rarely.

Sandrine & David Ausset
Beaucaire, Gard

Tel	+33 (0)4 66 01 14 61
Mobile	+33 (0)6 11 81 62 78
Email	contact@domaine-des-clos.com
Web	www.domaine-des-clos.com

Rhône Valley – Alps • Provence – Alps – Riviera

La Ferme du Nant

In summer, you rent one or both of the floors and self-cater; in winter, you have one whole beautiful catered chalet. Floor to ceiling windows span the front of the old house pulling in views that are pure Heidi. Downstairs is a cosily restored living area with a wonderful central fireplace, country dining table and big open kitchen. Upstairs, past a collection of ancient wooden sledges, are pine floors, halogen spotlights illuminating white walls, sandblasted timbers, big blue sofas. Two bedrooms are on the mezzanine – fun for kids – and there's a long, rustic, south-facing balcony to catch the sun. Furniture is a mix of Savoyard and modern with the odd giant pop-art portrait to add a sparkle. Bathrooms are white with mosaics. A trap door leads to a DVD cellar, a sloping garden has been reshaped to take a terrace and heated pool (the old cheese store makes great changing rooms) and the village is a six-minute walk downhill. The owners live on the top floor with their labrador; Susie also owns a horse – the riding is wonderful. *B&B also.*

Price	€840–€1,260 per floor (6–8 people) per week. Minimum 3 days. Catered in winter. Linen not included.
Sleeps	12.
Rooms	Ground floor: 3 twins/doubles; 2 bathrooms, 1 shower room. First floor: 3 twins/doubles; 3 shower rooms. Extra beds.
Meals	Restaurants within walking distance.
Closed	Rarely.

Susie Ward
La Chapelle d'Abondance,
Haute-Savoie

Tel	+33 (0)4 50 73 40 87
Mobile	+33 (0)6 75 81 91 96
Email	susie@susieward.com
Web	www.susieward.com

Ferme du Ciel

A place to catch your breath. well away from the summer crowds; you are high up over the pretty valley and Alpine town of Samoëns. The large chalet-style old farmhouse is happily renovated with soaring beams, a swish open-plan living space, shiny state-of-the-art kitchen and a huge fire to warm you on chilly evenings; balmier ones will entice you to eat on the terrace outside at a large wooden table. Bedrooms ooze style and comfort, with underfloor heating, bold patterned rugs, stripy curtains and white linen; all have sofabeds for children, and swanky bathrooms. A separate entrance leads to the small apartment, sweetly painted in baby blue with a tiny kitchen-in-a-cupboard, a compact modern shower room and its own patio. In the garden find a jacuzzi on one of several terraces, and a sauna too. A short drive will take you to plenty of restaurants and shops selling local honey, sausages and cheeses; work it all off with bracing hikes, cycling or horse riding. Your delightfully unobtrusive hosts are on hand to give advice, and this is perfect for big gatherings of family and friends.

Price	Winter: catered £660–£1,200 p.p. Summer: catered £600 p.p. Self-catered £260–£2,350 per week.
Sleeps	23.
Rooms	1 double, 4 twins/doubles each with double sofabed, 1 family room for 5; 6 bathrooms.
Meals	Fully catered in winter & summer; self-catered in May/June, September-December. Restaurants 3km.
Closed	Never.

Andrew & Su Lyell
Samoëns, Haute-Savoie

Tel	+33 (0)4 50 58 44 57
Mobile	+33 (0)6 21 19 74 83
Email	info@fermeduciel.com
Web	www.fermeduciel.com

Entry 261   Map 12

Le Château du Bérouze

Probably the finest house in Samoëns, the château is very old — the main part dates back to 1485 — yet it was once on the verge of being demolished. New Zealand journalists Jack and Jane came to the rescue, pouring love and talent into reviving old timbers and stones, then opened the large, extravagantly carved doors to guests. Up the stone steps to a first-floor apartment of elegant proportions, you find an ample, open-plan kitchen, a modern living room, a day room, three big bedrooms and two bathrooms, one with a steam cabinet. Lofty ceilings are a criss-cross of white-painted beams, lintels are ancient stone, floors rug-strewn, there's a gas-flame stove and big old radiators to keep you warm. The garden is every bit as lovely, with lush lawns, orchards and flowers, terrace and swimming pool. And… the house is partly moated, streams flow in and out, home to ducks and trout. It's a special place in every season: skiing and skating in winter, swimming, rafting and riding in summer, high hiking. Unspoilt Samoëns, its restaurants and bars, is a five-minute stroll, and your kind hosts will babysit if you ask them.

Price	£800-£2,000 per week.
Sleeps	8.
Rooms	2 twins/doubles, 1 quadruple, 2 sofabeds; 2 bathrooms.
Meals	Restaurant 200m.
Closed	Never.

Jack & Jane Tresidder
Samoëns, Haute-Savoie
Tel	+33 (0)4 50 34 95 72
Email	jane.tresidder@orange.fr
Web	www.chateauduberouze.com

Alps in Style - Chalet Esprit & Chalet Exige

Energetic, charismatic Toni and Jez moved to the great Grand Massif to live the dream: sunshine, snow and crisp mountain air. They live in an apartment in Chalet Exige with their two young daughters and are always on hand for guests — whether staying as B&Bers, or self-caterers or being looked after hotel-style. Whichever option you choose, they do it — brilliantly. Drop-offs, pick-ups, special food for fussy folk, children's high teas... all is possible. Walking distance from the sweet little ski village of Morillon — restaurants or shops — are the couple's twin chalets, spanking new and architect-designed. Warm cosy bedrooms are encased in pine; fabrics are violet, aubergine, cream; delicious beds zip and link; bathrooms are white; sitting rooms are big and inviting. Luxury comes in a hot tub on the balcony beneath starry skies; swanky TV rooms, ten-seater cinema and indoor games keep children merry. It's sleek, stylish and heart-warming all at the same time, great for families and foodies: Jez's menus are delicious. Outside: slides and swings in summer, snowmen in winter, forest views all year round. *Lift station 500m.*

Price	Winter: half-board from €475 p.p. Summer: self-catered from €1,650. Apt from €465. Prices per week. Ask about B&B/fully catered option.
Sleeps	33.
Rooms	Chalet Esprit: 2 twins/doubles, 2 triples, 2 family rooms for 4; s/c apt: 1 twin/double, 1 triple (summer only). Chalet Exige: 2 triples, 1 family room for 4. Extra beds & cots.
Meals	Winter: catered (half-board). Summer: self-catered. Flexible meal arrangements.
Closed	Rarely.

Toni & Jez Waite
Morillon, Haute-Savoie

Tel	+33 (0)4 50 90 31 10
Mobile	+33 (0)6 30 54 70 32
Email	info@alpsinstyle.com
Web	www.alpsinstyle.com

Chalet la Forêt

It was Mont Blanc and the fearsomely steep Aiguilles that put Chamonix on the map; and it is the Aiguille du Midi that towers above you here. Standing in a garden bordered by larch trees and river, in a village near big beautiful 'Cham', this lovely chalet comes with an unlikely history: built in 1950 by a Russian émigré whose son was the first Frenchman to scale Everest. Step in to discover a big kitchen-diner with a wood-burner, and two bedrooms with plump duvets, honeyed floorboards and patchwork quilts. Then it's up the stair to a spacious sitting room with a furnished balcony and inspirational views; further bedrooms too; and a fifth, sweet double tucked into the garden's mazot. Be delighted by cow hide rugs and cushioned sofas, DVDs, music, board games and books, vintage posters and fluffy white towels; be cosseted by a barrel-cabin sauna and a hot tub under the stars. It's friendly and fabulous, just like its owners. The ski lift is a mere 600m away and Chamonix, skiing's 'hardcore capital', is a five-minute drive or 25-minute stride… boutiques, bars, character, cobbles and delectable organic food.

Price	€1,600-€4,850. Catered €2,100 extra for 10. Prices per week.
Sleeps	10.
Rooms	4 twins/doubles, 1 double in mazot; 3 bath/shower rooms, separate wc.
Meals	Restaurants 5-minute walk.
Closed	Rarely.

Martha Tullberg
Chamonix, Haute-Savoie
Mobile	+44 (0)7545 575277
Email	bonjour@chaletlaforet.com
Web	www.chaletlaforet.com

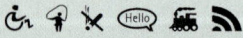

Villa Terrier

A grand old 1910 villa in the middle of big, bustling, beautiful Chamonix. Sporting a smart new stone roof with shiny copper pipes, it looks across to Mont Blanc and the vertiginous Chamonix 'needles'. Ceilings are high, old pine spans the floors, original cornicing beautifies the walls. The living room is charming with an elegant mirror above a carved stone fireplace, rose-pink sofas to sink into, grand lamps to read by, delightful curtains to draw across big windows; the kitchen is family big. Up the wide staircase to light, roomy bedrooms, one with a balcony, two with sloping ceilings. Some have huge bathrooms and, although fabulously new, a traditional French feel, with their claw-foot baths, big basins and fat iron radiators. White towels and bathrobes spread the mood of unashamed luxury. There's music and the internet, an indoor play area for children downstairs – an attic space for them under the eaves, too – lifts to the slopes and four-course dinners with wine. Plus sauna and pool for hot weather. Chamonix is the killer-black-run capital of Europe – and just as popular in summer.

Price	£1,750–£3,400 summer; £3,000–£6,000 winter. Catered £640–£850 p.p. summer; £685–£1,200 p.p. winter. Prices per week.
Sleeps	12.
Rooms	1 double, 3 twins/doubles, attic room for 4 children; 4 bathrooms, 2 separate wcs.
Meals	Self-catering or catered.
Closed	Rarely.

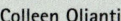

Colleen Olianti
Chamonix Mont Blanc, Haute-Savoie

Tel	+33 (0)4 50 55 83 08
Mobile	+33 (0)6 71 91 20 60
Email	sales@collineige.com
Web	www.collineige.com

Mazot Les Tines

Shaded by poplars rustling in the wind is this upstairs-downstairs little chalet. As the name implies, it was once a wood store – Colleen's. She is the owner, runs her own ski company, and lives across the garden. All is light and bright and stylishly decorated, with country furniture and modern checks. Downstairs is open plan with a roundly rustic dining table for four, a shower room with bathrobes, a washing machine and a kitchen with pottery and pine. The living area is cosy and charming: colourful textiles and prints grace pine-clad walls, there's a perfect red sofa, a little wood-burning stove, a stereo. The mezzanine is great for kids with its ladder to two single mattresses. A floor-to-ceiling window looks onto the garden, filling the space with light. Up the wooden spiral staircase is the bedroom with its balcony and magnificent mountain views. Outside stairs leads down to the garden where roses clamber up wooden walls, geraniums fill window boxes, creepers weave through a pile of stacked slates. You are on the edge of lovely Les Tines and a bus brings you to even lovelier Chamonix.

Price	€650-€1,250 per week.
Sleeps	4.
Rooms	1 double, mezzanine for 2; 1 shower room.
Meals	Restaurant 1km.
Closed	Never.

Colleen Olianti
Chamonix Mont Blanc, Haute-Savoie

Tel	+33 (0)4 50 55 83 08
Mobile	+33 (0)6 71 91 20 60
Email	sales@collineige.com
Web	www.collineige.com

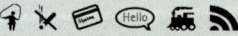

Les Mazots

It's a steep road to get here: views over the Mont Blanc ranges soar. In a quiet corner of Chamonix, this 1930s-built chalet is still only on its second careful owner. Charming Colleen has run the house as a B&B for over 15 years and now lets it for self-catering, too. The lovely house has a faded elegance, with much of the furniture left by the original owners: worn leather armchairs, sepia photographs of acrobats on dark panelled walls, shelves on the stairs crammed with old tomes – deeply atmospheric. Bedrooms are a good size, comfortably furnished and traditional; billowing duvets spread themselves on antique iron beds: sound sleep is guaranteed. The excellent modern kitchen has stainless-steel worktops and a large oven. Checked sofas sit under pretty reading lamps, the large wooden fireplace is decorated with candlesticks and French windows open onto the terrace where the hot tub beckons, and then it's down to the sloping garden and fruit trees. World-renowned for its ski domains, which are at your doorstep, Chamonix is also great in summer. *B&B also.*

Price	€1,900-€3,600 summer; €3,800-€7,500 winter. Catered €640-€850 p.p. summer; €700-€1,200 p.p. winter. Prices per week.
Sleeps	14.
Rooms	1 double, 5 twins/doubles, 2 singles; 6 bathrooms, separate wc.
Meals	Picnic €10. Dinner, with wine, €35. Chef on request.
Closed	Never.

Colleen Olianti
Chamonix Mont Blanc, Haute-Savoie

Tel	+44 (0)1483 579242
Mobile	+33 (0)6 71 91 20 60
Email	sales@collineige.com
Web	www.collineige.com

Entry 267   Map 12

La Marmotte Penthouse

The 1970s chalet-style building was given a facelift by a local architect in 2004 and the duplex penthouse has stacks of style, sweeping views and all you need to ski all day and collapse at night. There are soft sofas and flashes of cushion colour in the generous high-ceilinged living room; one sunny south-facing downstairs balcony where you can eat in summer. Floors are brushed oak, the kitchen is brilliantly equipped, bathrooms shine. Under chunky rafters, the compact bedrooms are deeply comfortable with built-in wardrobes, fluffy duvets, the best mattresses, wine-red wool carpeting and contemporary curtains. The master bedroom shares an east-facing balcony with the bunk-bedded room and... a stunning view of the National Park; the tiny mezzanine over the living space has beds for children. You are ideally placed for busy shops, bars and ski-lifts; a ski-booted hop away from the most sophisticated, far-reaching and interlinked skiing in the Alps and close to fishing, paragliding, golf and fabulous summer biking and hiking. *Free ski bus service links Courchevel 1850, 1650 & 1350.*

Price	£950-£1,780 per week.
Sleeps	6.
Rooms	1 double, 1 twin & pull-out single on mezzanine, 1 room with bunks & pull-out single, sofabed; 2 bath/shower rooms.
Meals	Chef on request. Restaurant 200m.
Closed	Rarely.

Ros & Jeremy Charles
Courchevel 1650, Savoie

Tel	+44 (0)20 8455 4554
Mobile	+44 (0)7788 741870
Email	jeremycharles1@hotmail.com
Web	www.rentapent.com

La Maroquinerie

The living here is simple, convivial, genuine. Sit on the sunny terrace (you are often above the cloud) with a drink and the post lady may join you, bringing her own bottle, or the neighbour may invite you for an aperitif by his *tonneau*. Or sit alone and look for eagles. Winding your way up the narrow mountain road after dusk, you will probably see deer, wild boar, foxes. Inside the ground floor of this 18th-century mountain village house, the dark rusty-red living room has beams and a huge slate fireplace you can sit in as well as cook in (logs provided), new pine flooring and old pine furniture, clocks, paintings, books and games. Also, a simple kitchen area (when Andrew is upstairs, he will cook for you – very nicely – if you ask). Each large double bedroom has a venerable shower cubicle and basin. Two minutes from cross-country skiing: you can ski back to the door in a good season and ski hire is right there. The mountain walks are wonderful: there are racquets in the house for snow walking, in summer you'll fight your way through the sheep and goats grazing wild.

Price	€300 per week.
Sleeps	4.
Rooms	2 doubles; 2 shower rooms, separate wc.
Meals	Occasional table d'hôtes. Restaurants within walking distance in summer (cross country skiing distance in winter).
Closed	December–January.

Elizabeth & Andrew Bamford
Montpascal, Savoie

Tel	+33 (0)4 79 59 79 60
Mobile	+33 (0)6 15 07 05 39
Email	info@chaletsalpes.com
Web	www.chaletsalpes.com

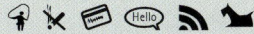

Salivet & La Sousto

Few places have it all but this must be one of them. Breathtaking mountain views, a lovely artistic owner and a fascinating, secluded old farm with a flock of sheep; honey-stoned Salivet stands where the cattle sheds and haylofts used to be. Jane, an English artist, lives next door; she and her farming husband have restored and furnished the place simply but beautifully with old beams, terracotta floors, whitewashed walls, stone fireplaces, wood-burning stoves and antique furniture. On summer nights you can sleep on the roof terrace; during the day sit beneath the wisteria, snooze on the lawn under the weeping willow or cool off in the springwater pool. La Sousto is similarly delightful and unspoiled. Jane sells honey and lamb and Merino wool, cooks fabulous meals on request (much organic) and will supply walking itineraries, maps and flower guides to this beautiful area. There's a bright, spacious art studio too and art teachers can bring groups: a perfect artist's haven. *Shared pool.*

Price	Salivet €750–€1,000. Sousto €450–€600. Prices per week.
Sleeps	12.
Rooms	Salivet: 2 doubles, 1 twin, 1 single, 1 single on mezzanine; 1 bathroom, 1 shower room, 2 separate wcs. Sousto: 1 double, 1 children's twin; 1 bathroom.
Meals	Dinner €20, on request.
Closed	Never.

Ethical Collection: Food.
See page 370 for details

Familie Höming
Truinas, Drôme

Tel	+33 (0)4 75 53 49 13
Mobile	+33 (0)6 99 29 27 78
Email	rimandoula@aol.com

Les Mûriers

Come for views, simplicity, peace. And lovely people: Jill is an artist and sculptor, her Danish husband is a raku specialist, and they've lived and worked here for over 30 years. The grass is unmown to preserve the wild flowers, the trees are full of birds, there are cherries in early June, beehives, herbs and truffles on the land and the springwater pool is hedged. Your private and secluded gîte has a shady rose-covered veranda, and big ochre floor tiles in the main room along with a sofa and two wicker armchairs, a big dining table, a country cupboard. There's an intriguing kitchen counter top, made by Jill's husband, depicting a relief map of the whole area. The bedrooms have open hanging space, pretty olive curtains, good sculptures by Jill. Slip down to the bottom of the garden with a glass of something chilled and watch the sun set over the vineyards and the hills. No sound – bar the neighbour's dog at supper time. You're up high here and it's a magical spot. Come in spring for the hiking, in summer for the music at Orange, all year round for the peace. *Shared pool.*

Price	€450–€550 per week.
Sleeps	3.
Rooms	1 twin/double, 1 single; 1 shower room, separate wc.
Closed	Never.

Jill Ratel
Venterol, Drôme
Tel   +33 (0)4 75 26 22 08
Email   dominique.ratel@wanadoo.fr

Château Colombier

Take the whole house! So wonderful for a big family gathering. But for smaller groups there are endless mix-and-match possibilities: an apartment under the eaves; one bedroom in the tower; a wheelchair friendly studio on the ground floor. The apartment, with a big salon and a kitchen on the landing, is self-contained; the rest share the big, golden-yellow, beautifully equipped kitchen with its table for 16. Unless you're in one big party, you'll be making new friends. Bedrooms are freshly painted to match their names – Lavender, Verveine, Apricot – and are simply and charmingly furnished: voile curtains, pretty brocante. Bathrooms are spotless and chic. Downstairs, where the walls are a metre thick and the ceilings vaulted, is the living room, cosy with a wood-burning stove, heaps of books, music and piano, a tapestry on the wall. Clare adores her *maison de maître*; it stands in a walled garden on the edge of the village, its views of orchards, woods and mountains changing colour with each hour. In summer you can splash in a lovely pool with a jacuzzi, or swim in the river five minutes down the lane.

Price	€400.
Sleeps	19.
Rooms	Apartment: 2 family rooms, 1 single; 1 bathroom, 2 shower rooms. Studio for 2-3 with wheelchair access. Also: 4 doubles, 1 twin, sofabeds; 1 bathroom, 3 shower rooms.
Meals	Meals on request. Restaurant 100m.
Closed	Never.

Clare Howard
Condorcet, Drôme

Mobile	+44 (0)7773 800741
Email	clare.howard@chateaucolombier.com
Web	www.chateaucolombier.com

Le Vieil Aiglun - Gîte du Couchant

Getting here is half the fun, up a steep, windy, well-tarred road, and your arrival at this ancient hilltop village is rewarded with an unforgettable panorama: most of Haute Provence spread out before you. An energetic, creative and very lovely Belgian family opens Le Vieil Aiglun's rustic doors for B&B in a huge barn; a dining room in a vaulted byre; a pool, a play area and these gîtes. Privately separate, your small house has two bedrooms, one up, one down, a well-planned kitchen/diner with a sofabed, a bathroom with two pretty white basins and an enclosed garden in the walls of an old ruin. Plus views of a Romanesque church on a hill, romantically floodlit at night. It's perfectly gorgeous inside: fresh white walls and rafters, plain linen curtains, red and orange bedcovers, Moroccan lights. After a hard day's sunbathing by the fenced pool (open June-September) book in for twice-weekly table d'hôtes. The long glamorous candelabra-lit table — with special low table for tinies — is stunning, and a huge open fire turns bad-weather days into the cosiest nights. *B&B also. Shared pool.*

Price	€650-€1,150 per week. Linen not included.
Sleeps	5.
Rooms	1 twin, 1 triple, sofabed in living room; 1 bathroom.
Meals	Meals on request.
Closed	Never.

Charles & Annick Speth
Aiglun, Alpes-de-Haute-Provence

Tel	+33 (0)4 92 34 67 00
Email	info@vieil-aiglun.com
Web	www.vieil-aiglun.com

Le Vieil Aiglun - Gîte du Levant

Once again, the local artisans have done a brilliant job. Once again, the interior sings: Annick has a joyous sense of style. Welcome to the Gîte du Levant, a house of comfort, charm and stupendous views. Inside is a large open-plan living space with the palest floor tiles, the softest stone walls and the subtlest fabrics — deep rose and soft grey. French windows fling open to a perfectly lovely terrace stuffed with herbs to delight your nose and palate. Light pours in to illuminate pretty metal dining chairs, modern sofas, a fireplace for the cooler months, touches of brocante. The kitchen is custom made from beech, its latticed cupboards holding pink and grey china, of course. The iron-balustraded staircase takes you up to serene bedrooms: the pale lilac room matches the trees in the garden, the other, spacious and cool, opens to a terrace — watch the sun rise (*le levant* — the east) from your bed. The bathroom is large, bright and welcoming. A pool-with-a-view and a charming play area, plus lots of outdoor space, add up to delights for all the family. *B&B also. Shared pool.*

Price	€1,100–€1,700 per week.
Sleeps	4.
Rooms	1 double, 1 twin; 1 bathroom, 2 separate wcs. Extra bed.
Closed	Never.

Charles & Annick Speth
Aiglun, Alpes-de-Haute-Provence

Tel	+33 (0)4 92 34 67 00
Email	info@vieil-aiglun.com
Web	www.vieil-aiglun.com

Les Granges de Saint Pierre

Everything in this remarkably converted 14th-century barn — once attached to the priory — is stylish and caring. Lavender-infused air, simple iron furniture, modern art, a fine use of colour, an inner terrace where lemons grow — it has a sense of peace and space. Arched doorways with new doors and ancient locks lead to big, light bedrooms with tiled floors and colourwashed walls. Bathrooms are sophisticated in rust-red and white. You have a sunny, lofty, white-beamed living room with cream drapes, canvas directors' chairs and big sofas in front of an even bigger fire. The kitchen is in the corner: terracotta-painted units, old country furniture, stripped floor. Rooms gather round a central terrace filled with geraniums, there's fruit in the orchards and chickens in the pen. Josiane, kind and intelligent, lives in the château next door where the magical pool half hides in a walled garden. Simiane la Rotonde, once the regional capital of lavender, is a gem: a hilltop village with a 16th-century market place, surrounded by vast purple fields. A heavenly place. *B&B also. Shared pool.*

Price	€670–€980 per week. Short winter breaks available, €150 per day.
Sleeps	6.
Rooms	2 twins/doubles, 1 double; 3 shower rooms.
Meals	Restaurant 100m.
Closed	Never.

Josiane Tamburini
Simiane la Rotonde,
Alpes-de-Haute-Provence

Tel	+33 (0)4 92 75 93 81
Mobile	+33 (0)6 63 68 13 48
Email	lesgrangesdesaintpierre@yahoo.fr

Snowgums - Apartments One & Two

Next to the apple and pear trees, Pippa has created a lovely level spot in the garden whence you may gawp at the views. But you'll catch them anyway from this charming old farmhouse, whose rustic walls and vaulted ceilings hold two big apartments done with cheerful covers on pale pine beds, cotton rugs on tiled floors, jolly towels in shining showers, lightness, brightness and comfort. The cupboards spill novels and games, there are cots and high chairs for the asking, the Chantemerle cable car is a five- minute drive by free ski bus and Pippa will child-sit if you'd like an evening out. Pippa, a Londoner raised in Australia, has that charming, relaxed manner you would expect and makes a stay here memorable. She has a deep love for the outdoor life and will point you in the direction of most of the area's activities — skiing, boarding, hiking, biking, rock climbing, parapenting, tobogganing. She buys local produce for the welcome pack and is totally involved with village life. There are heated floors for cosiness, a drying room for ski gear and a free shuttle bus up and down the valley. Brilliant value.

Ethical Collection: Environment.
See page 370 for details

Price	€480–€980 per week. From €240 for 3 days. Minimum 3 days.
Sleeps	6.
Rooms	Apartment One: 1 family room for 4, sofabed in living room; 2 shower rooms. Apartment Two: 1 twin, sofabed in living room; 1 shower room.
Meals	Dinner, 4 courses with wine, €25-€30. Chef on request. Restaurants 2km.
Closed	Never.

Pippa Curtis
Briançon, Hautes-Alpes

Tel	+33 (0)4 92 20 44 26
Mobile	+33 (0)6 78 39 65 73
Email	info@alpsholiday.com
Web	www.alpsholiday.com

Chalet du Laurau

A 70s ski chalet in a small estate of mountain properties, just outside the village and with panoramic views of the Serre Chevalier valley and slopes. For skiers it is perfect – regular buses to the lifts are a five-minute walk away. Ski guides can be organised…and you can ease aching limbs at the gorgeous new spa in Monétier. You enter through glass doors to the salon which glows with peach walls, sunny striped curtains and a merry wood-burner. There's a small snug with TV, games and books, and a kitchen with local hand-painted tiles, stone flagged floors and a good big family table. There are cone heart decorations, driftwood lights, wall hangings, pine mobiles and the feel of a real family home. Bedrooms are not huge but are fun and charming with red and white snowflake theme, decorations, old-fashioned skiers, alpine checks and hearts; bathrooms are modern with smart fittings and spotlessly clean. Walks from the house are wonderful and you can sunbathe on the terrace all year round. Summer activities are thrilling; rafting, kayaking, paragliding – or take a gentle ride up the mountain by cable car.

Price	€1,400–€3,600 per week.
Sleeps	10.
Rooms	3 doubles, 1 twin, 2 singles; 1 bathroom, 2 shower rooms, separate wc.
Meals	Restaurant 12-minute walk.
Closed	Never.

Nathalie Erard
Serre Chevalier, Hautes-Alpes

Tel	+33 (0)1 34 51 89 17
Mobile	+33 (0)6 64 70 17 63
Email	erardmi@wanadoo.fr
Web	www.chaletdulaurau.fr.nf

Maison Clarée

Cross-country skiers whizz from this lovely old farmhouse in Les Alberts village through the Vallée de la Clarée; the downhill mob find nearby Montgenèvre and Serre Chevalier; in spring, a multitude of flora and fauna reveals itself to hikers, bikers, kayakers, horse riders. Jo and Jacqui's family house has thick walls, arched doors and fabulous vaulted ceilings, while modern uplighters illuminate Jacqui's bright artworks and there are colourful rugs, throws and cushions galore. Groups relish the multitude of spaces: the cavernous living room with central pillar, piano and wine cave; the sociable, south-facing kitchen; the minimalist dining room. The master bedroom comes complete with carved armoire and original doors; there's also a self-contained double and twin at ground level; other twin rooms hide under the eaves. Children can ping-pong in the woodstore or scramble in the playground while parents relax on the terrace. Jacqui organises anything from ski mountaineering to a private chef — and also bread deliveries. Les Alberts is so charmingly small that not even a bakery exists in the village!

Price	£1,250–£2,500 per week.
Sleeps	12.
Rooms	3 doubles, 3 twins/doubles; 1 bathroom, 3 shower rooms.
Meals	Restaurant 1km.
Closed	Rarely.

Jo Greig
Montgenèvre, Hautes-Alpes

Tel   +44 (0)1434 689987
Email   jo@thegreigs.net
Web   www.maisonclaree.com

Les Marmottes

Serre Chevalier's white peaks parade past upstairs windows, Chantemerle's cheerful villagey life bustles around the old arched door, inside all is smiles and laughter. Hunkered down in the village near ski lifts and restaurants is the old family home of Denis (French, ski instructor, wine expert) and Karen (English, sporty, excellent cook). Straightforward and homely, the high-ceilinged living room has chocolate sofas around an open fire, red rugs and scatter cushions, masses of books, games, pictures, an honesty bar. Larch-clad bedrooms are named after the world's greatest mountains: Kilimanjaro is a deep ochre with African wall hangings, Ben Nevis has fun tartan curtains, Cortina's bright duvet is all snowflakes. But the heart is the open-plan kitchen and dining room – if you're lucky, Karen will cook for you in the evenings (Denis can arrange wine tastings). Outside, a terrace tumbles over with roses, climbers and charm. There's the whole village to wander, the National Parc des Ecrins to explore: skiing; hiking, biking and rafting. With everything so close, the only vehicle you don't need is a car.

Price	€1,490 per week.
Sleeps	12.
Rooms	2 doubles, 2 twins, 1 family room for 4 (double & bunks); 3 bath/shower rooms, 2 shower rooms.
Meals	Dinner, with wine, €23. Restaurants 3km.
Closed	Rarely.

Denis & Karin Lucas
Serre Chevalier, Hautes-Alpes

Tel	+33 (0)4 92 24 11 17
Mobile	+33 (0)6 70 11 08 32
Email	lucas.marmottes@wanadoo.fr
Web	www.chalet-marmottes.com

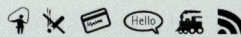

Les Romarins - Les Vignes, Le Studio & Côté Jardin

Sit on your terrace overlooking the garden with a glass of something cool to hand as you relish the tantalising aroma of spicy sausages on the barbecue. Then a pleasant stroll or horse ride through the vineyards? An excursion to lovely Vaison la Romaine and its Roman ruins? A night at the opera in Orange's magnificent Roman amphitheatre? A relaxing swim in the pool with views of Cairanne and rolling vineyards? Or just a quiet snooze in a shaded garden lounger before an outing to one of the region's many fine restaurants. You'll be spoilt for choice in this lovely secluded spot, a former wine estate just outside town, whose fine Côtes du Rhône villages regularly sweep the honours in wine competitions. There are three comfy, well-furnished apartments here, each with its own private terrace. White-tiled floors and pale walls highlight the clever use of colour (tan, yellow, russet, blue) in bedcovers, wall prints, cushions and kitchen/bathroom tiles. Simple bliss at its best, charming and peaceful.

Price	€240–€590 each per week.
Sleeps	8.
Rooms	Les Vignes: 1 double, 1 mezzanine double; 2 shower rooms. Le Studio: 1 double; 1 shower room. Côté Jardin: 1 double; 1 shower room.
Meals	Dinner, 4 courses with wine, €30. On request.
Closed	Never.

Mathieu & Myriam Schillinger
Cairanne, Vaucluse

Tel	+33 (0)4 90 30 77 72
Mobile	+33 (0)6 67 32 75 86
Email	romarins84@orange.fr
Web	www.romarins-gites-cairanne-provence.com

Les Convenents

Pure Provence: the views from your traditional stone mas are of vines, sunflowers and distant pines. Welcoming and warm Sarah, who does B&B next door, stocks the kitchen of the small gîte with basics – fruit, wine, olive oil – and often invites guests next door for a drink. She is also happy for you to share the pretty pool but if you prefer the privacy of your own sitting-out area (with barbecue) that's fine too. Inside, the feel is contemporary, light and bright; there's a dear little living/kitchen area with pale tiled floors, sandy walls, cheery blue and yellow curtains with matching cushions and throws, attractive cane armchairs, pale beams. The kitchen in the corner is cleverly designed to include oven, fridge and freezer. (If you need bigger pots and pans, you can borrow them.) Upstairs are two small but adequate bedrooms whose yellow and blue bedspreads, cushions and curtains echo the furnishings downstairs. There's ping-pong, boules and bikes to borrow, and Vaison la Romaine, with restaurants and Tuesday market, is happily nearby. *Sawday B&B. Shared pool.*

Price	€600–€800 per week.
Sleeps	4.
Rooms	1 double, 1 twin; 1 shower room. Cot & high chair.
Meals	Dinner with wine, €25, by arrangement. Restaurant 15-minute walk.
Closed	Never.

Sarah Banner
Uchaux, Vaucluse

Tel	+33 (0)4 90 40 65 64
Email	sarahbanner@wanadoo.fr
Web	www.lesconvenents.com

Les Petites Bergines

Within walking distance of a Provençal village is a chic retreat in a sea of vines. This is the second of three gîtes owned by the Bungeners, award-winning producers of organic wines. It's a solid 1970s construction that has been thoroughly, thoughtfully brought up to date; it is simply, resolutely modern. The bungalow has light white rooms and a lovely enclosed and well-treed garden; the big pool (shared with the gîte just up the hill) has a fabulous deck surround. There's a good-sized, super-equipped kitchen in black, wood and grey with fun touches (lamp pendants in red glass; a black, white and orange painting from the 60s) opening to a raised terrace with multi-coloured chairs: dine to a backdrop of birdsong and vineyard views. Bedrooms have scatter rugs, cocoa bedspreads, a painting each; no more. The keywords are simplicity, things natural, a love of the environment. Heating/air conditioning is low energy and the winery is organic; enjoy the tastings! In the sweet village is a hotel restaurant; in atmospheric Carpentras a Friday market; in Roaix a Michelin star. Fabulous.

Price	€550.
Sleeps	4.
Rooms	1 double, 1 twin; 1 shower room, separate wc.
Meals	Restaurant 500m.
Closed	Never.

Janet Bungener
Vacqueyras, Vaucluse

Tel	+33 (0)4 90 65 85 33
Email	gite@closdecaveau.com
Web	www.vacation-rentals-provence.com

Le Clos de Caveau

On an 18th-century farm, tucked between the wine-making cellar and the owners' house, is one of the most charming little gîtes in Provence. Wood from rustic doors and a polished armoire coexist with simple fabrics and beautiful tiles: kitchen counter a delicious shade of cornflower blue, floor tiles worn terracotta, bathroom tiles delicately white and blue. Bedroom walls are pale open stone; others are white plaster. With a sofabed in the sitting/dining room, a private terrace and a safe garden (shared, plus pool, with the owners) this would be just perfect for a family of three. There are vines everywhere, plenty of trees, and a stunning sweeping view over the vineyards to the Alpilles. As for the 50-acre domaine, the vines have been under organic cultivation since 1989 and the Bungeners' reds and rosés frequently win awards. You are minutes from pretty little Vacqueyras, 20 minutes from historic Orange; the Pont du Gard is a breathtaking must, and food markets and festivals abound. Not the place for conspicuous consumers but a dream for those who share the same values – and seek peace.

Price	€375–€650 per week. Short breaks available.
Sleeps	2.
Rooms	1 double, sofabed; 1 bathroom.
Meals	Restaurants 2km.
Closed	Never.

Janet Bungener
Vacqueyras, Vaucluse

Tel	+33 (0)4 90 65 85 33
Email	gite@closdecaveau.com
Web	www.vacation-rentals-provence.com

Flop House Palace

The backdrop is Mont Ventoux. Then the view stretches south over endless mountain woodlands to the vineyards of the Vaucluse, ending in the west with the jagged Dentelles de Montmirail chain: a full 180° panorama visible from anywhere in the beautifully planted pool and garden area, its colours changing with the light. This is balm to the soul. The outside is stunning but you must go inside: there's yet more style, clean and light, almost minimalist, in luscious whites, beiges, greys, ochres. Variegated chandeliers bring a rococo touch, all materials are natural – seagrass, pure Egyptian cotton, leather, stone. Then there's the Indian library, masses of paintings, sculptures and… books for all tastes. The owners know about renovating old houses, this is clear. You will love your bedroom, be it in the main house or the pool wing, the all-dancing kitchen, the earthy sitting room with the best hi-fi and DVD equipment. The region throngs with festivals, markets, ancient villages, artists' studios, but you may be blissful just staying in this utterly lovely place. *Village shops & restaurant walking distance.*

Price	€3,000–€4,500 per week.
Sleeps	11.
Rooms	Flop House: 5 double rooms, 1 bathroom, 4 shower rooms. Extra single bed.
Meals	Restaurant 1.2km.
Closed	Rarely.

Madeleine Ford
Bédoin, Vaucluse

Tel	+33 (0)4 90 35 03 91
Mobile	+33 (0)6 74 86 73 17
Email	provencesummers@hotmail.com
Web	www.provencesummers.com

Mas de Maître

Complete independence. The house, built in 1820, has its own drive, garden and shrubby pool area. Inside is a beamed, limestone-floored sitting room with a fireplace, comfy sofas and earthy colours, and a small extension, the perfect place to write a postcard home or read a book. Cooks will be happy in the kitchen with its plethora of white china, round table and extra large fridge. The dining room is kitted out in greys and whites, with lots of simple French antiques; there's another fireplace here and two large windows looking onto the garden. Curtains in all rooms are floor-length filmy white, beds have exquisite Egyptian cotton linen – all infinitely soft and romantic with restful garden views – and Italian-style bathrooms may tempt you to linger: stone surrounds, bronze taps, walk-in showers. The riding stables lie just outside the village, which even has a model railway for children. There is music and art in every little town as well as those famous antiques markets, museums, festivals and Roman ruins. Will you have time for wine-tasting and fine dining? *Yoga on request.*

Price	€1,700-€3,350 per week.
Sleeps	12.
Rooms	2 doubles, 1 single, 2 family rooms for 3 (1 double, 1 single); 1 bathroom, 4 shower rooms. Extra single bed.
Meals	Restaurant in village.
Closed	Rarely.

	Madeleine Ford
	Saint Didier, Vaucluse
Tel	+33 (0)4 90 35 03 91
Mobile	+33 (0)6 74 86 73 17
Email	provencesummers@hotmail.com
Web	www.provencesummers.com

Les Cerisiers

A lovely old stone farmhouse with sweeping views, Provençal décor and tomette floors, and a hostess who has "thought of everything", from perfect little poolside kitchen to fine linen. You have it all in a hamlet surrounded by vineyards, olive groves and cherry orchards – and your own private summer house and pool. Bedrooms have good big beds, white walls, beams. The year-round apartment and the bigger summer bedroom – it has a delicious Mediterranean feel – overlook the gardens fore and aft and Mont Ventoux beyond. Bath and shower rooms sparkle. (The two-bedroom/two-bathroom formula is only available May to early September.) Up its own outside staircase and bathed in sunny yellows and soft greens, the apartment feels big, bright and open. Enjoy sunsets on the terrace while sipping a cool Côtes de Ventoux. Visit Carpentras and its Friday market, Orange and its Roman amphitheatre for open-air opera, Avignon for the famous festival; history and art, architecture and music come alive here. Two minutes away is a grocer's shop that doubles as a part-time café. *Baby-friendly. Shared laundry. Chef & taxi available.*

Price	€400-€820 for 2; €1,200-€1,400 for 4 (May-Sept only). Prices per week. Ask about short winter breaks.
Sleeps	4.
Rooms	1 twin/double; 1 shower room. Also (high season only): 1 double; bath/shower room.
Meals	Restaurants 5-minute drive.
Closed	Never.

Tory Johnston
Carpentras, Vaucluse

Tel	+33 (0)4 90 41 77 34
Email	info@les-cerisiers.com
Web	www.les-cerisiers.com

La Saga

Stepping out of a narrow, winding street in the heart of Pernes you find yourself in a scene from the Arabian Nights – or might it be Petrarch? An enclosed courtyard holds a spring-fed pool, a wide terrace, greenery galore, a wooden pergola, romantic lighting: poetry that on a warm summer's night would melt the heart of the toughest pragmatist. From here into the 21st century: a cool haven of space with an airy feel, a minimalist décor, earth colours, natural fabrics, and plain good taste. Quirky touches, too. You'll want to stay a while to experience both worlds, the ice-cube lamps against the old stonework, the Art Deco style and the abstract art. Comfortable bedrooms have quiet style, the excellent kitchen has an extraordinary quantity of crockery, cutlery, platters and baskets, and the living area's 30s-style leather sofas open arms to a superior music system; the owner is a professional musician. Just up from the market square yet quieter than the countryside: no tractors, no roosters. Fine dining, festivals great and small, history, art and winegrowers are all around you.

Price	£900–£3,000 per week.
Sleeps	12.
Rooms	5 doubles, 1 twin; 2 bathrooms, 1 shower room.
Meals	Restaurant 500m.
Closed	Never.

Peter Beachill
Pernes les Fontaines, Vaucluse

Tel	+44 (0)870 446 0168
Mobile	+44 (0)7770 914928
Email	enquiries@la-saga.co.uk
Web	www.la-saga.co.uk

Le Mas de Miejour

Yours is the oldest part of this pretty Provençal farmhouse with your own entrance and garden with barbecue. Fred and Emma, craftspeople both, came here to bring up their children. They do B&B in the other half, Fred turns potter in the winter and Emma conjures up leather baby shoes. Passionate about wine, they are qualified sommeliers and can point you to the best vineyards. The farmhouse atmosphere is utterly restful. Well-equipped yet nicely old-fashioned and homely with its little windows and ancient tiles, the kitchen is dominated by an ancient bread oven, perhaps originally pillaged from the 12th-century château nearby. Up steepish steps are the salon, with comfy leather sofa and armchairs, and the bedrooms. The double bed is huge, the white-tiled bathroom is small but fine, the views are over the garden or fields; Mont Ventoux lies beyond. The land here is flat with a high water table so the garden, sheltered by trees and fields of tall maize and sunflowers in summer, is always fresh and green. You are welcome to share the lovely, fenced pool – and the wine knowledge. *Sawday B&B. Shared pool. Arrival 5pm-8pm.*

Price	€550-€1,250 per week.
Sleeps	5.
Rooms	1 double, 1 twin, 1 single; 1 bathroom.
Closed	November-February.

**Frédéric Westercamp
& Emmanuelle Diemont**
Le Thor, Vaucluse

Tel	+33 (0)4 90 02 13 79
Email	masdemiejour@orange.fr
Web	www.masdemiejour.com

Les Trois Cloches

A breath-catcher, inside and out. Perched high above the already perched village of Lioux, the house faces the dizzyingly sheer cliff that rises behind the village; beyond are the Lubéron hills and the Alpilles. Sit and gaze from the lovely sitting-room terrace or the master bedroom window. An 18th-century farmhouse with thick walls for summer cool and winter warm, renovated with care, taste and imagination - even the lighting is intriguingly original -, it is a harmony of old timbers, working fireplaces, tiles and polished wood against white walls. There are peaceful colour schemes, comfortable contemporary furniture, the occasional well-chosen antique and some definitely good modern paintings. Sleep happens in one fine big bedroom and two simpler smaller ones, ablutions in two modern bathrooms and communal things in the gorgeous kitchen, wonderful for convivial gatherings. A stream murmurs through the fountain in the generous terraced gardens, the pool lies discreetly low, the Lubéron regional park is all around and your cultured, literary landlords are delightful.

Price	€1,050-€2,200 per week.
Sleeps	6.
Rooms	1 double & double sofabed, 1 double, 1 twin; 2 bathrooms.
Meals	Restaurants 2-5km.
Closed	Never.

Jürgen Kreuzhage
Lioux, Vaucluse

Tel	+33 (0)4 90 05 70 03
Email	3cloches@free.fr
Web	www.3cloches.com

La Grande Bastide - Rosiers, Auvent, Grand Colorado, Petit Colorado

Through the brown iron gates and down the drive fringed with ancient oaks to the old bastide. The setting is stunning – hills to the east, valley to the west, hikers' heaven. Beyond the busyish road, you can walk or bicycle out into the multi-coloured landscape of the Colorado range, famous for its ochre pigments. These four gîtes, neat as new pins, separated by thick walls, stand apart from the owners' living quarters in a wing of the old house and share a huge pool and a walled courtyard garden full of roses with mulberry trees for shade. All is spotless and spacious; there are beams and new terracotta tiles, pale sofas, light-wood tables and chairs, new beds and linen, and a generous farmhouse table in each pristine kitchen. In contrast, the garden is a joyous multitude of jasmine, honeysuckle, lavender and roses. You are north of Sault, famous for its lavender and nougat, and south of Apt, whose all-day Saturday market is legendary. Peaceful Rustrel has a shop and a sprinkling of restaurants and bars; and your bread is delivered every morning. *Shared pool (closed low season).*

Price	Rosiers €800-€1,550.
	Auvent €520-€1,000.
	Grand Colorado €520-€1,100.
	Petit Colorado €450-€720.
	Prices per week.
Sleeps	16.
Rooms	Rosiers: 2 doubles, 1 twin; 2 bathrooms.
	Auvent: 1 double, 1 twin; 1 bathroom.
	Grand Colorado: 2 doubles; 1 bathroom.
	Petit Colorado: 1 double; 1 bathroom.
Meals	Restaurant 1km.
Closed	Never.

André & Yangbin Marini
Rustrel, Vaucluse

Tel	+33 (0)1 47 20 98 11
Mobile	+33 (0)6 82 96 17 69
Email	bin.yang@wanadoo.fr
Web	www.grande-bastide-provence.com

La Gardiole

The oldest of Bonnieux' two churches, crowning this perfect hilltop village, is surrounded by ancient cedars so huge they can be spotted for miles. Here, on the lower flanks of the hill, is an unexpectedly simple and inexpensive place to stay. Owned by the good people who run the town's small, lofty B&B, Le Clos du Buis, this is perfect for two. Your studio room is in the lower half of a newish stone building, the top floor is occupied but quite separate. Décor is neither stylish nor contemporary but simple and clean with a certain old-fashioned charm. You have a white-walled double room with flowery curtains and comfy beds, a small blue-tiled bathroom, a round dining table, a new sofa, and a small kitchen with shining pans and two rings. Views open wide to the Lubéron and your garden, with a cherry tree for shade, has a delightful private pool. Bonnieux is one of the less touristy 'perched villages', its steep, winding streets numerous enough to get lost in, its restaurants fashionable, its Friday market carnival-like in summer. *Sawday hotel. Two further houses for 4 & 6 in nearby Castellet.*

Price	€380–€600 per week. Linen not included.
Sleeps	2.
Rooms	1 twin/double, sofabed; 1 bathroom.
Meals	Restaurants within walking distance.
Closed	Never.

M & Mme Maurin
Bonnieux, Vaucluse

Tel	+33 (0)4 90 92 06 14
Email	contact@hotel-gounod.com
Web	www.leclosdubuis.fr

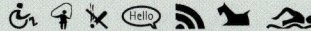

Jas des Eydins

Among organic vineyards and cherry orchards, with sweeping views to the Lubéron hills, a blissful retreat at the end of a private lane. These 18th-century stone buildings, once a sheepfold and part of a Provençal farm, were restored by their architect owner and his elegant art historian wife. There's a charming simplicity, a soothing, serene mix of country antiques and modern bits and pieces. You have a large, beautifully equipped kitchen and open-plan sitting room and three peaceful bedrooms (one in an adjoining building) shaded by a trellis of Banksia roses. On hot summer days, relax by the heavenly pool, enveloped in the scent of roses and lavender, or enjoy the big garden and revel in distant views of Mont Ventoux. In the evenings, dine on the covered terrace to the chirrup of the cicadas. There's a fabulous outdoor kitchen with chimney and built-in barbecue, too. Shirley and Jan live next door, are family-friendly and on hand if you need them, but leave you to relax in peace – perfect hosts. If you can bear to break away, there are some enchanting hillside villages to discover.

Price	€1,250-€1,950 per week.
Sleeps	6.
Rooms	2 twins/doubles, 1 twin; 2 bathrooms, 1 shower room. Extra twin in main house, with private entrance, on request.
Meals	Restaurant 3km.
Closed	November to mid-March.

Shirley & Jan Kozlowski
Bonnieux, Vaucluse

Tel	+33 (0)4 90 75 84 99
Email	jasdeseydins@wanadoo.fr
Web	www.jasdeseydins.com

Le Massonnet - Main House

A long drive lined with ancient plane trees brings into focus this large, exquisitely restored 16th-century flour mill. Then, through the wrought-iron gates and round the softly burbling fountain, you find charming hosts Claire and Thierry de Foy waiting to greet you. Everything here is comfort and top hospitality: two cosy green-blue bedrooms (for B&B or your extra family members), one connected to a snug peachy-beige studio for two. Then the big airy apartments, Lavande all in soothing blues, Colombier in warm earth colours, both a blend of old and new, with excellent fabrics and great garden views. Among the many original and quirky touches you will find two high points: the legendary, hand-made Apt wall tiles dotted here and there in their unbelievably beautiful deep blue and turquoise colours; and the massive original wooden flour mill whose top is the focal point of a large shared living room-cum-kitchen that is often used when groups take the whole property. All this just outside Apt, with the entire Lubéron region and its delightful hilltop villages an easy nip away. *B&B also. Shared pool.*

Price	Apartments €200-€730 per week. Extra bedrooms €52-€61 per day.
Sleeps	10.
Rooms	Cyprès: 1 twin; 1 shower room, separate wc. Lavande: 1 double, sofabed; 1 bathroom, separate wc. Colombier: 1 double, sofabed; 1 shower room. Two extra bedrooms on ground floor.
Meals	Restaurant 5km.
Closed	Never.

Thierry & Claire de Foy
Apt, Vaucluse

Tel	+33 (0)4 90 04 66 15
Email	info@lemassonnet.com
Web	www.lemassonnet.com

Le Massonnet - Garden Wing

The ground-floor, 'garden' wing of the main house has its own special feel. For one thing, the bedroom and two apartments all have their own private, well-furnished terraces with dreamy pergolas and a grandstand view of the huge, tree-studded garden dotted with flowers and shrubs, overlooking the Lubéron hills. The perfect spot for a lazy breakfast, a lively aperitif or a candlelight dinner for two. The apartments have medium-sized living rooms and – as throughout this superb place – a blend of old and new, simple lines, an airy feeling and well-equipped kitchens. Colours run to warm ochre, russet, gold and peach, natural fabrics predominate, and the keyword is quality. After some serious pool-sampling there's lots to get up to in this lovely region: colourful markets in one town or another every day of the week; walking, riding, wine visits, courses (art courses working with colour are a local speciality); festivals in Avignon, Aix-en-Provence and La Roque d'Anthéron, and many village mini-festivals. Plus fine eating choices everywhere, some just minutes away. *B&B also. Shared pool.*

Price	Apartments €495–€1,270 per week. Extra bedrooms €52–€61 per day.
Sleeps	6.
Rooms	Églantier: 2 twins, sofabed; 1 bathroom. Noisetier: 1 double, sofabed; 1 bathroom, separate wc.
Closed	Never.

Thierry & Claire de Foy
Apt, Vaucluse

Tel	+33 (0)4 90 04 66 15
Email	info@lemassonnet.com
Web	www.lemassonnet.com

Mas des Genêts

Set among vineyards and lavender fields just below the charming village of Saignon, perched like a fort on turrets of white rock, this one-up-one-down stone cottage is a sweet retreat in the popular Lubéron. Reached by a private drive, the pale-stoned extension (once a tractor shed) is part of an old farmhouse that has been skilfully converted by American-born Stephen and his English wife Meg. They live in the main part of the house and there's a twin-bedded ground-floor apartment for two next door. Each property has its own private terrace and lawn from which to take your fill of birdsong and big mountain views. Inside, original beams, new terracotta tiles, modern pine tables and chairs, books, puzzles and games… even underfloor heating for winter stays. There's a functional kitchenette in one corner and a sunny upstairs bedroom with a big brass bed, sloping beamed ceilings and blue and green floral blinds. Take the footpath to Saignon (about half an hour), or walk in the Lubéron hills: you can hike straight from the door. And don't miss the superb Saturday market in Apt.

Price	€420–€580 per week.
Sleeps	2.
Rooms	1 double; 1 shower room.
Closed	Never.

Meg & Stephen Parker
Saignon, Vaucluse

Tel	+33 (0)4 90 04 65 33
Mobile	+33 (0)6 89 22 24 73
Email	masdegenet@aol.com
Web	www.masdesgenets.eu

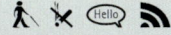

Ferme de la Platane

The magnificent 12th-century château of Ansouis dominates the skyline, the braided hills surround you, enchantment is in the air. Each of the secluded apartments in the old farmhouse is a delight, each has space. La Cour is reached through a courtyard garden, its terrace and pergola facing west; the approach to La Fenière and La Magnanerie is via an outside stone staircase, their terraces and living spaces (with magical views) are above, their bedrooms below. La Petite Maison is creeper-covered, with blue shutters and cream-coloured stone. Crisp sofas rub shoulders with country armoires, stylish walk-in showers with antique roll-top baths. Old limewashed walls and terracotta floors keep you cool. With the welcome bread and wine comes an information folder so you can plan how lively or laid-back you wish to be. The lazy pool beckons... as do the innumerable festivals, concerts and markets of this part of the Luberon (at least one for each day of the week). Pad through the vines to medieval Ansouis and that château (15 minutes) or take the car to lively Lourmarin (five). A delightful getaway.

Price	€650–€900 each per week.
Sleeps	8.
Rooms	4 apartments each with 1 twin/double; 1 bathroom.
Meals	Restaurant 1km.
Closed	November–April, except on request.

Rosemary & Peter Fraser
Ansouis, Vaucluse

Tel	+33 (0)4 90 09 80 89
Mobile	+33 (0)6 74 52 90 37
Email	rosemary@fermedelaplatane.com
Web	www.fermedelaplatane.com

Mas de la Boissiere

Deep in the Lubéron, with mountains as a backdrop, this 18th-century farmhouse stands sturdy and broad. And the bright spacious entrance hall perfectly reflects the smartly restored interior: Provençal floor tiles and original beams, fireplaces and stonework. The villa has six bedrooms, each with its own touch of colour: here earthy, there celestial. In some rooms teddies snuggle in mounds of throw cushions and beds are swathed in exquisite locally crafted boutis quilts: a delightful nod at unpretentious luxury. Wander from the kitchen to your own shimmering pool, rustle up a barbecue, sip a cool glass of wine, find a shady spot for a catnap. A boules pitch is lit at night, in case you fancy a game in the cool of the evening. By day, venture down to the nearby farmers' market, fill your baskets with fresh baguettes and goat's cheese and match your meals to your lifestyle — simple but undeniably pleasant. Caretakers are on hand but only if you want them to be, so bring along an intimate party of family or friends and enjoy serenity and seclusion at your own pace.

Price	€2,500–€4,950 per week.
Sleeps	12.
Rooms	3 doubles, 3 twins/doubles; 6 bathrooms.
Meals	Meals on request.
Closed	Never.

Georgina Causton
Cucuron, Vaucluse
Mobile   +33 (0)6 84 14 62 60
Email   georgina.causton@free.fr
Web   www.masdelaboissiere.com

Château de la Loubière - La Grange, Les Platanes, Sebastian's House

Space, peace and much to explore. Ten acres of parkland surround these three stone-built gîtes, outbuildings of the 16th-century château. While the kids make hay in the sun-drenched grounds, you can slip into the pool or gaze on the Provençal countryside. In a mad moment, you might even play tennis: a court lies hidden among the trees. Nicely separated, each gîte has been renovated by the McDougalls, who live in the château, to keep its Provençal charm intact. Rooms have exposed stonework, terracotta floors and fresh white walls, furnishings are bright and uncluttered and quirky features have been retained — one bathroom has an iron hayrack, another an old feeding trough. The open-plan living areas, some with fireplaces or beams, have sunny terraces for al fresco eating. Kitchens are modern and well-equipped, bedrooms light and breezy with pretty bedcovers and soft lamps. Toss a coin in La Grange for the bedroom with the terrace. There's walking, riding, the Lubéron National Park, festivals in Aix, restaurants in Pertuis. The delightful McDougalls can provide a babysitter.

Price	Grange €1,950-€2,600. Platanes €1,000-€1,350. Sebastian's House €900-€1,250. Prices per week.
Sleeps	20.
Rooms	Grange: 2 doubles, 1 twin, 2 twins/doubles; 3 bathrooms, 4 sep. wcs. Platanes: 1 double, 1 twin/double; 1 bathroom. Sebastian's: 2 doubles, 1 twin; 1 bathroom.
Closed	November-March.

Deb & Alec McDougall
Pertuis, Vaucluse

Tel	+33 (0)4 90 09 53 96
Mobile	+33 (0)6 24 51 81 05
Email	info@laloubiere.com
Web	www.laloubiere.com

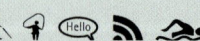

Mas des Tourterelles

Climb the steps to your veranda and let the views wash over you. All around, peace, greenery, the little pool tucked into the garden – and the bustling centre of Saint Rémy mere minutes away. The Aherns have thrown themselves into their new life in the Alpilles; Richard restoring the farmhouse with its honey-coloured stone, beams and tiles, Carrie adding the light and deceptively simple touches – pale walls, linen curtains, sisal carpets, splashes of colour. Bedrooms – you can 'add on' extra from the adjoining B&B – are restful spaces of white and grey with Vi-Spring mattresses, pretty bedcovers and striking photographs on the walls. Bathrooms are neat, well-planned oases of shiny white ceramics and limestone flooring. Relax in the elegantly simple sitting room, dine on the veranda with its view of the pool and the garden. There's also a smart dining table in your modern, well-equipped kitchen, though on some nights you might want to wander into town to eat. There's bags to do – the Van Gogh Museum, the Camargue, hiking in the Alpilles. Then return to your perfectly simple retreat. *B&B also. Shared pool.*

Price	€690–€2,025 per week.
Sleeps	2.
Rooms	1 double; 1 bathroom.
	Extra double & twin in house.
Meals	Restaurants within walking distance.
Closed	Never.

Richard & Carrie Ahern
Saint Rémy de Provence,
Bouches-du-Rhône

Tel	+33 (0)4 32 60 19 93
Email	richard.ahern@sfr.fr
Web	www.masdestourterelles.com

Appartement Quatre

A gem in the centre of one of France's loveliest towns — all fountains and leafy squares. The building dates from 1900 and was designed for the Carmelite nuns whose chapel stands next door. Step off a narrow pedestrian shopping street to ascend a wide and gracious stairway, then into an airy apartment for two. An immaculate façade, an inviting interior: linen curtains billow in the breeze, the scent of lavender fills the air. It feels immensely cool and peaceful up here. There are white tiled floors, shuttered windows, wicker furniture in the bedroom at the back, and a super big bathroom with a wild pink ceiling. The kitchen comes in green and blue and is well equipped, so it's off to the market in the morning — a three-minute walk — and back for a feast at night. In the living room are a huge white L-shaped linen sofa and a round antique dining table: lots of comfort, no clutter. Gabriele, a designer, is delightful. She will advise on just about anything, from where to get the best croissants to what's on at the opera. Perfect peace and great value for the area.

Price	€650-€850 per week.
Sleeps	2.
Rooms	1 double, 1 single on mezzanine (not for children); 1 bathroom.
Closed	Never.

Gabriele Skelton
Aix en Provence, Bouches-du-Rhône

Tel	+33 (0)4 90 75 98 98
Email	gabriele.skelton@orange.fr
Web	www.appartementquatre.com

Saporta

A great base for delving into the cultural depths of Aix-en-Provence: step outside to a parade of pedestrians, boulangeries, cafés, florists; the Cathédrale to your right, the Mairie to your left. Up in the spacious second-floor apartment, all is calm. You step straight from stairway to elegant 1930s-style salon: high ceilings, tall south-facing windows over a quiet courtyard, a splash of blue accentuating colours in the mosaic-tiled floor, abstract artwork, a fireplace. Arched dark wood doors lead to a cheery kitchen in red and deep grey. Eat here around a contemporary table, light streaming through a rooftop window. Glass doors conceal the bedroom suite, a zen-like space with its pale colours, king bed, sofa behind a voile divider and tall window catching the morning light. As the owners' pied-à-terre it's fully equipped with all practicalities, including modern gadgets if you really must work. The Roman city's cobbled streets were made for walking so don't even consider a car: within an easy stroll lie vibrant markets, festivals, fountains, gardens, a lively student population, cultural activities galore.

Price	€580–€780 per week. Cleaning €30.
Sleeps	2.
Rooms	1 double, sofabed in sitting room; 1 bath/shower room.
Meals	Restaurants nearby.
Closed	Never.

Ralf Maurer & Brigitte Brienne
Aix en Provence, Bouches-du-Rhône

Tel	+33 (0)4 90 46 51 34
Mobile	+33 (0)6 14 03 52 48
Email	mail@provenceliving.com
Web	www.provenceliving.com/aix.html

La Maison du Faïencier

Step in from the village square and be catapulted into the early 17th century. This captivating house has belonged to three master potters; ateliers still exist in the village. The living area is a cool sweep of the palest terracotta, the kitchen has a 'French Aga', the welcome pack is one of the best we've seen. Beneath a vaulted ceiling, a majestic staircase transports you to huge dreamy bedrooms that bring instant seduction: sisal floors, pale timbers, delicate ironwork, generous wicker. Some have slanting skylight windows, others overlook the garden. Stonework has been left exposed where possible, old walls stand at jaunty angles, hand basins have been crafted to fit into uneven walls, showers have 'sunflower' heads. Ron has kept the soul of the place intact but introduced a designer feel to the interiors, and a smattering of bright colour in tiles and textiles. Stone martins nest in the courtyard, the garden is sweet with lilacs, apricots and figs, the pool resembles a Roman bath and the village offers market, shops, bars and restaurants. Head for the deep Verdon Gorges and watery adventures! *B&B also.*

Price	€2,295-€2,995 per week. Additional 70m² salon 15% of rental price. Towels €10 p.p. per week. End-of-stay cleaning €185.
Sleeps	10.
Rooms	5 twins/doubles; 1 bathroom, 4 shower rooms. Extra beds.
Meals	Meals on request.
Closed	Never.

Ron Alldridge
Varages, Var

Tel	+33 (0)4 94 77 81 01
Mobile	+33 (0)6 19 96 58 82
Email	alldridge@wanadoo.fr
Web	www.lamaisondufaiencier.com

Pimaquet - La Magnanerie (The Silkworm House)

Tucked into the hillside, two old stone houses. Their owner, Mimi, once a university lecturer, now a painter, lives in one of them. La Magnanerie (The Silkworm House) – the rock on which it was built still visible indoors – did indeed house silkworms in the 18th-century, when the industry flourished. It climbs the hill in four half storeys, each level with a terrace, under the shade of a majestic oak. Bedrooms have valley views and a gentle mix of old furniture; bathrooms are bright and beautiful with handmade tiles; and the kitchen is charming and nicely equipped. The large main terrace is the perfect spot for enjoying an angelic chorus of birdsong, a spectacular sunset, a brilliant star-studded sky; in the winter a log fire in the living room adds a cosy glow. Behind the house is a Roman canal, fast-flowing and pristine, for which Mimi pays €20 a year to use. In a protected valley, it's a dreamy place to laze on languid summer days, in gardens shady with mulberry trees, oleander and buddlea. Then down to the cooling river Bresque to swim, paddle or read. Find shops, markets, restaurants in old Carcès and Entrecasteaux.

Price	£120–£600 per week. Linen not included.
Sleeps	6.
Rooms	2 doubles, 1 twin; 3 bathrooms. Cot.
Meals	Restaurants 6–13km.
Closed	Never.

Debbie Badger
Entrecasteaux, Var

Tel	+44 (0)1722 341990
Email	djbadger@ntlworld.com

Bastide Oleander

Tout privé; the 15th-century stone house hides in a cloud of olives and oaks pierced by a long, winding track. But there's no hiding the views, which slide out over a gorgeous Provençal panorama before splashing into the Mediterranean. The house has had a marvellous makeover, in which old beams, fireplaces and tomettes are joined by modern travertine bathrooms and a superb new marble kitchen and balconied master bedroom. The Holworthy family's personal touch is evident in the handmade ceramics and blend of Edwardian English and classic French – a sleigh bed in one room, a walnut armoire, antique dressers, a touch of brocante, a sitting room alive with art and fresh flowers, a dining table under a curving ceiling. The whole house is beautifully looked after. Outside, olives, oleanders, agaves fight for space, a heated swimming pool teases you down from the stone-flagged terrace; or settle on loungers with meat from Lorgues' Tuesday market smoking on the barbecue. Thick walls are oblivious to summer's heat or wintry chills – in the former case, let children loose on nearby aquaparks, or join the Riviera set.

Price	£1,850–£3,350 per week.
Sleeps	10.
Rooms	3 doubles, 2 twins; 1 bathroom, 3 shower rooms. Cot.
Meals	Restaurants 5km.
Closed	Never.

Crispin & Trikia Holworthy
Lorgues, Var

Tel	+44 (0)1590 683554
Email	trikia@bastideoleander.com
Web	www.bastideoleander.com

Château Roubine - Le Mas des Candeliers

A deep passion for wine pervades this authentic *mas*, buried in an ancient vineyard whose swirling Van Gogh colours transform with Provence's changing seasons. The stone building, where vineyard workers once rested, has been enhanced through careful renovation and divided into three self-contained units. Clairette has a king bed and brocante feel, Mourvèdre is wheelchair accessible with a stylish wet room, Tibouren's mezzanine is perfect for lovers, or families (with Syrah), with a huge bed, free-standing bath and simple twin bedroom below. The vineyards invade: a palette of greens, plums, aubergines, reds; long linen curtains framing stunning views, a touch of fresh lavender, a flower bud. Outside: a fountained Roman pool and garden rampant with roses, oleander, olives. Taste wines, learn about the wine-making process (13 varieties of grape are grown here), arrange a cookery course; if you're lucky, a concert will take place. Spin around to a dizzying panorama of vineyards, forest, verdant vegetation: to the south lies the Mediterranean, to the north the Gorges du Verdon. Above, after nightfall, a blanket of stars.

Price	€459.
Sleeps	8.
Rooms	Mourvèdre: 1 double; 1 shower room.
	Clairette: 1 double; 1 shower room.
	Syrah: 1 twin; 1 shower room.
	Tibouren: 1 double; 1 bathroom.
Meals	Chef on request. Restaurants 3km.
Closed	Never.

Madame Riboud–Rousselle
Lorgues, Var

Tel	+33 (0)4 94 85 94 94
Email	com-roubine@orange.fr
Web	www.masdescandeliers.com

Entry 305   Map 16

Bastidon Saint Benoît

Pine, rosemary, thyme and lavender fill the air in this corner of the Var. With the olive trees, oaks and broom that range around this sunny one-storey house, they bring welcome relief from hot summers. The fresh, light interiors sing with Provençal colour; there are cool terracotta floors, large picture windows and Anne-Marie's joyous stencil work – sprinkled on walls, bedhead and lampshades – to add to the breezy feel. Kitchen and bathroom are roomy and modern while the large sitting/dining room – log fire for cooler months – opens to the terrace; shaded by a pine tree and roll-down awning, this is a lovely spot for dining and lounging. It sits above a neat garden that manages to squeeze in a lawn, an exotic palm and a children's swing. There are also shared boules, ping-pong and pool, but please avoid using the pool at meal times; the owners, former Sawday B&B hosts, are a warm, welcoming couple. Perfectly pitched, half-way between the Verdon Canyon and the Îles du Levant, close to the beaches and water sports of Lac de Sainte Croix, you are brilliantly placed. *Shared pool.*

Price	€500–€700 per week.
Sleeps	2.
Rooms	1 double, sofabed in sitting room; 1 shower room.
Meals	Restaurant 2km.
Closed	Never.

Jean & Anne-Marie
Pinel Peschardière
Flassans sur Issole, Var

Tel	+33 (0)4 94 04 01 04
Mobile	+33 (0)6 33 81 13 27
Email	bastidonsaintbenoit@orange.fr
Web	www.giterural-provence.com

Bastide des Hautes Moures - Gîte Anis

A track deep in the Var forest leads to this exquisite 1780s sheepfold. Attached to the main house, it stands in a hollow amid 14 acres of gnarled scrub oak surrounded by cypresses, roses and lavender. Birds sing, butterflies shimmer. The cottage has been brought back to life in spectacular fashion, a monument to Catherine's flamboyant style and her love of colour; she is also an assiduous seeker of antique and brocante finds. You have a vast, lofty, open-plan kitchen/living room, and an enchantingly pretty bedroom with floral canopied bed and yellow Provençal quilt. The bathroom is charming, the kitchen superb. Antoine was a restaurateur so if you don't want to cook, he will: stuffed vegetables, bass, foie gras, fine breads and jams. You can breakfast with the B&B guests if you prefer, for a small extra charge. Outside is your own little stone terrace with white wrought-iron tables and chairs. It's an easy drive to Aix where there's masses to do – once you've raised yourself from the teak loungers that flank the big saltwater pool. *Sawday B&B. Shared pool. Third gîte available for 2.*

Price	€500–€990 per week.
Sleeps	2.
Rooms	1 double; 1 shower room. Extra bed.
Meals	Table d'hôtes €32, on request. Restaurant 5km.
Closed	Never.

Catherine & Antoine Debray
Le Thoronet, Var

Tel	+33 (0)4 94 60 13 36
Email	infos@bastidedesmoures.com
Web	www.bastidedesmoures.com

Bastide des Hautes Moures - Lodge Kaomi

The old pool house has been spectacularly converted into a discreet, single-storey refuge for two. From a concealed terrace, your views are to the saltwater pool, a piece of beautifully landscaped garden and the wooded hills. Step into the stone-flagged living area and be happy; the owners have gathered some wonderful things on their travels giving an 'out of Africa' feel. Sofas, a low table and a wrought-iron screen divide the cosy dining corner from the kitchen which, with its stone sink set into a white lava worktop and its wide window drawing the eye to the distant hills, is one of most delectable we've seen. Muslin curtains round the four-poster bed float softly in the breeze, the linen is crisp, the bed wide and firm, the shower room has an antique console embracing its basin. Catherine, young and soignée, looks after B&B and gîte guests with imagination and warmth, chef Antoine knows about the eateries in the area and the whole place could scarcely be more peaceful. All this, and the wondrous Abbey of Le Thoronet almost next door. *Sawday B&B. Shared pool. Third gîte available for 2.*

Price	€600–€990 per week.
Sleeps	2.
Rooms	1 double; 1 shower room. Extra bed.
Meals	Table d'hôtes €32, on request. Restaurant 5km.
Closed	Never.

Catherine & Antoine Debray
Le Thoronet, Var

Tel	+33 (0)4 94 60 13 36
Email	infos@bastidedesmoures.com
Web	www.bastidedesmoures.com

Number One - 1st & 2nd Floors

Again, in the four middle-floor apartments of this marvellous ensemble, we have aristocratic old bones dressed in clean-cut modern fashions and bathed in the eternal light of Provence. The lovely original wrought-iron banister leads up, and up, the many wide stairs to the four doors. Inside, original terracotta covers the floors, there is space, light and the same gracious minimalism founded on total respect for the building's fine classical proportions. Living areas are lit by the elegance of the high 19th-century windows overlooking the pretty square while bedrooms, crisp and quiet, are behind, set back from the sleepy bustle down below. Design and quality are keywords here: kitchens are quietly superb, bathrooms, large or small, are works of art in themselves. Creative contemporary furniture and local antiques blend with original beams and fireplaces, decorative touches are just a couple of pots, a tribal mask, a few pebbles. The surprise of such stylish urban comfort in a little old Provençal village is vastly stimulating. *Tennis at owner's house, 10-minute drive.*

Price	€400-€1,100 per week.
Sleeps	8.
Rooms	Each apartment: 1 twin/double, double sofabed; 1 bath/shower room. The two apartments on each floor can connect.
Meals	Restaurants 100m.
Closed	Never.

Arja Suddens
Mons, Var

Tel	+33 (0)4 94 76 35 15
Mobile	+33 (0)6 19 39 37 80
Email	arja.suddens@wanadoo.fr
Web	www.numberonemons.com

Number One - Ground & Top Floors

If you long for the unexpected, the sudden jolt of contrast, this is for you; if you love undemonstrative luxury, it's for you too. Elegant 17th-century architecture and gentle all-white interiors hold suave leather furniture, a few choice pieces placed just so – a giant vase, a piece of antique textile, an old Provençal triple settee – and always, quantities of restful space. Step in from the sights and shapes of timeless Provence to what could be 21st-century Milan. On the ground floor, coloured furniture and a working fireplace glow against the white walls, tall windows give onto the plane tree and the light of the square, bold Italian-style furniture, utterly contemporary and deeply comfortable, enhances the space; the bedroom seems humble in contrast. The lofty top-floor apartment under the eaves has a big fabulous terrace looking across Mons to the endless hills and the sea. Come back inside to a bright, luxurious living space for two where you may want to stay for ever. Kitchens and bathrooms are, of course, in sleek modern harmony with the rest. *Ground-floor meeting/reception room for 12. Tennis court short drive.*

Price	€400–€1,100 per week.
Sleeps	4.
Rooms	Ground floor apt: 1 double; 1 shower room.
	Top floor apt: 1 double; 1 bathroom.
Meals	Restaurants 100m.
Closed	Never.

Arja Suddens
Mons, Var

Tel	+33 (0)4 94 76 35 15
Mobile	+33 (0)6 19 39 37 80
Email	arja.suddens@wanadoo.fr
Web	www.numberonemons.com

La Ferme de Guillandonne

This enchanting 200-year-old farmhouse is the height of country-hideaway chic. Earthy, stylish and magical, it is bordered on one side by a stream. You are wrapped in ten acres of countryside. Rows of lavender run along one side of the pool while on the other a tunnel of wisteria leads down to a sun-trapping terrace. The interior is equally satisfying. Walls are washed in traditional colours – cool yellows, cosy reds, pale greens. There are old beams and a big arched window gives onto the terrace. One of the bedrooms has a magnificent high ceiling and a window that looks out onto a Chinese mulberry tree, another an original open fireplace and views over the pool. Marie-Joëlle, a former English teacher, and her husband, an architect, have renovated with a happy respect for the spirit of the place, for its history and the landscape that envelops it. You are in one of the loveliest parts of the Var and villages here have musical events running throughout the summer. This is a *bona fide* classic, a very special place. Don't miss it. *Sawday B&B.*

Price	€1,000–€2,300 per week.
Sleeps	6.
Rooms	2 doubles, 1 twin; 2 bathrooms, 2 shower rooms (1 with separate entrance). Extra bed.
Meals	Restaurants within walking distance.
Closed	Never.

Marie-Joëlle Salaün
Tourrettes, Var

Tel	+33 (0)4 94 76 04 71
Mobile	+33 (0)6 24 20 73 09
Email	guillandonne@wanadoo.fr

Les Mérelles - Cottage

Wrapped in jasmine, wisteria and roses, this house is straight out of a story book. Snug amid two hectares of Mediterranean gardens, it is private yet enjoys the benefits of the main house: swimming pool, shady or sunny garden spots, views to the mountains, woodland to explore, herbs from Regina's organic garden. Step through French windows into a large, elegant space, both bedroom and living room. With rocking chairs, pale walls and green quilting, views to garden or forest, muslin drifting at the windows, it's an enchanting haven. The kitchen, a pearl of creative practicality, is ingeniously hidden by curtains; the shower room is classy and big. Another pretty room acts as bedroom or study. Eat outside – there's a private garden – or at a choice of nearby restaurants, or join your hosts for a Provençal meal. Charming and cultured Germans with excellent English, they will also do your laundry. Walk from the grounds to alpine foothills – great for gliding or golf. Explore coastal towns and enjoy markets and summer festivals. A very special den for two or three. *Shared pool.*

Price	€900.
Sleeps	3.
Rooms	1 twin/double, 1 single; 1 shower room.
Meals	Meals on request. Restaurant 15-minute walk.
Closed	Never.

Peter & Regina Westrick
Callian, Var

Tel	+33 (0)4 94 47 72 21
Mobile	+33 (0)6 82 39 52 39
Email	regina.westrick@wanadoo.fr

557 Chemin des Hautes Cottes

Committed Francophiles, the Yorkes have lavished quantities of TLC on their big 'neo-Provençal' house and terraced garden. It's a seductive hideaway in a cocoon of luxuriant vegetation, like a balcony hanging over the glorious scenery. Inside there is space and an almost palpable sense of calm. Artist Morag has a flair for colour and impeccable, unpretentious taste: gold, turquoise, blue, brick-red and white are married with Indian cottons, local antiques (a wedding cupboard is proudly dated 1832), good kilims and personal mementoes – the house of a family you would like to know better. Her enchanting and colourful paintings decorate the walls, the lime-green sofa before the open fireplace is almost edible, there are all the books on Provence you may need. Plus fine big bedrooms, pretty Salernes-tiled bathrooms, a perfect family kitchen to prepare for the stupendously gleaming antique refectory table. Then choose the pool or a secret corner in the luscious garden, or go for water sports of every description on Lac de Saint Cassien, or walking in the hills behind Callian. *Village 10-minute walk.*

Price	£800–£2,100 per week.
Sleeps	8
Rooms	2 doubles, 2 twins; 3 bathrooms, 1 shower room, separate wc.
Meals	Restaurants 10-minute walk.
Closed	Rarely.

Robert & Morag Yorke
Callian, Var

Tel	+44 (0)1403 790311
Mobile	+44 (0)7860 559445
Email	robert.yorke@btinternet.com
Web	www.callian.co.uk

Entry 313   Map 16

Le Madison

From first-floor windows, an expanse of sky. Below, green fairways, trees and distant hills. The communal pool is out of sight, the motorway a distant hum, the golf course beckons… here is peacefulness, light and space. Your three-bedroom apartment in this gated, pink and white 'village' is probably one of the largest and surely the most immaculate. Slip a CD into the state-of-the-art music centre, slide open the glass doors to the almost wraparound balcony, roll down the electric shade, unfurl on a white-cushioned lounger. The owners have employed the most talented artisans and have decorated to their own design. The result is a spare, sweeping, luxurious décor with a red and cream theme and oriental touches. Everything is crisply, perfectly new: the pale quarry tiles, the creamy drapes, the Turkish carpet, the de Dietrich oven, the huge TV (plus videos for kids). And when you've tired of the fine linens and the silk cushions, there's the sea two miles away, and Nice, Mougins, Saint Tropez. Not forgetting three tennis clubs and innumerable golf courses… the nearest lapping at your feet. *Shared pool.*

Price	€1,500–€2,100 (£1,000–£1,400 sterling) per week.
Sleeps	6.
Rooms	3 twins/doubles; 2 bathrooms, 1 shower room, 1 separate wc.
Meals	Restaurants within walking distance.
Closed	Rarely.

Ennis & Barry Bartman
Mandelieu, Alpes-Maritimes

Tel	+44 (0)1582 769728
Mobile	+44 (0)7831 636644
Email	mandelieu@bdbartman.co.uk
Web	www.rivieragolf.info

Les Princes d'Orange

Longing to do it as the French do? This is exactly the sort of place that Parisians hope to escape to for the month of August, a modern Riviera apartment on a gated estate set in manicured grounds with well-clipped lawns and beds of sweet-scented flowers. It is pretty, spotless and conveniently positioned but the highlight is the vast balcony and its magnificent views down the Côte d'Azur with alpine foothills rising behind – you can see Italy on a good day. It is a perfect spot, one that encourages great sloth, and it faces south-east, so expect to breakfast lazily in the sun, under the awning if it gets too hot. The interior swims with light from full-height windows, you live with fabulous views, big old-gold sofas, a glass dining table on marble floors, white walls, a queen-size bed dressed in pure cotton. The beach and the old town are both within walking distance (about 15 minutes), though buses pass frequently if you prefer. The old town is a must: café culture, a maze of narrow streets, a covered market, pretty squares, a cathedral and a château. Exceptional. *Not suitable for children. Arrival Saturday.*

Price	£400–£600 per week.
Sleeps	2.
Rooms	1 double; 1 bathroom.
Closed	Never.

Sian & James Wroe
Antibes, Alpes-Maritimes

Tel	+33 (0)4 94 73 58 26
Email	james.wroe@orange.fr
Web	www.orangedazur.co.uk

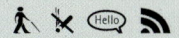

Villa Gardiole & La Petite Maison

Between Cannes and Nice, a gated, two-hectare hideaway and hillside paradise, built in the 1950s – the owners' house plus two charming villas. Most rooms lead to the garden, a glorious expanse of grass, trees and potager (yours to poach), a discreet lake-like pool, a wooden pergola, a serene all-glass weights room (that opens up in warm weather), swings, slides, treehouse, hammocks and bamboo forest. And your dining courtyard too. Inside the larger villa, rustic terracotta floors, a polished country dresser, a regiment of copper pans, a touch of trompe l'œil – the feel is immaculate Provençal. Downstairs, a pale green-check sofa, a working chimney and an open country kitchen; upstairs, a gaily canopied bed. The smaller villa has a wonderful feel of space and light, elegant blue and white bedroom, perfect linen and a collection of hats on a wall. Madame Severgnini can arrange a maid, a cook, a yoga teacher, a personal trainer, a gardening course with an expert, Italian cookery with her. The Brague National Park starts from the back door and there are cultural and sporty distractions galore. Fabulous! *Shared pool.*

Price	€2,000-€4,000 per week.
Sleeps	9.
Rooms	Villa Gardiole: 2 doubles, 1 twin, 1 single; 4 bathrooms. La Petite Maison: 1 double & child's single; 1 bathroom.
Closed	Never.

Ignazia Severgnini
Biot, Alpes-Maritimes

Tel	+33 (0)4 93 65 55 08
Email	severgnin@aol.com
Web	www.villagardiole.com

Domaine de Pierrefeu - Apartment

Valbonne is a lively village with restaurants, shops, galleries and heaps of Provençal charm. There's a weekly Friday market for great food and – on the first Sunday of the month – antiques and brocante. Here is a modern house in its own vast grounds, at the end of a quiet cul de sac set back from the road, with a garden to roam and a good pool – yours during the day while the charming owner is at work. Your ground-floor apartment is small but cosy, with white walls, floral curtains, a sofa with a throw and French windows opening to a covered terrace and delightful mosaic-tiled table. Lovely in summer; and you have all you need to knock up a meal in the kitchen, pretty with its creamy pink tiles. The bedroom is traditionally furnished, the bathroom is large and lovely, with plenty of space to fit your things. This would be a delightfully cool apartment even in the height of summer, and the pool area is surrounded by loungers, flowering shrubs and palm trees for shade… all you hear is birdsong. So peaceful, and the village just a seven-minute walk.

Price	€450–€650 per week.
	Two-day bookings out of season.
Sleeps	2.
Rooms	1 double; 1 bathroom.
Meals	Restaurants 1–2km.
Closed	Never.

Caroline Duval-Flahault
Valbonne, Alpes-Maritimes

Tel	+33 (0)4 93 12 90 47
Mobile	+33 (0)6 67 00 85 43
Email	cduvalflahault@wanadoo.fr

La Bergerie & Le Cabanon

The soft stone walls of these two sweet cottages keep you cool in the hottest weather. In the sheepfold, enjoy your morning coffee at the old manger – now a breakfast bar – or on the terrace, and watch the sun come up over high-perched Bar sur Loup, a 20-minute walk away. Surrounded by grass, oaks, olives, pines and rocky-peaked mountains, this is a blissfully peaceful and natural place. Sylvie, an actress, and sporty Pascal (they met hang-gliding), have restored and decorated in a stylish but informal way. Floors are bleached wood, timber ceilings are painted, there are simple, charming touches and the Bergerie bedroom has fabulous views. The Cabanon has the extra seductions of washing machines, a pretty terrace and a piano; the Bergerie has a new bathroom. The owners and their three children make you feel warmly at home but don't intrude. Come for cherries in May, fireflies in June: a spring and summer paradise. It's a short hop to the coast if you fancy the snazziness of the Riviera; gentler forays might include visits to the stunning hilltop villages of the area – or just loll by the pool.

Price	€350–€700 each per week.
Sleeps	5.
Rooms	Bergerie: 1 double, sofabed in dining room; 1 shower room. Cabanon: 1 double, 1 small child's room; 1 shower room.
Closed	Never.

Sylvie & Pascal Delaunay
Le Bar sur Loup, Alpes-Maritimes

Tel	+33 (0)4 93 42 50 08
Email	chemindelachenaie@hotmail.com
Web	www.chemindelachenaie.com

La Maison de Laurence

One of the loveliest places in this book, utterly authentic and sure of itself, with that special air that attracts the artist and the writer. It is a place to chance upon, as if the house were too modest to seduce you in advance. The lucky ones who do will find an old Provençal stone farmhouse standing beneath the protective gaze of Le Baou, a sugar-loaf mountain. You are surrounded by peace and Laurence's luscious terraced garden; beyond are the suburbs of Vence. Your top-floor apartment is reached via open stone steps and a super private terrace, shaded by an ancient olive tree. Laurence, warm, cultured and full of life, lives on the ground floor, her equally delightful son lives above her. Bedrooms are simple and cosy, beds dressed in fine linen. One has whitewashed walls and a beautiful 18th-century 'built-in' cupboard, the other an antique desk and views through trees. There's a long refectory dining table in the kitchen with rush-seated chairs, and a tiny but adorable sitting room. Stroll down to the swimming holes and waterfalls of the Cagne river — audible from the house after heavy rainfall. *Parking on road.*

Price	€400–€550 per week.
Sleeps	4.
Rooms	1 double, 1 twin; 1 bathroom. Child's bed.
Meals	Restaurant 3km.
Closed	Never.

Laurence Thiebaut
Vence, Alpes-Maritimes

Tel	+33 (0)4 93 58 13 95
Mobile	+33 (0)6 24 62 76 39
Email	lamaisondelaurence@hotmail.com
Web	www.lamaisondelaurence.com

Mas Josephine

The TGV stops at Nice and a local bus soon drops you off at Vence for a 20-minute yomp to this pretty, modern Provençal house on a steep slope, ideal for a couple; views are over cypresses, terracotta roofs, the mountains of the Col de Vence and the sea in the distance. Your apartment joins the end of the house, but has its own entrance through a smart metal gate. Be calmed by the white open-plan living area with its black wrought-iron table and chairs; a Maroc sofabed and cheerful throws add a touch of southern French colour. Sleep soundly in a simple, pine-furnished bedroom, with cream linen curtains and smooth floor tiles. The drop-dead gorgeous bar kitchen has everything you'd expect, so foodies will be happy; on sunny days take it all outside to the terrace, and a snooze in a garden hammock (there are many quiet spots). Joëlle offers cookery courses and lessons in Provençal style cookery, sourcing from local food markets: take home your spoils at the end of the day. In winter keen skiers can use the owner's lodge, just one hour away, within the week for the same price. Cool!

Price	€450.
Sleeps	2.
Rooms	1 double; 1 shower room.
Meals	Restaurant 1km.
Closed	Never.

Joëlle Deville
Vence, Alpes-Maritimes

Tel	+33 (0)4 93 24 30 64
Mobile	+33 (0)6 15 79 24 72
Email	joelle-deville@wanadoo.fr
Web	www.mas-josephine.fr

Nice Noble Apartments

From a flower-filled balcony, high up in an 18th-century apartment block on the Place du Justice, you can scan the rooftops of Old Nice. (Stand on tip-toes and you can see the sea.) Off the street, between cafés where the lawyers and their clients meet, is an elegant wrought-iron and glass door with a brass plaque. Enter the hall and let the lift transport you to the fourth floor. Kara Noble and Pam Demacon have renovated Fresco (named after the gorgeous old fresco on its ceiling) and Carrara (named after the marble on the bathroom floor) in such a way that they interlink for two parties. Each apartment is filled with light: romantic Fresco, with its old honeycomb tiles, cosy sofa and scatter cushions, and homely but luxurious Carrara, with its full kitchen and antique pieces. Expect crisp cotton on very comfortable beds, air conditioning for summer nights, double glazing for quiet, books, magazines, art, brocante. Pam is gardienne and is charming. Step out of the door: the flower and veg market is up the road; walk straight ahead: you find promenade, beach and glittering sea. A special address.

Price	Fresco €500–€600.
	Carrara €700–€950.
	Together €1,100–€1,400.
	Prices per week.
Sleeps	6.
Rooms	Fresco: 1 twin/double; 1 shower room.
	Carrara: 2 twins/doubles; 2 bathrooms.
	Apartments connect to create
	Frescarra for 6.
Closed	Never.

	Kara Noble
	Nice, Alpes-Maritimes
Mobile	+33 (0)6 25 89 69 53
Email	pam@nobleapartments.com
Web	www.nobleapartments.com

Les Cloîtres

Overlooking Sospel's 600-year-old cathedral, this historic building was probably one of the original monastic or university buildings clustered round the bishop's throne, and your big bright apartment must be one of the most extraordinary you will find. All the walls, all the ceilings are frescoed, a 20th-century local artist's two-year labour of love. The rooms – two bedrooms (one with French windows to the courtyard), library/sitting and dining rooms – are vast with soaring ceilings, polished wood and honeycomb tile floors. With the Hollands' antique furnishing, the atmosphere is old-style grand yet comfortable and totally undaunting. The excellent kitchen has a door onto the wide terrace for cool dining. When Sospel, a wonderful leafy backwater in the hills, was an Italian town it was favoured by the clergy – and their wealth. It is still lively, in a civilised way (good choice of restaurants), and a great base for fabulous walking, kayaking, fishing and paragliding. The fleshpots of the coast beckon from below and the huge and famous Friday market in Vintimiglia is just a 25-minute drive. *Children over 10 welcome.*

Price	€450-€650 per week.
Sleeps	4.
Rooms	2 doubles; 1 bathroom, 1 shower room.
Meals	Restaurant nearby.
Closed	Never.

Brett & Caroline Holland
Sospel, Alpes-Maritimes

Tel	+33 (0)4 93 91 44 23
Mobile	+33 (0)6 24 86 77 96
Email	brett.holland@bpb.barclays.com

Photo: istock.com

Many of you may want to stay in environmentally friendly places. You may be passionate about local, organic or home-grown food. Or perhaps you want to know that the place you are staying in contributes to the community? To help you we have launched our Ethical Collection, so you can find the right place to stay and also discover how each owner is addressing these issues.

The Collection is made up of places going the extra mile, and taking the steps that most people have not yet taken, in one or more of the following areas:

• **Environment** Those making great efforts to reduce the environmental impact of their Special Place. We expect more than energy-saving light bulbs and recycling – in this part of the Collection you will find owners who make their own natural cleaning products, properties with solar hot water and biomass boilers, the odd green roof and a good measure of green elbow grease.

• **Community** Given to owners who use their property to play a positive role in their local and wider community. For example, by making a contribution from every guest's bill to a local fund, or running pond-dipping courses for local school children on their farm.

• **Food** Awarded to owners who make a real effort to source local or organic food, or to grow their own. We look for those who have gone out of their way to strike up relationships with local producers or to seek out organic suppliers. It is easier for an owner on a farm to produce their own eggs than for someone in the middle of a city, so we take this into account.

How it works

To become part of our Ethical Collection owners choose whether to apply in one, two or all three categories, and fill in a detailed questionnaire asking demanding questions about their activities in the chosen areas. You can download a full list of the questions at www.sawdays.co.uk/about_us/ethical_collection/faq/

We then review each questionnaire carefully before deciding whether or not to give the award(s). The final decision is subjective; it is based not only on whether an owner ticks 'yes' to a question but also on the detailed explanation that accompanies each 'yes' or 'no' answer. For example, an owner who has tried as hard as possible to install solar water-heating panels, but has failed because of strict conservation planning laws, will be given some credit for their effort (as long as they are doing other things in this area).

We have tried to be as rigorous as possible and have made sure the questions are demanding. We have not checked out the claims of owners before

making our decisions, but we do trust them to be honest. We are only human, as are they, so please let us know if you think we have made any mistakes.

The Ethical Collection is still a new initiative for us, and we'd love to know what you think about it – email us at ethicalcollection@sawdays.co.uk or write to us. And remember that because this is a new scheme some owners have not yet completed their questionnaires – we're sure other places in the guide are working just as hard in these areas, but we don't yet know the full details.

Ethical Collection online

There is stacks more information on our website, www.sawdays.co.uk. You can read the answers each owner has given to our Ethical Collection questionnaire and get a more detailed idea of what they are doing in each area. You can also search for properties that have awards.

Ethical Collection in this book

On the entry page of all places in the Collection we show which awards have been given.

A list of places in our Ethical Collection is shown below, by entry number.

Environment
65 • 72 • 111 • 136 • 158 • 159 • 194 • 197 • 208 • 209 • 221 • 233 • 237 • 241 • 247 • 250 • 251 • 276

Community
145 • 197 • 208 • 209 • 247

Food
111 • 188 • 194 • 237 • 250 • 251 • 270

Photo: La Roseraie, entry 110

Climate Change   Our Warming World   £12.99

"Climate Change presents in a clear and unique way the greatest challenge facing humanity. It is illustrated with telling photography and sharply written text. It is both objective and passionate. To read it is to know that urgent action is needed at every level in all societies." Jonathan Dimbleby

Climate Change is the greatest challenge facing humanity today. In the coming decade a tipping point may be reached triggering irreversible impacts to our planet. This book is not just for scientists or academics, it is for everyone concerned about the future of the earth.

Also available in the Fragile Earth series:

Ban the Plastic Bag A community action plan **£4.99**
One Planet Living A guide to enjoying life on our one planet **£4.99**
The Little Food Book An explosive account of the food we eat today **£6.99**

To order any of the books in the Fragile Earth series call +44 (0)1275 395431 or visit www.fragile-earth.com

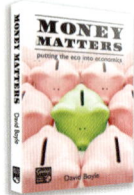

Money Matters
Putting the eco into economics £7.99

This well-timed book will make you look at everything from your bank statements to the coins in your pocket in a whole new way. Author David Boyle sheds new light on our money system and exposes the inequality, greed and instability of the economies that dominate the world's wealth.

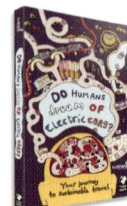

Do Humans Dream of Electric Cars? £4.99

This guide provides a no-nonsense approach to sustainable travel and outlines the simple steps needed to achieve a low carbon future. It highlights innovative and imaginative schemes that are already working, such as car clubs and bike sharing.

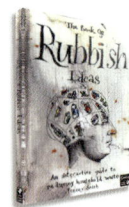

The Book of Rubbish Ideas £6.99

Every householder should have a copy of this guide to reducing household waste and stopping wasteful behaviour. Containing step-by-step projects, the book takes a top-down guided tour through the average family home.

The Big Earth Book
Updated paperback edition £12.99

This book explores environmental, economic and social ideas to save our planet. It helps us understand what is happening to the planet today, exposes the actions of corporations and the lack of action of governments, weighs up new technologies, and champions innovative and viable solutions.

What About China? £6.99
Answers to this and other awkward questions about climate change

A panel of experts gives clear, entertaining and informative answers arguing that the excuses we give to avoid reducing our carbon footprint and our personal impact on the earth are exactly that, excuses.

Have you enjoyed this book? Why not try one of the others in the Special Places series and get 35% discount on the RRP *

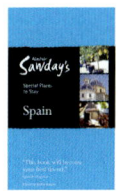 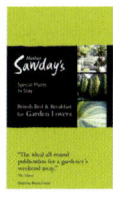  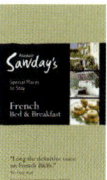 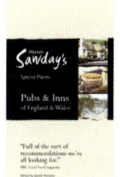 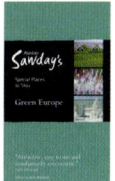

British Bed & Breakfast (Ed 14)	RRP £14.99	Offer price £9.75
British Bed & Breakfast for Garden Lovers (Ed 5)	RRP £14.99	Offer price £9.75
British Hotels & Inns (Ed 11)	RRP £14.99	Offer price £9.75
The Cotswolds (Ed 1)	RRP £9.99	Offer price £6.50
Devon & Cornwall (Ed 1)	RRP £9.99	Offer price £6.50
Scotland (Ed 1)	RRP £9.99	Offer price £6.50
Wales (Ed 1)	RRP £9.99	Offer price £6.50
Pubs & Inns of England & Wales (Ed 7)	RRP £15.99	Offer price £9.75
Go Slow England	RRP £19.99	Offer price £13.00
Ireland (Ed 7)	RRP £12.99	Offer price £8.45
French Bed & Breakfast (Ed 11)	RRP £15.99	Offer price £10.40
French Châteaux & Hotels (Ed 6)	RRP £14.99	Offer price £9.75
French Vineyards (Ed 1)	RRP £19.99	Offer price £13.00
Go Slow France	RRP £19.99	Offer price £13.00
Paris (Ed 1)	RRP £9.99	Offer price £6.50
Italy (Ed 6)	RRP £14.99	Offer price £9.75
Go Slow Italy	RRP £19.99	Offer price £13.00
Spain (Ed 8)	RRP £14.99	Offer price £9.75
Portugal (Ed 4)	RRP £11.99	Offer price £7.80
India & Sri Lanka (Ed 3)	RRP £11.99	Offer price £7.80
Green Europe (Ed 1)	RRP £11.99	Offer price £7.80
Morocco (Ed 3)	RRP £9.99	Offer price £9.10

*postage and packing is added to each order

To order at the Reader's Discount price simply phone +44 (0)1275 395431 and quote 'Reader Discount FSC'.

If you have any comments on entries in this guide, please tell us. If you have a favourite place or a new discovery, please let us know about it. You can return this form or visit www.sawdays.co.uk.

Existing entry

Property name: _____

Entry number: _____ Date of visit: _____

New recommendation

Property name: _____

Address: _____

_____

Tel/Email/Web: _____

Your comments

What did you like (or dislike) about this place? Were the people friendly? What was the location like? What sort of food did they serve?

_____

_____

_____

_____

Your details

Name: _____

Address: _____

_____

_____ Postcode: _____

Tel: _____ Email: _____

Please send completed form to:
FSC5, Sawday's, The Old Farmyard, Yanley Lane, Long Ashton, Bristol BS41 9LR, UK

Quick reference indices

Wheelchair-accessible
At least one bedroom and bathroom accessible for wheelchair users. Phone for details.

Limited mobility
At least one bedroom and bathroom accessible without steps.

Swimming
River, lake or beach within 500m.

Short Breaks

Can be booked for short breaks.

Quick reference indices

Photo: La Basse Lande, entry 104

Photo: The Beachhouse, entry 136

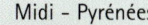

Midi - Pyrénées ❶

❷ **Barrau**

❸ Bliss for those who wish to leave creature comforts behind and lose themselves in the hills. The main house, where Jennifer lives, is 30 yards away. Secluded on a 15-acre hillside estate with two private sitting-out areas, one filled with lavender and figs, Barrau is perfect for a couple or a solo traveller. And trees, long views and wildlife. Deer and badgers live on the land, 42 species of butterflies have been identified, nightingales sing, the odd salamander scampers by and beehives dot the landscape. Your retreat, a former house for the pigs and hens that goes back to 1890, has been renovated simply. It's rather like camping but without the tent and with a bathroom. You have a pine-floored room with rugs and a plain table, a cupboard, a radio/cassette player, two beds and two easy chairs, a tiny painted-brick shower room and a corridor kitchen. Charming Jennifer lives simply and happily, is passionate about her "wildlife guests" and an expert on the local churches and brocante fairs too. Beneath pollution-free night skies, the tree frogs will sing you to sleep.

❹	Price	€200-€350 per week. Heating not included.
❺	Sleeps	2.
❻	Rooms	1 twin; 1 shower room.
❼	Meals	Dinner, 3 courses, €15. On request. Restaurant 20-minute drive.
❽	Closed	December-March.

	Jennifer Boncey
	Esparsac, Tarn-et-Garonne
Tel	+33 (0)5 63 26 12 72
Email	boncey@wanadoo.fr
Web	www.haumont.com

Ethical Collection: Environment; Community. See page 370 for details ❾

❿

Entry 197   Map 14 ⓫